VRIJE UNIVERSITEIT TE AMSTERDAM

THE PSALM CITATIONS IN THE EPISTLE TO THE HEBREWS

Academisch Proefschrift

TER VERKRIJGING VAN DE GRAAD VAN DOCTOR IN DE GODGELEERDHEID, OP GEZAG VAN DE RECTOR MAGNIFICUS MR. I. A. DIEPENHORST, HOOGLERAAR IN DE FACULTEIT DER RECHTSGELEERDHEID, IN HET OPENBAAR TE VERDEDIGEN OP VRIJDAG 10 FEBRUARI 1961 DES NAMIDDAGS 1.30 UUR IN HET WOESTDUIN-CENTRUM, WOESTDUINSTRAAT 16, TE AMSTERDAM-WEST

DOOR

SIMON KISTEMAKER

GEBOREN TE SINT MAARTEN (N.H.)

WIPF & STOCK · Eugene, Oregon

Wipf and Stock Publishers
199 W 8th Ave, Suite 3
Eugene, OR 97401

The Psalm Citations in the Epistle to the Hebrews
By Kistemaker, Simon
Copyright©1961 by Kistemaker, Simon
ISBN 13: 978-1-60899-721-3
Publication date 6/23/2010
Previously published by Wed. G. Van Soest N.V., 1961

CONTENTS

ACKNOWLEDGMENTS 9

INTRODUCTION 11

Chapter I THE TEXTUAL IMPLICATIONS
    1. Introduction 13
    2. Direct Quotations 17
    3. Conclusions 57

Chapter II THE HERMENEUTICAL PRINCIPLES
    1. Principles 61
    2. Application. 71
    3. Conclusions 88

Chapter III THE EXEGETICAL METHODS
    1. Plan and Perspectives 96
    2. Psalm 8:4–6 102
    3. Psalm 95:7–11 108
    4. Psalm 110:4 116
    5. Psalm 40:6–8 124
    6. Conclusions 130

Chapter IV THE THEOLOGICAL MOTIFS
    1. Christ's Superiority 134
    2. Historical Background 140
    3. Scriptural Authority 146
    4. Conclusions 150

LIST OF ABBREVIATIONS 152

BIBLIOGRAPHY 153

INDEX OF BIBLICAL PASSAGES 160

ACKNOWLEDGMENTS

The task of writing words of thanks fills me with a sense of dependence and joy. Throughout my academic career I have experienced the guidance, care, and providence of God; now at the close of my university training my gratitude, my honor and praise, are directed first of all to my heavenly Father.

I wish to take this opportunity, Professor Dr. R. Schippers, to thank you for consenting to be my promotor; for your encouragement and advice during the course of my study; for your keen insight and kind words of correction; and for the interest you have shown in the subject matter of this dissertation. A word of appreciation is directed to those professors of the Free University who showed their readiness, their devotion and interest, in presenting stimulating and enjoyable lectures for the benefit of the Foreign Students group.

When I think of my training received at Calvin College and Seminary, in Grand Rapids, Michigan, my gratefulness is addressed to all those who have been influential and instrumental in the molding of my academic life. Of the Seminary professors I wish to mention Dr. R. Stob and extend a word of acknowledgment to him. He introduced me to the riches of the Epistle to the Hebrews; he ushered me into a period which opened perspectives for extensive study in this New Testament book.

My wife, Jean, has been of invaluable aid and support to me. She has been a source of encouragement from day to day; she joyfully shared the life of a student. After her mother had passed away, she voluntarily offered to take upon herself the full responsibility of caring for a double family. This thesis is dedicated to her and to the memory of her mother.

In grateful recognition we remember the visible tokens of friendship which we received during our stay in Amsterdam, and especially during this last year. In particular I thank all my friends who have willingly offered their services in the typing, correcting, and proofreading of this dissertation. My thanks are extended especially to Mr. and Mrs. Tjitze Baarda for their interest, readiness and valuable suggestions, but above all for their warm friendship.

Last of all I wish to express my gratitude to the librarians of the Universiteits Bibliotheek, Bibliotheca Rosenthaliana, Theologisch Instituut, and the Vrije Universiteit. They have given unsparingly of their time, have tried to obtain the needed literature, and have contributed their share to my pleasant memories of Amsterdam.

INTRODUCTION

Something which draws the immediate attention of the reader is the abundance of psalm citations in the Epistle to the Hebrews. In the first chapter five out of the seven quotations are taken from the Psalter. Also in the other chapters passages out of the book of Psalms represent an important share in the number of OT citations quoted. Undoubtedly the question will be raised what the author's purpose has been in expressing himself by means of citations from this particular OT book. Was it perhaps because of the familiarity ascribed to the Psalter? Was it because the Psalter was in vogue as the book of praise? If this is the case, we may assume that the unknown writer of the Epistle has adapted his citations to the comprehensibility of his audience.

Of this dissertation, devoted to these psalm citations, it is chapter one, which is concerned primarily with this assumption. The purpose of this chapter is to learn whether the direct quotations in Hebrews were used in worship services, and whether the OT passages were familiar to the first recipients of the Epistle. At times we have resorted to textual variants in supporting the assumption made. However, we have not taken up the citations *qua* text; such study has been performed by commentators, and recently by K. J. Thomas, in his unpublished dissertation *The Use of the Septuagint in the Epistle to the Hebrews*, (University of Manchester), 1959.

Ever since the discoveries of the Dead Sea Scrolls the study of this literature has brought to light its immense value for a better understanding of the NT. Various thoughts and concepts found in the one body of literature are echoed in the other. Further, certain hermeneutical principles employed by the writers of the Scrolls (and especially of the commentaries on Biblical books) have also been the working tools for some NT authors. In fact the *Midrash pesher*, peculiar *e.g.* to the commentary on Habakkuk, is the method adopted by the author of the Epistle to the Hebrews. Of course it should be borne in mind that the study of the recently discovered documents is still in its introductory phase. However, with the available information we have made an attempt to apply the hermeneutical principles of this literature to our study. This pursuit is submitted in the second chapter.

In chapter three the characteristics of the *Midrash pesher* applied in the Epistle to the Hebrews are considered. The features of the *pesher* belong in particular to those four psalm citations (Pss. 8:4–6; 95:7–11; 110:4; 40:6–8) which appear to dominate the entire Epistle. All other citations are more or less subservient to these four passages, which follow one another in subsequent order. The author has given evidence of this order by presenting summary statements; summarizations are worked out in detail as the discourse progresses. In his exegesis of the psalm citations, the writer envisions fulfilment of promise and prophecy in the coming of the Son of God; and he intertwines the general message expressed by the psalm passages with the gospel of Jesus Christ. Thus his exegetical methodology is controlled by the fulfilment of the OT.

The choice in psalm citations reveals the author as a talented literary scholar who is able to disclose his thoughts in well-chosen words. The quotations in the first two chapters of his Epistle serve the theological motif of stressing the difference between the Son and the angels. Another theological motif is found in the historical background which the psalm citations reflect. A third motif concerns the question of scriptural authority attributed to the OT passages quoted. These theological motifs represent the fourth chapter. It is to be understood that in this final chapter only those theological matters are discussed which have been prompted by our consideration of the psalm citations.

Throughout our study we have tried to approach the first recipients of the Epistle in the time and world of thought which was theirs. Our interest has centered around the early Christian's familiarity with, and understanding of, the citations quoted, exegeted, and adapted by the author. Anachronistically we might say: if the "footnotes" to the Epistle should have been lost, we have attempted to restore some of them.

Chapter I

THE TEXTUAL IMPLICATIONS

1. Introduction

Proportionately, the Gospel according to Matthew may have more direct quotations from the OT than the other Gospels; the Epistle to the Romans may excel the other Pauline Epistles in citing passages from the OT; the Apocalypse, in alluding to the OT, may tower high above the other writings attributed to John; but it is the Epistle to the Hebrews which surpasses all the books of the NT canon in its direct and indirect use of the OT.[1] It should be clearly understood that the authors of the various NT books did not introduce and apply the quotations from the OT in a scientific manner, with literary accuracy characteristic of our day. Rather the OT passages were embodied in the Gospels, in the Epistles, in the Acts, and in the Apocalypse in order to bear witness to the fulfilment of the Old Covenant in the New. Of all the four Gospels it is Matthew's which appeals to the churches in Palestine. Paul's Epistle to the Romans, enhanced by quotations and reminiscences of the OT, was addressed to the Church at Rome with its many converts out of Judaism. The Revelation of John, the one and only prophetic book in the NT, is directed *e.g.* to the seven churches of Asia Minor at the close of the first century A.D. And it is the author to the Hebrews [2] who addresses his Epistle with all its OT citations

---

[1] "De tous les écrits du Nouveau Testament, l'épître aux Hébreux est celui qui compte proportionellement le plus grand nombre de citations formelles de l'Ancien Testament et surtout de réminiscences ou allusions (certains chapitres sont presque des centons de textes bibliques)." L. Venard, "Psaumes," *Mélanges*, p. 253.

[2] In our study we shall employ the term *the author to the Hebrews*, though at times for stylistic reasons a synonym may be used. Granted that the expression is a bit cumbersome, we are of the opinion that it is more suitable for our purposes than the use of "Hebrews" to express the author and "*Hebrews*" to indicate the Epistle; for this terminology is apt to be confusing. Vs. F. C. Synge, *Hebrews*, p. vii.

and allusions to the Jews acquainted with the Scriptures written in the Greek tongue. In appealing to the seed of Abraham, the authors employ the books of the OT which were known to the Jews in Palestine as well as in the Diaspora.

Besides quoting from his favorite book, Isaiah, in the Epistle to the Romans, Paul cites nearly as many quotations from the book of Psalms. Of the 53 direct quotations, 16 are taken out of Isaiah and 13 (14, counting Ps. 107:26, in 10:7) from the Psalter. In his first Epistle to the Corinthians, Clement of Rome, quoting from a great number of OT books, cites from the Psalter far more than from any other book.[1] Also the Epistle to the Hebrews is indicative of the fact that about one-third of the direct quotations are drawn from the book of Psalms.

It is apparent that in the first century A.D. the writers of the NT Scriptures, as well as Clement of Rome, used the Psalter not only for substantiating ideas, but — what seems even more important — for citing something which was familiar to the eyes and ears of the readers and hearers of their letters. "The early Church [2] was not such a bookish community. The main current of its life and thought seems to have been carried by oral tradition, at least to the end of the first century...."[3] Although the author to the Hebrews may display exquisite literary ability, this does not imply that all the recipients of his letter were talented in reading and writing. Much was communicated by word of mouth; much had to be remembered. It is not surprising at all that the author, in an attempt to reach perfect communication, strengthens not only his whole Epistle with quotations from the Psalter known in the liturgy of the Church: indeed in his first

---

[1] According to the *Index Locorum Veteris Testamenti* of I Clem. in *Patrum Apostolicorum Opera* (ed. O. de Gebhardt, A. Harnack, Th. Zahn, pp. 144f.), the Psalms are referred to and quoted 34 times; Genesis, 17 times; Isaiah, 14 times; Job, 11 times; all the other books, less than 10.

[2] By the expression *the Early Church* we designate the Christian community belonging to the period of the middle of the first to the end of the second century A.D. Since the recipients of the Epistle to the Hebrews were Christians of the second generation (Heb. 2:3), we believe that they are a fair representation of the Church in the latter part of that first century. Extra-biblical authors of that period have been designated as *Early Church Fathers*.

[3] C. H. Dodd, *Acc. to the Scr.*, p. 29.

chapter he avails himself of five passages from the Psalms and one from the Hymn of Moses (Deut. 32).[1]

However, it was not only the Psalter which the Early Church derived from the services held in the Temple and Synagogue. There were also the Scripture lessons, the liturgical texts, and the congregational prayers.[2]

> ... There are some elements in the musical liturgy of Christianity and Judaism which stem from a common source. ... The common elements are: (1) The scriptural lesson ... to be read or recited regularly and periodically. ... (2) The vast field of psalmody. ... (3) The litany or the congregational prayers of supplication and intercession, especially on fast-days, which from time immemorial, have been used as important media of musical and religious expression. (4) The chanted prayer of the priest or precentor.[3]

Our investigation of the text will not merely be limited to the text itself. Such study has been performed by most of the commentators whose works may be consulted.[4] Instead, we shall concern ourselves with the use made of the individual quotation, and consequently with its evident familiarity among the believers.

---

[1] It is B. F. Westcott who comprehensively remarks: "The large proportion of passages taken verbally from the Greek Psalter points to the familiar use of the Book both by the writer and by the readers. Under this aspect the absence of verbal coincidences with the Psalms apart from quotations from them is remarkable." *Comm.*, p. 473.

The Epistle to the Hebrews, which is rich in direct quotations from the Psalter, is almost devoid of reminiscences from the Psalms. Heb. 11:26 shows, the word "reproach," which finds resemblance in Pss. 69:9; 89:50,51. Also Heb. 12:14 with the phrase "follow after peace" corresponds to its counterpart "seek peace, and pursue it" in Ps. 35:14. The expression "a sacrifice of praise" (Heb. 13:15) is vaguely similar to the words "a sacrifice of thanksgiving" in Ps. 50:14,23. These three places in Hebrews represent all the allusions to the Psalms.

[2] The book of Acts is replete with instances in which the Apostles and believers continue the practices to which they were accustomed in Temple and Synagogue, *e.g.* Acts 3:1; 17:2.

[3] E. Werner, *Sacred Bridge*, p. 26; and cf. I. Elbogen, *Gottesdienst*, pp.494ff.

[4] The most recent treatment of the text has been performed by K. J. Thomas in his unpublished dissertation *The Use of the Septuagint in the Epistle to the Hebrews*, 1959. Also see the elaborate study of the text by C. Büchel, "Der Hebräerbrief und das Alte Testament," *TSK*, 1906, pp. 508–591.

It is rather difficult to determine the exact number of direct quotations in the Epistle to the Hebrews. Counting all the citations marked as direct in Dittmar's valuable work on the compilation of OT quotations in the NT, we come to a total of 34 in all.[1] Spicq, in his introductory volume, presents a neat tabulation of *Citations formelles ou tacites* and surpasses Dittmar in bringing the total number to <u>36</u>.[2] Although Padva discusses 34 direct quotations in all, yet in his conclusion he speaks of only 29 passages which the author to the Hebrews has used in his Epistle.[3] While Michel mentions 32,[4] Venard counts 29 or 30 explicit citations.[5] Last of all, Westcott properly compiles, in the order of the books of the OT, the quotations which are directly introduced, 24 in number. He adds another 5 passages "which are used verbally though not formally quoted," thus showing a total of 29 citations.[6]

Our "range of quotations" will be quite similar to that of Westcott, with the exceptions that Gen. 14:17ff. and Deut. 9:19 will be added, and that our tabulation will be according to the order in which the passages occur in the Epistle. We will <u>not</u> discuss the allusions found in this letter, for they do not contribute substantially to the purpose of our study.[7]

Though recognizing that the author to the Hebrews did not intend to give scientific proof whenever he employed a verb of saying followed by a quotation, we still think it best to regard as direct the passages with an introductory formula. Thus we get 26 in number, and add another six which, though lacking the introduction, are exact in wording. This brings the total to 32 citations; we count the combined quotation in Heb. 10:37–38 double. There are two quotations which may be called "border

---

[1] Cf. W. Dittmar, *Vetus Testamentum in Novo*.

[2] C. Spicq, I, *Introd.*, p. 331.

The difference in number (Dittmar 34 and Spicq 36) is accounted for by the inclusion of Heb. 7:1,2 (Gen. 14:18ff.) and Heb. 10:12 (Ps. 110:1) in Spicq's list of direct quotations.

[3] P. Padva, *Les Citations*, p. 100.

[4] O. Michel, *Comm.*, p. 81.

[5] Venard, "Psaumes," *Mélanges*, p. 253.

[6] Westcott, *Comm.*, pp. 469ff.

[7] Spicq, I, *Introd.*, pp. 332f., counts a total of nearly 80 reminiscences; Venard has 50; and Westcott, 47.

line cases" — Gen. 47:31 (Heb. 11:21) and Deut. 4:24 (Heb. 12:29). However, on the basis of introduction and faithfulness to the LXX or MT, we have classified them as reminiscences.

For textual sources in this study we have used Kittel for the MT, Rahlfs for the LXX, and Nestle for the Greek NT.[1] Whenever recourse is had to an English translation, we have followed the American Standard Version.

2. Direct Quotations

Psalm 2:7 (Heb. 1:5a; 5:5)

The Psalms of Solomon, composed during the first century B.C. and used generally in local synagogues,[2] testify that the second Psalm, out of which the author to the Hebrews has taken his first quotation, was understood messianically.[3] Although Targum Jonathan may give evidence of this same type of interpretation,[4] yet in later years, when the controversy between Christianity and Judaism waxed hot, the Rabbis poured quite a different meaning into the term *Anointed*.

---

[1] R. Kittel, *Biblia Hebraica*³; A. Rahlfs, *Septuaginta*⁶, Vol. I, II, (Stuttgart); *Septuaginta, Societas Scientiarum Gottingensis*, (ed. A. Rahlfs); E. Nestle and K. Aland, *Novum Testamentum Graece* ²³. We have also consulted F. Field, *Hexaplorum*, Vol. I, II. Recognizing that the numbering of chapters and verses differs in the MT and its Greek version and English translations, we have followed the numbering customary in the English Bibles. Wherever it has been necessary to refer to the numbering of the LXX version, the chapters and verses have been designated as such.

[2] E. Kautzsch, *Die Apokryphen*, II, pp. 127f.

[3] "... The Son of David, ... let Him reign over Israel thy servant, ... so as to destroy the wicked from thy inheritance : and to break their pride like the potter's vessel; to break with a rod of iron all their firmness." Ps. Sal. 17,23ff., ed. R. Harris and A. Mingana, *The Odes and Psalms of Salomon*, pp. 430f. For Rabbinic references see Str.-Bill., III, pp. 675ff.

[4] "Vermutlich hat auch der Targum Ps 2 messianisch gedeutet; denn die spätere Zeit hat bei dem "Gesalbten" Jahves kaum an etwas anders als an den messianischen König gedacht." Str.-Bill., III, p. 675. A. Vis, *Mess. Psalm Quotations*, pp. 22f., enumerates the messianic and non-messianic interpretations of Ps. 2 in Jewish literature. He concludes that the Church has been the primary agent in attributing a messianic interpretation to the psalm. However, Vis should have mentioned and discussed the reference in the Psalms of Solomon; instead he neglects it entirely.

The NT writings reflect this messianic interpretation in all the quotations and references from Ps. 2. Whereas the first two verses of this psalm, quoted in Acts 4:25, apply the term *Anointed* to Jesus, Acts 13:33, in citing verse 7 with the rubric, "it is written in the second psalm," employs the quotation to explicate the resurrection of Christ. In Hebrews we find this text with the rubric of what God "said" (1:5) or "spoke" (5:5). While several references to the verses 2, 8, and 9 are found in Acts and Revelation, allusions to verse 7 are provided by Matthew, Mark, Luke, Hebrews, and II Peter.[1]

Three Early Church Fathers[2] place the quotation in quite different settings. Clement of Rome, introducing it by "the Master says thus," renders it within the context of a large portion borrowed from Heb. 1. Though Irenaeus joins the verse with Ps. 110:1, Justin Martyr puts it twice in the scene of Jesus' baptism, which may be an indication of a textual tradition prevalent within the Early Church.[3] The LXX reading of Ps. 2:7 is given in the Western text (Codex D, Itala, Justin, Origen) of Lk. 3:22. "... It is conceivable that Luke gave the full form here as in Acts 13:33, and that the prevailing textual tradition assimilated it to Mark 1:11."[4]

The quotation which is identical to the LXX and faithful to the MT, consists of two parts. While the first half, except for the word order and the definite article before υἱός, is also found in Mark and Luke, the second is indicative of another tradition.

---

[1] Cf. the *Index Locorum* in Nestle, *Novum Testamentum Graece*[23], p. 662.

[2] In our investigation of the OT quotations located in the writings of the Early Church Fathers we will limit ourselves mainly to Clement of Rome, Justin Martyr, and Irenaeus (with the occasional reference to Barnabas), because they represent and bring to a close the first period of the history of Church and dogma. Whereas Irenaeus still belongs to the conservative sphere, Clement of Alexandria and Tertullian usher in a new period of Church history. Cf. J. L. Koole, *De Overname van het OT*, pp. 9, 16–51. We have consulted Irenaeus, *Opera*, Vol. I (ed. A. Stieren); Irenaeus, *Apostolische Verkondiging* (ed. H. W. Meyboom), which will be abbreviated hereafter by I-IV and Epid. respectively. For Justin Martyr we have followed *Opera*, Vol. I, (ed. E. J. Goodspeed), abbreviated as Dial. The First Epistle of Clement and the Epistle of Barnabas have been consulted in the edition *Apostolic Fathers*, Vol. I, of the Loeb Classical Library (*LCL*) series.

[3] The passages are located in I Clem. 36,4; Just. Dial. 88,103; Iren. Epid. 49.

[4] Dodd, *Acc. to the Scr.*, p. 32.

Matthew, Mark, Luke, and II Peter have the reading "in whom I am well pleased," but the Western text of Luke quotes the LXX version. Also the Ebionite Gospel reveals this other tradition by having wording comparable to Lk. 3:22 and to the *varia lectio* of this verse.[1] The accompanying scheme may aid us in noticing the word order of the presented readings.

Mt. 3:17	Mk. 1:11 Lk. 3:22	Eb. Ev. 3	Ps. 2:7 (LXX) Lk. 3:22 (*v. l.*)
οὗτος	σὺ	σύ μου	υἱός μου
ἐστιν	εἶ	εἶ	εἶ
ὁ υἱός	ὁ υἱός	ὁ υἱός	σύ
μου	μου	—	—
ὁ ἀγαπητός	ὁ ἀγαπητός	ὁ ἀγαπητός	—
ἐν ᾧ	ἐν σοὶ	ἐν σοὶ	—
εὐδόκησα	εὐδόκησα	εὐδόκησα (καὶ πάλιν)	—
		ἐγὼ	ἐγὼ
		σήμερον	σήμερον
		γεγέννηκά	γεγέννηκά
		σε	σε

By means of this tabulation it will be seen readily that the Early Church used different phraseology to express the words spoken at the time of Jesus' baptism. It is most likely that in the Greek-speaking communities the tendency developed toward associating the LXX reading of Ps. 2:7 with the baptism scene. Although we know that Paul, in preaching at Antioch, applied this verse to the resurrection of Jesus, this does not remove the fact that all of Ps. 2:7 — in accordance with the *varia lectio* of Lk. 3:22 — may be applied to the baptism of our Lord.

II Samuel 7:14 (Heb. 1:5b)

As further proof for the superiority of the Son over the angels the author quotes a text out of II Sam. 7. The quotation is preceded by the words "and again," which is a formula not only

---

[1] M. R. James, *The Apocryphal NT*, p. 9; W. Michaelis, *Apokryphen Schriften*, p. 128; E. Hennecke, *Ntl. Apokryphen*, p. 103; H. U. Meyboom, *Evangeliën buiten het NT*, pp. 33f.

current in haggadic Midrash,¹ but also found in Philo and the Early Church Fathers; it is even used in the Fourth Gospel (John 19:37) and in the Pauline Epistles (Rom. 15:10-12, I Cor. 3:20).

Although the passage refers to King Solomon, it is evident that this prophecy could never be fulfilled in his person. In the LXX version the text in II Sam. 7:14 and its parallel in I Chron. 17:13 are preceded by the phrase ἀναστήσω τὸ σπέρμα which points to a successor who will be raised up after the death of David.²

In the NT Luke records that the angel Gabriel comes to Mary and tells her, by referring to II Sam. 7, that Jesus will fulfill the words of this passage (Lk. 1:32,33). Also the people involved in the controversy concerning Jesus' prophethood knew the OT Scriptures: "Hath not the scripture said, that Christ cometh of the seed of David . . . ?" (John 7:42). This knowledge could only be derived from the pericope out of II Sam. 7. The apostle Paul uses a paraphrase of the quotation in II Cor. 6:18, but it appears that he is not interested in the messianic interpretation, since certain elements out of Isa. 43:6 are interwoven in the text. "And he that sitteth on the throne," who makes all things new, applies the quotation slightly modified to the believer who "shall inherit these things" (Rev. 21:7).

It is evident that the passage was well-known in the Early Church.³ Since the prophecy could only be fulfilled in its entirety by Jesus, the Son of God, it is but natural that it was understood as messianic (cf. Mt. 12:42). The words of Nathan the prophet were originally meant for Solomon, yet Jesus through his work on earth had completely overshadowed this historic person.

Deuteronomy 32:43 (Heb. 1:6b)

The Hymn of Moses, divided in six portions,⁴ was used in the service of the Temple and sung by the Jews of the Diaspora, where it received the same standing as the Psalms of David. It was a well-known hymn, for IV Maccabees, written during

---

¹ Hebrew וְיָעוּד; Aramaic וְתוּב. Cf. Spicq, II, *Comm.*, p. 16. Philo, *Quis rer. div. haer.* (xxiv) 122, *LCL*, Vol. IV, p. 342; *Leg. Alleg.* III, (ii) 4, *LCL*, Vol. I, p. 302. References to the Early Church Fathers are numerous.

² G. Harder, "Septuagintazitate," *Theologia Viatorum*, p. 33.

³ Also Justin Martyr (Dial. 118) quotes the verses 14-16 of II Sam. 7, and places the passage in the context of several quotations from the OT, *e.g.*, Ps. 110:4; Isa. 57:2; Dan. 7:26; and Ezk. 44:3.

⁴ Elbogen, *Gottesdienst*, p. 169.

the first century A.D., records that the mother of the seven sons reminds them to learn the Hymn of Moses.[1] Philo calls it the "Great Song," or the "Greater Song," of Moses.[2]

Of all the chapters in Deuteronomy, the NT writers quote and refer to the 32nd more than any other. Not only the author to the Hebrews quotes the hymn (Heb. 1:6; 10:30), but also Paul in his letter to the Romans (10:19; 12:19; 15:10). References to it are made in Rom. 11:11; I Cor. 10:20,22; Phil. 2:15; Lk. 21:22; Rev. 6:10; 10:5; 18:20; 19:2. The fact that John sees the victorious ones in heaven singing the song of Moses (Rev. 15:3) perhaps reflects liturgical use in the Church on earth.[3]

The Hymn of Moses included in the Odes following the Greek Psalter presents the reading in Deut. 32:43b (Odes) which is identical to the quotation in Heb. 1:6b. This reading is testified by the LXX Codex A (except for the addition of the definite article preceding the noun ἄγγελοι), 55, and Justin Martyr.[4]

---

[1] "The mother of the seven children also uttered these righteous sayings to her children : ... When these sons were grown up, their father died ... Nor indeed did he forget, in his instruction, the song that Moses taught, which says, 'I kill and I make alive; for that is thy life and the length of thy days.'" IV Macc. 18:6,9,18, and 19. (Ed. and transl. M. Hadas, *The Third and Fourth Books of Maccabees*, pp. 239ff.). Also cf. H. Schneider, "Die biblischen Oden im christlichen Altertum," *Bibl.* 30 (1949), p. 31.

[2] When referring to the work of Philo, we have depended on the edition and translation of the *LCL*. Philo, *Quod det. pot.*, (xxx) 114, *LCL*, Vol. II, pp. 278f.; Philo, *Leg. Alleg.* III, (xxxiv) 105, *LCL*, Vol. I, pp. 370f.; Philo, *De Plant.*, (xiv) 59, *LCL*, Vol. III, p. 398. Cf. Schneider, *Bibl.* 30 (1949), pp. 31ff. This Hymn was used in the Temple and the Synagogue on equal standing with the Psalms of David, and its concluding verses were even considered and interpreted messianically in Jewish circles. Cf. F. Delitzsch, *Comm.*, p. 38; E. Böhl, *Die Alttestl. Citate*, p. 263; F. W. Grosheide, *Comm.*, p. 69.

[3] "Die himmlische Liturgie wird wohl auch an dieser Stelle ein Abbild der irdischen Liturgie der Urchristen sein; also werden die ersten Christen die Ode des Moses in einer freien, christlichen Nachgestaltung gesungen haben." Schneider, *Bibl.* 30(1949), p. 35.

[4] Just. Dial. 130. Although Westcott is mistaken in saying, "But the exact phrase is found in the Vatican text of an addition made to the Hebrew in Deut. 32:43 by the LXX version..." (only Codex F and the Lucian recension of the LXX agree with the reading in Hebrews and Just. Dial.), he is correct in commenting : "If (as seems correct) the gloss was found in the current text of the LXX in the apostolic age, it is most natural to suppose that the writer of the Epistle took the words directly from the version of Deuteronomy." *Comm.*, pp. 19f; also see J. Moffatt, *Comm.*, p. 11.

On the other hand, Codex A (LXX) in Deut. 32:43b (Odes) may have received the definite article under influence of Ps. 96:7 (LXX), where the same wording is found, and which may provide an explanation for the additional οἱ in the reading of Codex Alexandrinus.

Since the LXX passage of Deut. 32:43b does not have a known Hebrew text as basis, it may well be that the second line of Deut. 32:43 (Odes) has been brought about by interpolation from Ps. 97:7 (MT).[1] This line is in harmony with Ps. 97:7, for the Hebrew reading also lacks the definite article before the word אלהים.

With the aid of the following columns the various changes may be verified.

Heb. 1:6b	Deut. 32:43b	Deut.32:43b(Odes) Cod. A, 55, Just. M.	Ps. 96:7 (LXX)	Ps. 97:7 (MT)
καὶ	καὶ	καὶ	—	—
προσκυνη-σάτωσαν	προσ...σάτωσαν	προσ...σάτωσαν	προσκυνή-σατε	השתחוו
αὐτῷ	αὐτῷ	αὐτῷ	αὐτῷ	לו
πάντες	πάντες	πάντες	πάντες	כל
ἄγγελοι	υἱοὶ	(οἱ) ἄγγελοι	οἱ ἄγγελοι	אלהים
θεοῦ	θεοῦ	θεοῦ	αὐτοῦ	—

Of course by checking the above columns the obvious conclusion may be drawn that the quotation (Heb. 1:6b) and Deut. 32:43b (Odes) correspond. In view of the agreement between Heb. 1:6b and the Deut. passage, testified by the reading of 55 and Justin Martyr, and flanked by the support of Ps. 97:7, it may be assumed that the quotation has been part of the Hymn

---

[1] "... Qumran has provided us with a Hebrew text which ... gives both halves (c d) of the second line of v. 41. This new text ... has so much in common with our Greek that it represents its *Vorlage*, both where the Greek is superior to our Hebrew and where it is not. ... The most astonishing among the instances is the line borrowed from Ps. 97⁷ in exactly the same form, but with the initial ו. We may therefore assume that the whole of the Greek verse 43, with the exception of lines 2f., was translated from a Hebrew text. ... Last verses of hymns are easily interpolated from other parts of Scriptures," P. Katz, "Quot. from Deut." ZNW 49 (1958), p. 219. Cf. also his *Philo's Bible*, pp. 21, 144; and Z. Frankel, *Vorstudien zu der Septuaginta*, pp. 66f.; P. Winter, ZAW 67, NF 26 (1955), p. 48.

of Moses (Odes), which was securely incorporated in the liturgy of the Church.

Psalm 104:4 (Heb. 1:7)

This nature psalm was quite familiar to Jewish ears. It was a psalm used in the liturgy of the Synagogue on Friday evening and on the Sabbath morning.[1] Both the NT writers and the Early Church Fathers give evidence that this psalm was not unknown. In the Synoptics all three Evangelists make reference to verse 12 (Mt. 13:32; Mk. 4:32; Lk. 13:19), while the Apocalypse describes the great multitude praising God by the use of verse 35 (Rev. 19:1,3,6). Verse 4 is found in I Clem. 36,3 within the context of a Scripture portion borrowed from Heb. 1; in Irenaeus III,30,1 it is interwoven in a passage referring to the creation of heaven and earth.

For several reasons the author to the Hebrews has employed the LXX version. First, Targum Jonathan already indicates that some difficulty prevailed in the correct understanding of the double objects with the Hebrew verb עשה. The LXX was partaker of this same tradition, for instead of having the correct translation of the Hebrew text, "Who maketh winds his messengers," it has switched the two objects like Targum Jonathan, and reads, "Who maketh his angels winds."[2] Also the author to the Hebrews uses the wording of this tradition known to his readers. Second, the last two words of the quotation deviate from the LXX reading of the Codices ℵ B. Whereas Heb. 1:7 reads πυρὸς φλόγα, the two Codices have πῦρ φλέγον. Codex A^c (LXX) may either show a transitional stage, or, what seems more logical, may perpetrate an error by giving the words πυρὸς (φλέγα!).[3] The reading πυρὸς φλόγα seems to be an integral part of the NT language. By checking its usage in the NT Scriptures we learn that πῦρ is found with the word φλόξ six times (Acts 7:30,

---

[1] Werner, *Sacred Bridge*, p. 150.

[2] "Dafür ist bezeichnend, dass nicht bloss die LXX (und ihnen folgend der Hebräerbrief), sondern auch die altrabbinischen Gelehrten durchaus der Fassung folgen." Str.-Bill., III, p. 678.

[3] Katz, *ZNW* 46 (1955), p. 135, calls the variant in Codex A (LXX) a backreading of Heb. 1:7. Also see Grosheide, *Comm.*, p. 70; and Thomas, *Use of the Septuagint*, p. 83.

φλογὶ πυρός; II Thess. 1:8, πυρὶ φλογός; Heb. 1:7, πυρὸς φλόγα; Rev. 1:14, φλὸξ πυρός; Rev. 2:18, φλόγα πυρός; Rev. 19:12, φλὸξ πυρός), but πῦρ is never found with the modifier φλέγον. Third, it is clear that the author did not try to give his own translation of the MT, but presented the text which was prevalent in the Early Church. In the worship services "one singer only chanted the psalmody, as it is stated unanimously by the Church Fathers."[1] For reasons of proper balance and rhythm the term πυρὸς φλόγα, harmonizing with the preceding πνεύματα, may have been part of the liturgy of the Church.

Though we must recognize the literary qualities of the author, especially in balanced constructions and varying introductory formulas,[2] we should be willing to give credit where credit is due. Since the writer of Hebrews apparently has borrowed a quotation which was in vogue in the Early Church, it seems best to accredit the proper wording of the text as known in that day to the liturgy of the Church.

Psalm 45:6–7 (Heb. 1:8–9)

The Jewish Rabbis designated this psalm as a nuptial hymn composed for the occasion of the marriage of a king of Israel. Yet, Targum Jonathan, in paraphrasing the third verse, ascribes it to the Messiah: "Thy beauty, O king Messiah, is greater than that of the sons of men."[3] Also the Early Church Fathers give ample indication that it circulated in the Church. Justin Martyr, and also Irenaeus, quote the verses 6 and 7 three times (Just. Dial. 63,56,86; and Iren. III,6,1; IV,33,11; Epid. 47).

The text, except for a few details, is identical to the LXX. The deviations in Hebrews consist of the addition of the article τῆς; the switch of the article from the second to the first ῥάβδος; the

---

[1] Werner, *Sacred Bridge*, p. 131. "The term psalmody is understood to mean a type of musical setting which is governed by a coordination of syntactic and melodic accents," *Ibid.*, p. 129.

[2] For a scholarly compilation of literary devices in Hebrews see Büchel, *TSK*, 1906, pp. 508–511.

[3] Our translation of Targum Jonathan on Ps. 45:3. Cf. Str.-Bill., III, pp. 679f. Vis, *Mess. Psalm Quotations*, p. 46, concludes that the psalm was originally non-messianic. But see Delitzsch, *Comm.*, p. 33, who calls it "ein Messiaslied der Gemeinde."

replacing of σου by αὐτοῦ; and, finally, the addition of the conjunction καί, which may have been the cause of these minor differences. All in all, the addition of the connective brings about a balanced structure of the two clauses.

It is easy to regard the reading αὐτοῦ as an error of an early copyist,[1] but since it is attested by the MSS P[46] ℵ B, the word may be original. If αὐτοῦ is taken as the correct reading, we must explain the antecedent of the word. Since in both clauses the copula is lacking, we may consider ὁ θρόνος σου and ἡ ῥάβδος τῆς to be subjects of the respective verbs.[2]

Besides these observations we should notice that in the first clause the 2nd pers. sing. is expressed while in the following clause it is the 3rd pers. sing. It is the additional connective that separates the two clauses, with the result that in the first one the vocative ὁ θεός strengthens the 2nd pers. sing. by its very exclamation, and in the second the genitive αὐτοῦ upholds the 3rd pers. sing. In other words, two particular thoughts are mentioned: one addressing the Son directly as God, and the other in the form of an afterthought referring to the kingdom of the Son. While the conjunction "and" balances the two clauses, it also places them over against each other in order to call attention to the content of the individual statements.

The next clause resumes the same subject — 2nd pers. sing. — and continues it until the end of the quotation. Although the

---

[1] This is the opinion of H. Windisch, *Comm.*, p. 16, but since P[46] has strengthened the reading of the Codices Vaticanus and Sinaiticus, we may not dismiss a variant as a possible error when in all probability it represents the original text. Also Thomas, *Use of the Septuagint*, p. 22, takes αὐτοῦ as the text employed by the author to the Hebrews. Having accepted this reading, Thomas tries to solve the question of its antecedent. He concludes that the possessive pronoun must refer to the appellation *God*, and that this name should be translated as a nominative. Thus he translates Heb. 1:8, "*Thy* (the Son's) throne is God (the Father) . . . *and* the scepter of uprightness (the Son's) is the scepter of his (the Father's) kingdom." This solution for the antecedent appears quite acceptable, were it not for the fact that the addition of the conjunction "and" fits remarkably well into the pattern of the author's recurring expressions *and again, and*. The use of the conjunction "and" may be considered equivalent to "and" in Heb. 1:10 (also see Heb. 2:13; 10:30; 10:38).

[2] "The article sometimes distinguishes the subject from the predicate in a copulative sentence." H. A. Dana and J. R. Mantey, *Grammar*, p. 148.

Son has been given the appellation "God," he is ordained into office by God himself. Hence "thy God" (Heb. 1:9b) should not be taken as a vocative, but rather as the nominative; "therefore God, thy God, hath anointed thee with the oil of gladness above thy fellows." [1]

Psalm 102:25,27 (Heb. 1:10–12)

In Jewish interpretation this psalm described the unchangeableness of God, who has created heaven and earth. However, also in the Early Church it was not unknown, for Irenaeus expressly uses a quotation found in the *"centesimo primo psalmo"* (Iren. IV,3,1).[2]

It is evident that the author to the Hebrews, prompted by his introduction (1:2,3), wants to apply this particular quotation to Christ. He replaces the pronoun σύ by making it the first word in the sentence where it receives all the emphasis necessary. What formerly was brought to bear upon Yahweh, may now be said of Christ.

The question may be raised whether the unknown writer knew the Hebrew language and whether he has used it in these verses. Although the verb διαμένεις is in the present tense,[3] while the LXX shows the future which corresponds to the MT, the author is not attempting to render another translation, for he supposedly wrote the verbal form without the accent mark. But if the author had the ability to employ the Hebrew, why did he not show it in this quotation? If he were acquainted with the Hebrew tongue, he could have corrected the LXX at several places. First there is the addition of κύριε; next we find the plural ἔργα instead of the singular; and also the conjunction καί is added before ὡσεί. Apart from a few minor deviations caused by reasons of emphasis and style, the LXX version known in the Early Church, is cited and not a new translation of the MT.

The MSS P⁴⁶ ℵ B A D* 1739 arm, which in this combination

---

[1] Cf. Westcott, *Comm.*, p. 26.

[2] We may assume that the LXX numbering of the psalms must stem from an early date.

[3] Delitzsch, *Comm.*, p. 36, intimates that it is not necessary to indicate the future tense by means of an accent, "da διαμένεις das hebr. Fut. mindestens ebenso gut ausdrückt."

are quite important, show that the addition of ὡς ἱμάτιον belongs to the text. If this reading is original, we may see the literary scholar at work. By adding the extra words the author is balancing three clauses, each having a verb with a noun. If we take the reading ἑλίξεις to be correct, the first part of verse 12 displays three different verbs with two nouns — ἱμάτιον alternating. The sentence is given a more flowing style without changing the meaning. The verb ἑλίξεις may have been an allusion to a similar text in Isa. 34:4 in the LXX version, where the same verb is used — "and the skies roll up like a scroll."

Psalm 110:1 (Heb. 1:13)

In early Rabbinic literature which treats the period contemporaneous with the rise of Christianity, Ps. 110 was applied to Melchizedek who blessed Abram. According to Justin Martyr, the Jews of his time assigned the psalm to King Hezekiah (Dial. 33,83). Yet the question is posed, how was it understood in Church and Synagogue at the time the apostles went forth from the city of Jerusalem? And the unequivocal answer is, messianically. After the conflict between Christianity and Judaism began to take on harsher forms, various Scripture passages were reinterpreted in Jewish circles. The revising of Ps. 110 may be ascribed to Rabbi Ishmael ben Elisha, who died *c.* 150 A.D. Due to his vigorous activity messianic interpretations were taboo in the Synagogue for more than two centuries.[1] Yet, in spite of this restriction, Jewish literature is not silent on the messianic purport of this psalm. Apocalyptic writings of that age make references to the Chosen One sitting on the throne of glory; cf. Enoch 45,3; 51,3; 55,4; 61,8; 62,3–5; 69,27–29.[2]

Also the Early Church Fathers afford ample proof of the messianic nature of Ps. 110. Clement of Rome, recording the

---

[1] Str.-Bill., IV, 1, pp. 452–465, especially pp. 453, 459f. In his "Exkurs: Der 110. Psalm in der altrabbinischen Literatur" Billerbeck convincingly proves that this psalm was considered messianic in Jewish circles during the first century A.D. Vis, *Mess. Psalms Quotations*, p. 78, attributes the messianic interpretation of Ps. 110 to the early Christians. "But in so doing their inference was historically incorrect and Jewish tradition gave them no precedent for their exegesis of the Psalm."

[2] Michel, *Comm.*, p. 59.

first verse of this psalm in the context of a passage borrowed from Heb. 1, quotes it with Ps. 2:7, showing most clearly its messianic tenor (I Clem. 36,5). Justin Martyr cites it not only at several places in his Dialogue with Trypho (32,33,36,56,82, and 127), but even in his Apology (I,45). Irenaeus shows evidence of it in all his writings (II,28,7; III,6,1; III,10,6; III,12,2; III,16,3; Epid. 48 and 85). For completeness' sake, Barnabas 12,10 should be mentioned yet. Truly, Ps. 110:1 takes a most prominent place in the writings of the Early Church Fathers.

The NT authors show thorough familiarity with this verse by referring to it indirectly in the Synoptic Gospels, in the Pauline Epistles, and in Hebrews.[1] It is quoted directly in all three Synoptics, Mt. 22:44, Mk. 12:36, and Lk. 20:42–43, in Acts 2:34–35, and in Heb. 1:13. In the Gospel accounts Jesus applies this psalm to himself by teaching the Pharisees an exegetical lesson based on Ps. 110:1. All those present silently agreed to the interpretation given. If another explanation had been prevalent, the Pharisees would have been quick in replying. Now they were silent.

In addition to the correct wording according to the LXX, the phrase ἐκάθισεν ἐν δεξιᾷ was also known in the Early Church. It may be that the form δεξιᾷ originated under influence of the MT which has the singular. The author to the Hebrews uses both constructions in his Epistle. However, a more important textual tradition should be noted in the last part of the quotation. While Matthew and Mark are the only ones to use the word ὑποκάτω, Luke has the word ὑποπόδιον, which is the reading identical to the LXX, Hebrews, and the Early Church Fathers (cf. Lk. 20:42–43 and Acts 2:34–35). This is the second time that Luke gives evidence of another textual tradition current within the Church (cf. Lk. 3:22 v. l. and Acts 13:33). Hebrews appears to be in the stream which, perhaps, may be classified as that of the more Hellenistic type. Since this is the tradition to which the recipients of the Epistle to the Hebrews were

---

[1] Allusions to this text are found in Mk. 14:62; Acts 7:55; Rom. 8:34; and it is echoed in Eph. 1:20; Col. 3:1; Heb. 1:3; 8:1; 10:12; 12:2; and I Pet. 3:22. "It seems clear, therefore, that this particular verse was one of the fundamental texts of the *kerugma*, underlying almost all the various developments of it, and cited independently in Mark, Acts, Paul, Hebrews, and I Peter." Dodd, *Acc. to the Scr.*, p. 35.

accustomed, it is understandable that the author approaches them in their own terms.

Psalm 8:4–6 (Heb. 2:6–8a)

In the Synagogue this psalm was known to express the frailty of man. According to the Rabbis the angels used its words to air their contempt for human beings when Moses went up to receive the Law at Mount Sinai.[1] Ps. 8 "is not, and has never been accounted by the Jews to be, directly Messianic."[2] Also from the side of the Early Church Fathers we meet nothing but utter silence.

Yet the NT authors reveal that the psalm was understood in a Christological sense. Not only does Jesus apply the second verse to himself when he answered the Pharisees (Mt. 21:16); also Paul and the author to the Hebrews give the sixth verse a decidedly messianic tone when they cite it in connection with Ps. 110:1 (I Cor. 15:25,27; Eph. 1:20,22; Heb. 1:13 and 2:6–8). That these authors depended on each other for source material and interpretation is entirely out of the question. "The probability is that (Paul) and the author to the Hebrews follow a common tradition."[3]

For this quotation in the Epistle to the Hebrews the LXX has been employed. The reading $τί$, which is a faithful translation of the MT, appears to be the original word.[4] Except for the omission of the clause "and didst set him over the works of thy hands," the whole quotation is word-for-word identical to the

---

[1] Str.-Bill., III, p. 681.

[2] Westcott, *Comm.*, p. 42.

[3] Dodd, *Acc. to the Scr.*, p. 33. He also mentions the allusion to I Pet. 3:22, but since this reference has been classified as an echo of Ps. 110 (see p. 35), possible evidence for Ps. 8 seems rather vague. Likewise Rev. 5:12, which Dodd calls "remoter influence of this *testimonium* in the hymn to Christ," is very weak attestation of Ps. 8.

[4] G. Zuntz, *The Text of the Epistles*, pp. 48f., contends that the reading $τίς$ is needed to substantiate the Christological interpretation, but the proposed reading is weak, and the passage itself does not need this additional support. Similar comments are expressed by Thomas, *Use of the Septuagint*, p. 217 and esp. p. 219.

LXX.¹ Of course it is true that the LXX at some places in this passage is not too accurate in giving the exact rendition of the Hebrew text. The author does not seem to be interested in retranslating the Hebrew, if he had any knowledge of this language; for Ps. 8 is known to his readers in its Greek translation of the LXX. The Hebrew word מְעַט which in Ps. 8 can only have the meaning of degree may be understood of time in chapter 2 of this Epistle. The word אלהים has been translated by ἀγγέλους — which is also the case in Targum Jonathan with the Aramaic equivalent מלאכיא. Aquila, Symmachus, and Theodotion have returned to the proper rendering, θεόν. In the Early Church the phrase "Son of Man" was generally used to designate Christ; yet at all times the nouns were preceded by the definite articles — ὁ υἱὸς τοῦ ἀνθρώπου.² Be that as it may, the author applies the quotation to Christ, thereby indirectly showing that Jesus in his human state is the υἱὸς ἀνθρώπου. As a last example, the omission of the two conjunctions in Heb. 2:7 may be mentioned. In the

---

¹ Moffatt is of the opinion that the author "left it out as incompatible with 1:10...." *Comm.*, p. 22. Thomas, *Use of the Septuagint*, p. 37, remarks that the writer of the Epistle could not use the line from Ps. 8:6a (LXX 8:7a) due to his quoting from Ps. 102 previously: "... the author had already said that 'the Son' had participated in the act of creation (1:10). To avoid this difficulty, he left this phrase out of the quotation."

² Except for John 5:27 the phrase occurs with the definite articles in the Gospels, when referring to Christ. Hence E. Böhl's claim, that the words υἱὸς ἀνθρώπου "die gewöhnlichste Benennung Christi in den Evangelien waren," is unfounded, *Die Alttestl. Citate*, p. 274. F. J. Foakes and K. Lake, *Beginnings*, I, I, p. 380, note that the phrase *Son of Man* (with the definite articles) does not occur in the Epistles of Paul. Hence they pose the question: "Is not this because he was too good a Grecian to translate *Bar-naṣha* by so impossible a phrase as ὁ υἱὸς τοῦ ἀνθρώπου, and rendered it idiomatically by ὁ ἄνθρωπος ?" This question, however seems to be enough for Thomas, *Use of the Septuagint*, p. 34, to assume that the author to the Hebrews in quoting Ps. 8 understood the terms *man* and *son of man* to refer to Christ, for he suggests: "If this is true, then in this quotation from Psalm 8 are two parallel terms for the self-designation of Jesus...." The term *son of man* (without the definite articles) in Dan. 7:13 is a prophecy referring to Christ, and as recorded in Mt. 24:30; 26:64 par. fulfilled by Christ. But Ps. 8 or any of the places in Ezekiel, where the phrase occurs, may not be placed on the same level with Dan. 7:13, because Christ has never identified himself as clearly with these references as with Dan. 7:13. See F. W. Grosheide, *Zoon des Menschen*, (1921), p. 15.

MT we find a ו before תחסרהו, likewise before כבוד. Perhaps for stylistic reasons the LXX and Hebrews have not included the Greek counterpart.

Psalm 22:23 (Heb. 2:12)

The messianic import of Ps. 22 is echoed throughout the NT in a series of quotations and references.

> The psalm as a whole was clearly regarded as a source of testimonies to the passion of Christ, and His ultimate triumph, and probably from an early date, since it is woven into the texture of the Passion-narrative, and used in writings almost certainly independent of one another. Once again, the sufferings are described as if those of an individual, but with verse 22 interest shifts to the *ecclesia*, and the poem culminates in the proclamation of the universal kingdom of God.[1]

The Jews in the Synagogue of old sang this psalm — and especially the last verses — as messianic only to express their hope in the repentance of all Gentiles, without mentioning the person of the Messiah. In all early Rabbinic literature there is no indication that Ps. 22 was considered messianic. This may be due to the violent reaction against Christianity, for a Christological interpretation was lacking until the beginning of the 10th century.[2]

When in fact God is the speaker in the first chapter of Hebrews, the quotations found in 2:12 and 13 are put in the mouth of Jesus. The words of Ps. 22 spoken by Jesus are a faithful translation of the MT and are identical to the LXX version, except for the first word. Instead of giving the LXX wording "I will tell" the author has chosen the word "I will declare," which corresponds to the MT.[3]

---

[1] Dodd, *Acc. to the Scr.*, pp. 97f.

[2] Str.-Bill., II, pp. 574ff. Already Justin Martyr (Dial. 97) indicates that the Jews in his days had rejected the messianic interpretation of Ps. 22.

[3] Padva's plea for the Hebrew verb אבשרה ("I will proclaim") as basis for ἀπαγγελῶ, because "on raconte une histoire, une nouvelle, mais on ne raconte pas un nom," is put to non-effect. According to Brown, Driver, Briggs, the verb ספר in the Piel is used for rehearsing a name or praise in Ex. 9:16; Ps. 9:15; Ps. 96:3; Ps. 102:22; I Chron. 16:23; Jer. 51:10 (28:10 LXX). In all these places the LXX translates this Hebrew verb with a form of the verb ἀγγέλλω. Whenever ספר is used with the accusative

Again we are faced with the question whether the writer of this Epistle had any knowledge of the Hebrew tongue. At this point we cannot come to a conclusive answer, for we do not know whether *1)* the word ἀπαγγελῶ goes back to a Hebrew verb other than אספרה of the MT, or whether *2)* the author renders his own translation or else the Early Church used this psalm with the word ἀπαγγελῶ as part of its liturgy. Since the Easter vigil can approximately be dated rather early, it may be that Ps. 22 was sung before or after the reading of Scripture portions.[1]

Isaiah 8:17 — II Samuel 22:3 (Heb. 2:13a)

Seldom are the words of Isa. 8:17 cited in Jewish literature, and when they are found the reference is only to the prophet himself.[2] The Early Church Fathers as well as the NT are silent in respect to this text; only in Heb. 2:13 the verses 17 and 18 of Isa. 8 are quoted.

Although the truth of this observation cannot be denied, we must not be blinded by one detail. If the context of the quotation's source is taken into consideration, much light will be spread upon the passage in question. There is not merely an abundance of references to verses out of chapters 6 to 9 of Isaiah throughout the NT Scriptures, but many a verse is quoted directly.

The reflection of the hymn of the seraphim (Isa. 6) in Rev. 4:8 may even be an indication of possible liturgical use in the Early Church. The verses 9 and 10 of Isa. 6 are quoted in Mt. 13:14,15 and parallels, as well as in Acts 28:26,27, where Luke cites it as a last quotation of the apostle Paul directed against the Jews.

---

alone and it refers to the rehearsing of praise, then the Greek διηγέομαι is used as well as a form of ἀγγέλλω. It is rather simplistic to say with Riggenbach and Moffatt that the author to the Hebrews used a synonym; references are given to Judges 13:6 and Ps. 55:18, but in these two passages the Hebrew verb in question is not employed. Padva, *Les Citations*, p. 49. Brown, Driver, Briggs, *Lexicon*. E. Riggenbach, *Comm.*, p. 51 n. 28. Moffatt, *Comm.*, p. 33.

[1] Melitus of Sardes, who died *c.* 195 A.D., refers in an Easter Vigil sermon to the reading of Scripture portions out of the book of Exodus. Schneider, *Bibl.* 30(1949), p. 37.

[2] Str.-Bill., III, p. 683.

Isa. 7 provides the words of verse 14 which Matthew uses to illustrate the fulfilment of this messianic prophecy. In Isa. 8:8,10 the keyword "Immanuel" is given, which has its roots in the prophecy of 7:14, and finds its echo in the NT. Verse 14 of chapter 8, which refers to the stone of stumbling, is quoted in combination with Isa. 28:16 in Rom. 9:32,33, where it receives a definite messianic coloring. Also the author to the Hebrews furnishes the Christological interpretation when he quotes the verses 17 and 18 of Isa. 8. The application of Isa. 8:23; 9:1 to the ministering Christ is most clearly shown in the Gospel according to Matthew (4:15–16). "...Isa. 6:1—9:7 may have formed, for early Christian students of the Old Testament, a single complex unit of prophecy." [1]

In early Christian literature of the first two centuries references to the reading of Scripture portions are few and in the form of mere factual statements. "Why this silence and this lack of detailed explanation in an age which, as a whole, was not averse to loquacious reports? Although the Jewish sources are a little more explanatory, they too, are far from verbose. The answer is that one does not discuss well-known matters of fact: the Old Testament pericope was firmly embedded in the liturgy of the Synagogue, which in turn served as the general pattern for the primitive Church." [2]

The word order of the quotation is slightly different in Heb. 2:13 than in the LXX version. This may be due to the addition of the pronoun ἐγώ which, by taking all the emphasis, has drawn the main verb to itself. The essential meaning of the text remains the same; there is only a shift of emphasis.

The words according to the LXX version are also found in the Hymn of David recorded in II Sam. 22. Since this hymn is still found in a list of biblical odes registered by Origen,[3] it evidently was in general use among the Early Christians. Gradually, because of the doublet in Ps. 18, it was eliminated from the liturgies of the Church.

---

[1] Dodd, *Acc. to the Scr.*, p. 81; also pp. 78f.
[2] Werner, *Sacred Bridge*, p. 58.
[3] Schneider, *Bibl.* 30(1949), pp. 51f; *GCS*, Orig. Vol. 7, pp. 501f.; Orig. Vol. 8, pp. 27f., 80–83.

Isaiah 8:18 (Heb. 2:13b)

Although there is a possibility that the author cited the verses 17 and 18 of Isa. 8 from memory, we may not lose sight of the fact that familiarity with the passages perhaps stems from regular use in the worship services. Since the connecting formula "and again" is a natural literary device of the writer to the Hebrews, its presence between the two quotations may not be regarded as a possible slip on the part of an early scribe.[1] The author calls attention to a well-known text which may be drawn from two sources (Isa. 8 and II Sam. 22), and continues with a second quotation taken from one of them. A similar mode of operation is found in Heb. 10:30.

The word order is identical to that of the LXX; yet there are a few MSS of the LXX version which, in faithfulness to the MT, have the reading ἔδωκέν μοι. Seeing that the translations of Aquila, Symmachus, and Theodotion have rendered ὁ κύριος for the Hebrew יהוה in this text, we may raise the question whether the author's ὁ θεός shows mere conformity to the LXX, or whether perhaps ὁ θεός was used for exegetical reasons.

Numbers 12:7 (Heb. 3:2,5)

The quotation in Heb. 3:2 and 5 is neither direct nor is it identical to the LXX version in word order. Although the reference to Num. 12:7 is only found once in the NT, its words, however, were quite well-known among the early Christians. Since the Early Church Fathers allude to its phraseology repeatedly,[2] as a saying associated with Moses, we may assume that the text circulated in the Early Church.

In the reference the word θεράπων plays an important role. It is a unique title of honor ascribed to Moses and should be distinguished clearly from synonyms like δοῦλος, οἰκέτης, and

---

[1] Singe, *Hebrews*, p. 17, is of the opinion that "A scribe took the first half to come from II Sam. 22:3 . . . . Thinking that there were two citations, one from II Sam. and the other from Isaiah, in a moment of misguided pedantry he separated the two with the words 'and again.' But Hebrews intended the passage to stand as a single quotation."

[2] I Clem. 17,5; 43,1; 51,5; Just. Dial. 46,56,79,130; Iren. III,6,5. Specifically I Clem. 4,12; 43,1; 51,3,5; 53,5; Barn. 14,4.

παῖς. Whereas θεράπων is often found in connection with Moses in the OT, the word is nowhere used in the NT except in Heb. 3:5. In the literature of the Early Church the noun is always applied to Moses. We may assume that Irenaeus (III,6,5) had the same word in mind when he translated it by *servus*. It is readily seen that this indirect saying appropriated for itself a significant place in the Early Church.[1]

Psalm 95:7-11 (Heb. 3:7-11)

Except for the Epistle to the Hebrews all the NT books are silent in respect to the 95th Psalm. Nor are there any references to it in the writings of the Early Church Fathers.

Yet its use in the Synagogue was well-established, for the psalm was regarded as a preamble of services on Friday evening and Sabbath morning. This practice undoubtedly stemmed from the Temple ritual which in later years was gradually taken over in the Synagogue. Pss. 95 and 96 were known as the psalms of the invitation to worship.[2]

It is an accepted fact that the quotation had a LXX version as basis and not a Hebrew text. This can be proven at several places, e.g., the use of ἐάν, the plural καρδίας instead of the singular, the translation of the names Massah and Meribah to abstract nouns, the plural ἔργα instead of the singular, the use of ἀεί and πλανῶνται, ὡς for אשר, and εἰ for אם. In all these deviations the quotation in Hebrews is identical to the LXX.

Nevertheless, the wording of Heb. 3:7-11 shows some variations to the LXX version of Ps. 95:7-11. The harsh anacoluthon ἐδοκίμασαν is removed by ἐν δοκιμασίᾳ; the spelling τεσσαράκοντα has become τεσσεράκοντα current in NT times;[3] the phrase

---

[1] On the authority of P. Drews the term πιστὸς θεράπων is to be found in the Apost. Const. and exists as a liturgical formula. *Untersuchungen über die sogen. klementinische Liturgie*, pp. 49f.

[2] Werner, *Sacred Bridge*, p. 131; Elbogen, *Gottesdienst*, pp. 82, 108, 113. Also from the earliest Christian liturgies it may be ascertained that the 95th Psalm was used in worship services on Sundays when the Eucharist was celebrated (cf. Werner, pp. 145, 157).

[3] "The spelling τεσσεράκοντα for τεσσαράκοντα is adopted in all NT occurrences of the word, but it is by no means common in the papyri during i-iii/A.D." J. H. Moulton and G. Milligan, *The Vocabulary of the Greek Testament*, p. 631. Also see Moulton, *Grammar*, Vol. I, pp. 45f. A. T. Robertson, *Grammar*, p. 183.

τῇ γενεᾷ ἐκείνῃ, which is never found in NT language, has been replaced by the familiar τῇ γενεᾷ ταυτῇ;[1] and the literal translation καὶ αὐτοί has yielded to the smooth αὐτοὶ δέ. All these variations, perhaps brought about by constant usage in the Synagogue and probably the Early Church, have given the quotation a polished form molded by the language spoken in that day.

We may conclude at this point that the various textual divergencies are not so much the work of the author, but most likely have been brought about by constant usage in places of worship. It appears plausible that the writer has taken the quotation in its present form out of the ritual of worship services conducted in the Greek tongue.

Genesis 2:2 (Heb. 4:4)

Again, except for the Epistle to the Hebrews, the NT and the Early Church Fathers make no reference to the quotation out of Gen. 2. Yet it had a definite place in the Synogague service on Friday evening, which marked the beginning of the Jewish Sabbath.[2]

The contention that the author selected this text for the sake of the word κατάπαυσις, which is also found in Ps. 95:11, is a bit one-sided.[3] He may have been motivated in the choice of this verse by the word κατάπαυσις, but it seems more acceptable that the writer borrowed from an existing ritual in which Ps. 95 and Gen. 2:2 were used.[4]

---

[1] Especially Jesus in his discourse uses this phrase exclusively, *e.g.*, Mt. 11:16; 12:41, 42, 45; Mk. 8:12; Lk. 11:29.

[2] "Gen. 2:1-3, which on Friday evening is not cantillated according to the scriptural accents, but chanted in one of the most typical prayer modes of Judaism." Werner, *Sacred Bridge*, pp. 515f. Cf. Elbogen, *Gottesdienst*, pp. 110, 115; Padva, *Les Citations*, pp. 63, 100; Spicq, I, *Introd.*, p. 336.

[3] The key-word κατάπαυσις in Ps. 95:11 and Gen. 2:2 naturally strengthens Harder's hypothesis, but if the author to the Hebrews depended on a key-word, more evidence for the phenomenon would be expected in this Epistle. G. Harder, "Septuagintazitate," *Theologia Viatorum*, pp. 35f., 40. Also see Michel, *Comm.*, p. 112, "Durch die exegetische Methode des Stichwortes werden beiden Zitate miteinander verknüpft."

[4] "Ps. 95 et Gen. 2:1-3 se trouvent dans les recueils de prières du Samedi soir dans le même ordre que dans nôtre épître." Padva, *Les Citations*, p. 63.

As the primary speaker in the 95th Psalm is God, so the subject of Gen. 2:2 is ὁ θεός. Since this text begins with the subject ὁ θεός, and the quotation is taken from the last part of Gen. 2:2, it is natural to supply the subject when half the passage is cited. Seeing that Philo in referring to this text has the same addition,[1] we may either speak of normal procedure in applying grammatical rules, or we may conclude that both authors have drawn the quotation from a common source.

Gen. 2:2 is identical to the LXX version except for the addition of ἐν. This is rather insignificant, for the time expression τῇ ἡμέρᾳ is found with and without the preposition at various places in the LXX.

Psalm 110:4 (Heb. 5:6; 7:17,21)

Once again the author shows the close relationship between Ps. 2 and Ps. 110. Whereas in chapter 1 of his Epistle the series of seven quotations begins with Ps. 2:7 and ends with Ps. 110:1, here the fourth verse is quoted, separated from Ps. 2:7 by the introductory formula, "as he saith also in another" (ἑτέρῳ sc. ψαλμῷ).

The 110th Psalm and especially its fourth verse is fundamental to the Epistle. The first part of this verse is only found in 7:21; the second half is quoted several times (5:6; 7:17,21).

Except for the omission of εἰ, the quotation is taken verbally out of the LXX. In spite of the fact that P[46] shows the reading εἰ in all the three places where the text occurs, this does not take away the authority of the *lectio magis ardua*. The addition of εἰ may have occurred under influence of the LXX version.

Hoskier, for all the labor spent on his learned project to prove that the reading ἐπευξ in P[46] is the correct word in Heb. 5:6 rather than ἱερεύς, has failed to notice that ἐπευξ, presumably derived from ἐπεύχομαι, and translated "precentor," is a hapax legomenon in all known Greek literature.[2]

---

[1] Cf. Michel, *Comm.*, p. 111.
[2] H. C. Hoskier, *Text of the Epistle to the Hebrews in the Chester Beatty Papyrus*, pp. 3ff. It is Zuntz who asks the sobering question, "Was the scribe used to Latin P and mixed it up with Greek P?" Zuntz, *The Text of the Epistles*, p. 253 n. 7.

Genesis 22:16,17 (Heb. 6:13,14)

Gen. 22, which records the sacrifice of Isaac, was a passage known to Jew and Christian alike. It was read not only on the Jewish New Year's day, but also during the services of the early Christian Easter vigil. "... The Christological overtones prevail by far over the Jewish tradition, but the Isaac portion evidently dates back to ancient and genuine customs of the Synagogue." [1]

While Gen. 22:17 is directly quoted by Clement of Rome (I Clem. 32,2) and Justin Martyr (Dial. 120), definite allusions to it are found even in the NT itself. The Song of Mary and the Song of Zachariah reflect something of the ancient promise given to the patriarch Abraham (cf. Lk. 1:55,73).

In as much as the Greek translators have correctly rendered the Hebrew יהוה by κύριος, the author introduces the quotation with ὁ θεός, thereby indicating that it was God who swore and gave his promise to Abraham. The substitution of the personal pronoun σε for τὸ σπέρμα σου, may either be caused by citing from memory,[2] or — what seems more in harmony with the literary qualities of the author — may have been brought about by a desire to balance two clauses with identical endings.

Genesis 14:17–20 (Heb. 7:1,2)

As a historical background to his exposition of Ps. 110, the author reaches back to facts recorded in the 14th chapter of Genesis concerning the mysterious personage Melchizedek, king of Salem and priest of God Most High.

The unknown writer of the Epistle neither introduces the words of Gen. 14 as a quotation, nor does he show punctilious conformity to a LXX text. On the contrary, he displays a remarkable freedom in his usage of the passage. Although he seems to draw his material from the LXX, version to which he remains quite faithful the word order in Heb. 7:1,2 is rather mingled. However, while the LXX has the reading Ἀβράμ, the author presents the spelling

---

[1] Werner, *Sacred Bridge*, p. 88; cf. also pp. 79, 87, 123; Schneider, *Bibl.* 30(1949), p. 37.

[2] Büchel, *TSK*, 1906, p. 524, commenting on von Soden's interpretation says, "vielleicht was auch das messianisch klingende σπέρμα hier störend," which, of course, may be a reason. We believe that for the sake of literary construction the author rendered the present reading.

'Αβραάμ, by which he betrays NT usage of the first century A.D. This is the spelling throughout the writings of the NT and the Apostolic Fathers; the word 'Αβράμ is not found anywhere in the literature mentioned.¹

Exodus 25:40 (Heb. 8:5)

Although this quotation is not cited excessively, still there are indications that, apart from the Jewish sources which furnish information,² it was known in Synagogue and Church. It occurs in three bodies of literature. First, it is not only quoted in the Epistle to the Hebrews: also Stephen in his speech indirectly refers to the words of this text (Acts 7:44). In spite of Stephen's oblique reference, the two citations show substantial agreement. Second, Philo quotes it with certain deviations from the LXX, yet his citation agrees with Hebrews in the use of πάντα (Leg. Alleg. III,33).³ Third, Irenaeus gives the full quotation once (IV,14,3),⁴ but refers to the words of this passage several times (IV,19,1; V,35,2; Epid. 9). We may check word order and changes best with the aid of the following tabulation.

MT	LXX	Heb. 8:5	Acts 7:44	Philo	Irenaeus
וראה	ὅρα	ὅρα			
ויעשה	ποιήσεις	ποιήσεις	ποιῆσαι		facies
—	—	πάντα	—		omnia
כ	κατὰ	κατὰ	κατὰ	κατὰ	iuxta
תבניתם	τὸν τύπον	τὸν τύπον	τὸν τύπον	τὸ παράδειγμα	typum eorum
אשר	τὸν	τὸν	ὃν	τὸ	quae
אתה	δεδειγμένον	δειχθέντα	ἑωράκει	δεδειγμένον	vidisti
מראה	σοι	σοι		σοι	
ב	ἐν	ἐν		ἐν	in
הר	τῷ ὄρει	τῷ ὄρει		τῷ ὄρει	monte
				πάντα	
				ποιήσεις	

---

¹ E. Goodspeed, *Index Patristicus*, p. 1.
² Str.-Bill., III, pp. 702ff. "It was taught: R. Jose b. Judah says, An ark of fire and a table of fire and a candlestick of fire came down from heaven; and these Moses saw and reproduced, as it is written, 'And see that thou make them after their pattern, which is being shown thee in the mount.', Menachoth 188, *BT*, pp. 187f.
³ Philo, *Leg. Alleg.* III, (xxxiii)102, *LCL*, Vol. I, p. 370.
⁴ Irenaeus, *Opera*, Vol. I, p. 600.

We come to the conclusion that though the quotation in Hebrews has been drawn from a LXX text, it differs in respect to the words πάντα and δειχθέντα. It is rather easy to assert on the basis of these variants that the author must have cited from memory.[1] But if we notice that the word πάντα occurs in Hebrews as well as in Philo and Irenaeus, it is better to ask whether the authors have taken the quotation from a common source than to accuse the writer of the Epistle to the Hebrews of a failing memory. The fact that Codex F, the Lucian recension, and a few other MSS of the LXX have the addition of πάντα, is not too weighty; for this reading may have been influenced by either Philo, Hebrews, or Irenaeus. The wording δειχθέντα in the Epistle rather than δεδειγμένον of the LXX is hardly worth mentioning.[2] It is more important to observe that the author, if he had any knowledge of the Hebrew language, would have given evidence at this point.[3]

The introductory formula for this quotation is not only short, but also unique in this Epistle — γάρ φησιν with ὁ Θεός as the understood subject of the verb. However, the use of φησίν is found only once in Hebrews. Since the Apostolic Fathers employ this verb to introduce a divine speaker or a quotation from the Scriptures, the archaic English "quoth he" may be a suitable equivalent of φησίν.

Jeremiah 31:31–34 (Heb. 8:8–12)

According to Strack-Billerbeck the prophecy concerning the New Covenant in Jer. 31:31–34 is seldom quoted in the Midrash of early Rabbinic times.[4] Since we have seen that in the conflict with Christianity the Rabbis tended to reinterpret and avoid passages with Christological content, we do well to investigate the usage of this prophecy in the Early Church.

Before turning to the NT we shall focus our attention on the Early Church Fathers. The prophecy seems to be rooted in the

---

[1] Vs. Büchel, *TSK*, 1906, p. 572.
[2] Cf. Delitzsch, *Comm.*, p. 336.
[3] "Surtout ce qui nous induit à penser que l'auteur n'avait pas connu le texte massor., c'est que le mot πάντα ne corrige rien." Padva, *Les Citations*, p. 75.
[4] Str.-Bill., III, p. 704.

thinking of Justin Martyr, for, besides quoting parts of the passage rather accurately (Dial. 11), he also refers to it at several places (Dial. 24,34,43,67,118,122). Irenaeus alludes to parts of Jer. 31:31,32 in a discussion on the covenants (IV,9,1), yet quotes the whole prophecy verbatim in Epid. 90. Conclusively we may say that Justin and Irenaeus display a remarkable familiarity with the passage.

Also in the NT, knowledge of the prophecy in Jer. 31 is brought to light with unmistakable clarity. Though the verses are quoted *in extenso* in Heb. 8:8–12 and in summary form in Heb. 10:16,17, allusions to the passage are found in numerous places.[1] First, it is echoed in the Synoptic pericopes of the institution of the Lord's Supper (Mt. 26:28; Mk. 14:24; Lk. 22:20). Second, Paul clearly alludes to Jer. 31:31ff. when he describes the cup which is "the new covenant." Third, a faint relation to the prophecy of Jeremiah may be gleaned from the verses 12 to 14 in I John 2.

> Although, therefore, there is only one place where the prophecy of the New Covenant is expressly cited as from scripture, it seems clear that it was widely influential in the Church from an early date, since it has not only influenced Paul, Hebrews and the Synoptic tradition, and possibly the Johannine tradition too, but probably had a place in primitive liturgical forms.[2]

Therefore, on the assumption of a possible liturgical usage of Jer. 31:31–34, we shall investigate the text in Hebrews in as far as its wording deviates from the LXX version. The verbal form φησίν is avoided and replaced by the more common λέγει (8:8,9,10; 10:16). Without any actual change in meaning, the phrase διαθήσομαι διαθήκην is given some variation by the synonymous forms συντελέσω and ἐποίησα (8:8,9). Other stylistic improvements are διδούς, which agrees with the MT, instead of the cumbersome διδοὺς δώσω which stems from a Hebrew infinitive absolute; ἐπιγράψα for γράψω (8:10); and the contraction of κἀγώ. We are doing injustice to the author's literary abilities when we say that "these minor changes may be partly due to

---

[1] Dodd sets forth certain features of the passage, which are found in the NT Scriptures. They are "a) the law written on the heart; b) the intimate relation of God and His people; c) knowledge of God, and d) forgiveness of sins." *Acc. to the Scr.*, p. 45.
[2] *Ibid.*, p. 46.

the fact that he is quoting from memory."[1] Since this is the longest quotation in the entire NT, it is a bit out of place to expect memory work at this point.

May the stylistic improvements of the text be accredited to the author, or were they brought about by general usage in the Church? If we assume that the Jeremiah passage occupied a place in the liturgy of the Church, the conclusion may perhaps be drawn that not the author but the Church at worship has been responsible for the wording of the quotation in Heb. 8:8–12.

Exodus 24:8 (Heb. 9:20)

This Exodus quotation appears to be closely associated with the formulas pertaining to the Lord's Supper recorded in the Synoptic Gospels and in the explication of this Institution in I Cor. 11.[2]

It is not improbable that the words which Jesus used at the institution of the Lord Supper may have influenced the citation; however, there is no proof.[3] Also possible use of the quotation during the celebration of the Eucharist in the liturgy of the Early Church may be assumed but cannot be proven. Yet the first words of the text in Heb. 9:20 depart from the LXX version and come close to the Synoptic and Pauline formulas "for this is my blood of the covenant" (Mt. 26:28), and "this cup is the new covenant in my blood" (I Cor. 11:25).

The opinion may be held that the author relied on memory,[4] but it is better to assert that he adapted the quotation — whether

---

[1] Moffatt, *Comm.*, p. 110. The grammar in verse 9 is not entirely correct. Moulton in following Blass calls the use of the genitive absolute violent, but adds that "the construction was probably suggested immediately by the original Hebrew." *Grammar*, Vol. I, p. 74. But cf. Baruch 2:28 where the same construction is found. Westcott, *Comm.*, p. 222; Riggenbach, *Comm.*, p. 230 n. 36.

[2] W. D. Davies, *Paul and Rabbinic Judaism*, p. 251, calls attention to the fact "that Jesus had thought in terms of a New Covenant instituted through His Death.... He may even have actually expounded His thoughts at the Last Supper to this effect." Also see W. Manson in *Jesus the Messiah*, p. 146.

[3] "Men heeft vermoed, dat de woorden, die Jezus gebruikte bij de instelling van het avondmaal, invloed op den tekst van Hebr. hebben gehad. Dat is niet onmogelijk, maar niet te bewijzen." F. W. Grosheide, *Comm.*, p. 216; and cf. Windisch, *Comm.*, p. 74.

[4] Advocated by Padva, *Les Citations*, p. 81.

he took it from the liturgical ritual of the Early Church remains an open question — to the context of Heb. 9. This is perhaps shown by the reading ἐνετείλατο instead of διέθετο, but certainly by the departure from κύριος to ὁ θεός.

Psalm 40:6–8 (Heb. 10:5–7)

Our sources of information in respect to this passage are only limited to the NT and to Irenaeus. Beginning with the first mentioned, we find that the author to the Hebrews quotes the text in full in 10:5–7 with context quotations in 10:8–9. Next, the words προσφορὰν καὶ θυσίαν of Ps. 39:7 (LXX) are allusively used by Paul in Eph. 5:2. Granted that the recipients of the Epistles of Paul and the unknown author were acquainted with the words of Ps. 40:6–8, we must pose the question what the passage meant to the early Christians, who were far removed from the practice of offering bloody sacrifices.

> The actual sacrifices were replaced either by the recitation of the divine statute and order of the respective offering, or by spontaneous or "regulated" prayer. These noble substitutes for the sacrifice were emphasized and reinterpreted innumerably. Long before the cessation of the sacrificial cult the psalms had expressed the substitution in poetic language: Sacrifice and offering ... Ps. 40:6–8, 10.[1]

Both Paul and the author of the Epistle to the Hebrews interpret the reference to Ps. 40:6 to the love of Christ, who "gave himself up for us, as an offering and sacrifice to God" (Eph. 5:2). Also Irenaeus resorts to this quotation [2] in a discourse on the true sacrifice to God. He directs the attention of his readers to the offering of obedience and love to God.

Though the source material for the passage from Ps. 40 is indeed scanty, the presence of the references intimates that the verses 6 to 8 of this psalm were not entirely unknown in a context of offering true sacrifices of love to God.

By comparing the text used by Irenaeus which is in accord with the LXX, to the one employed in Heb. 10, we learn that there

---

[1] Werner, *Sacred Bridge*, p. 23.
[2] Irenaeus, *Opera*, Vol. I, p. 608, (IV, 17,1), "*Sacrificium et oblationem noluisti; aures autem perficisti mihi: holocausta etiam pro delicto non postulasti.*"

were two versions in regard to the words *body* in Hebrews and *ears* in Irenaeus.¹ The rendition of Irenaeus receives all the necessary support, for it is similar to the MT and Targum Jonathan. The translation in Hebrews, however, may have been brought about by dittography: if the second *sigma* in the phrase ἐθέλησας ὠτία is doubled, it is not improbable that the extra letter has resulted in the formation of the word σῶμα. Moreover, instead of the verbal form ᾔτησας, which is the verb used in the LXX, the author to the Hebrews has employed the word εὐδόκησας. Yet in the various MSS of the LXX a variety of translations is given for the Hebrew form שאל at this place.² The Greek εὐδόκησας is more expressive than the Hebrew שאל. There may be somewhat of a connection between the several verbs denoting *desire, request,* and *wish* found in Ps. 39:7–9 (LXX). Thus, while ἐβουλήθην is omitted at the end of the quotation in Hebrews, the use of the more suggestive εὐδόκησας may find some justification. On account of the omission of the verb ἐβουλήθην the phrase "as it is written of me in the roll of the book" has become a disjunctive clause. The pronoun μου, which modifies the vocative ὁ θεός, has been omitted.

All these textual differences in Heb. 10:5–9 indicate that the author has had recourse to a text akin to a LXX version,³ and that he adapted the quotation to some extent to the purpose of his discourse — the true sacrifice of love and obedience exemplified by Jesus Christ in the offering of his body once for all.

---

[1] Cf. Riggenbach, *Comm.*, p. 300 n. 15; Grosheide, *Comm.*, p. 229; According to Rahlfs, *Psalmi*, p. 144, the LXX witnesses for ὠτία are La ᴳ Ga and the interpreters α′, σ′, θ′, ε′, as well as the transliteration from the Hebrew (testified by the Syriac). The remaining LXX MSS have the reading σῶμα. Also see Böhl, *Die Alttestl. Citate*, pp. 288f.

[2] The LXX reading in the various MSS is indeed colorful: ᾔτησας B, *postulasti* Laᴳ Ga MT, ἐζήτησας א R Luc Z T Tht Sy He A 1219, *petisti* La Aug, ἠθέλησας 55, ηὐδόκησας bo sa 2013, cf. A. Rahlfs, *Psalmi*, p. 144. Also see Thomas, *Use of the Septuagint*, pp. 111ff.

[3] Padva, in commenting on this quotation, draws a twofold conclusion. First, the author has no knowledge of, or at least does not occupy himself with, a Hebrew text. Second, he follows a Greek text verbally. Hence the divergencies could not be ascribed to a faulty memory. *Les Citations*, p. 84.

Deuteronomy 32:35a (Heb. 10:30)

Introduced by a rather indefinite formula, "for we know him who said," this quotation is taken out of the Hymn of Moses. It may have been known to the faithful as they sang the words in the Synagogue of the Diaspora as well as in the Early Church, or it may have circulated among them as a proverbial saying. The NT, the LXX, and the MT are all witnesses to a change in a textual tradition. It is best to follow this trend by using the accompanying table.

LXX Philo [1]	Sam. Pent.	MT	Targ. Onk. Targ. Ps. Jon.	Targ. Jer.	Heb. 10:30 Rom. 12:19
ἐν ἡμέρα ἐκδικήσεως	ליום	לי	הדמי פורענותא ואנא	דידי היא נקמתא ואנא	ἐμοὶ ἐκδίκησις ἐγὼ
ἀνταποδώσω	ושלם וישלם	נקם	איישלים	הוא דמשלם	ἀνταποδώσω

We learn that the Samaritan Pentateuch and the LXX version agree as contrasted to the rest of the witnesses cited. The reading ἐν ἡμέρα ἐκδικήσεως is reflected in an allusion adduced by Luke. Jesus, in his discourse about the destruction of Jerusalem, says, "for these are the days of vengeance (ἡμέραι ἐκδικήσεως)," (Lk. 21:22). The change in the textual tradition may have been caused by the loss of the last two letters of the word ליום, so that the remainder לי most definitely refers to God.

> This proves that the corruption of the Hebrew was in existence in N.T. times, was welcome as giving strong emphasis to the genuinely biblical idea of God's absolute sovereignty, and therefore ousted the version preserved in the Samaritan and the LXX which now looked obsolete and weak.[2]

While the LXX has departed from the Hebrew noun ישלם already by translating it into the future indicative, a further development is found in the Targums with which the NT writers

---

[1] Philo, *Leg. Alleg.* III, (xxxiv)105, *LCL*, Vol. I, pp. 370f. Büchel, *TSK*, pp. 575–588, in his attempt to prove that the author to the Hebrews must have frequented the works of Philo extensively cites only those OT quotations in Philo which strengthen his contention. He, perhaps conveniently, omits this reference.

[2] Katz, "Quotations from Deut.," *ZNW*, 49(1958), p. 220.

agree. The Targumic inclusion of ואנא preceding the verbal form "I shall pay," is also shown, without the conjunction καί, in Romans and Hebrews.

It may be that the phraseology which the Targums and the NT writers have recorded, prevailed in an oral tradition, and that the quotation, which was considered divinely spoken, circulated as a proverbial saying.[1]

The author to the Hebrews leaves the speaker indefinite, when in fact Paul in Rom. 12:19 adds the words λέγει κύριος — something which never happens otherwise in the Pauline Epistles.[2]

Deuteronomy 32:36a – Psalm 135:14a (Heb. 10:30)

Once again the author to the Hebrews draws a quotation from the Hymn of Moses, which, as we have seen in the discussion of Heb. 1:6b, belonged to the liturgy of the Early Church. Besides being part of this liturgical hymn, the 36th verse is identical to Ps. 135:14a. That this psalm was not unknown during the latter part of the first century A.D. is borne out by allusions to its verses in Rev. 19:5; 9:20. Conclusively, we may assert that the text did not sound unfamiliar in the ears of the early Christians.

The words cited are identical to those of the LXX which shows a correct translation of the MT at this place. Only the causal ὅτι of the LXX, כי in MT, has been omitted in Hebrews, but this may be due to the introductory formula "and again."

---

[1] The commentaries have collected all the Deuteronomy texts in the Epistle to the Hebrews, analyzed them, and concluded that in respect to the book of Deut. the author must have used another text than we possess. Cf. Riggenbach, *Comm.*, p. xxxvi and p. 328 n. 13; Michel, *Comm.*, p. 237 n. 1. However, Katz in his learned article has ably refuted this generalization: "To group them together as the commentaries do, is meaningless. The assumption that they stand for a Greek different from the LXX is unwarranted." *ZNW*, 49(1958), p. 221. F. Delitzsch's approach to this particular text (Deut. 32:35a) is worthy of consideration: "vielleicht war das Citat in dieser Form ein stereotype Bestandtheil der Kirchensprache geworden." *Comm.*, p. 499. Also Thomas, *Use of the Septuagint*, p. 122, concludes: "In any case, it is evident that the author did not make the changes himself, since this form was already in existence."

[2] Padva, *Les Citations*, p. 89. Also see E. E. Ellis, *Paul's Use of the OT*, pp. 111f.

Isaiah 26:20 and Habakkuk 2:3,4 (Heb. 10:37–38)

Without an introductory formula the author adduces a combination of two quotations taken out of Isa. 26 and Hab. 2 respectively. Both passages were used in Synagogue and Church alike.

Isa. 26 represents one of the 9 canticles taken out of the OT and Apocrypha, and which were chanted or read in the worship services of the early Synagogue.[1] Gradually these biblical hymns disappeared out of the ritual till only Ex. 15 and Deut. 32 were left. Why were most of the canticles removed from the older liturgies of the Synagogue? The answer is to be found in connection with the spirit prevailing in the early Synagogue. "The decisive criterion, of course, depended on the aptness of some of these canticles for a Christological interpretation.... Isa. 26 likewise was eliminated, probably because the verses 17–19 were propitious to Christological interpretation...."[2] In the Early Church the verses 9–20 had been selected for use in the morning or evening prayers, because verse 9 in the LXX version introduces the pericope with the words, "my spirit seeks thee very early in the

---

[1] The Early Church was in possession of a list of 9 canticles, most of which were derived from the liturgy of the Synagogue. This list was supplemented with an additional 5 hymns. The 9 canticles are listed under the heading *Novem odae ecclesiae graecae*, and the remaining 5 are classified under *Odae aliae*, in Septuaginta Vol. X, *Psalmi cum Odis*, (ed. A. Rahlfs), pp. 341–365, and in A. Rahlfs' *Septuaginta*, Vol. II, following the Psalter. The canticles under the first heading are: *1*) Song of Moses (Ex. 15:1-19); *2*) Hymn of Moses (Deut. 32:1-43); *3*) Prayer of Hannah (I Regn. 2:1-10); *4*) Song of Habakkuk (Hab. 3:2-19); *5*) Song of Isaiah (Isa. 26); *6*) Prayer of Jonah (Jonah 2:3-10); *7*) Prayer of Azariah (Dan. 3:26-45); *8*) Prayer of the three men (Dan. 3:52-88); *9*) Prayer of Mary (Lk. 1:46-55) and Prayer of Zacharias (Lk. 1:68-79). And the 5 hymns listed under *Odae aliae* are: *10*) Ode of Isaiah (Isa. 5:1-9); *11*) Prayer of Hezekiah (Isa. 38:10-20); *12*) Prayer of Manasseh; *13*) Prayer of Simeon (Lk. 2:29-32); and *14*) Gloria. Although the list was not drawn up immediately at the dawn of the Christian era, we may be certain that the hymns circulated among the early Christians for quite some time before they were recorded in the present order, and that many of these hymns were sung in the churches near the end of the first century A.D. already.

[2] Werner, *Sacred Bridge*, p. 140.

morning, O God, for thy commandments are a light on the earth."[1] Also Paul in his Epistle to the Ephesians reflects a certain measure of acquaintance with this song. In Eph. 5:14 he cites the words of a hymn which most likely represents an adaptation to, or a borrowing from, the 18th verse of Isa. 26 in the LXX version.[2]

Since the words ὅσον ὅσον also appear in Greek profane literature,[3] they seem to have been used as a colloquial expression. Yet here they are preceded by μικρόν — a word which Jesus used twice in his farewell address to his disciples (John 14:19; 16:16). The whole phrase is joined to two verses out of the second chapter of Habakkuk's prophecy.

The author to the Hebrews has given the combined quotation[4] a decidedly messianic interpretation considered from an apocalyptic point of view. This is not only clear from the intent of the first two chapters of the book of Habakkuk, but the very third verse of chapter two was interpreted by the Jewish Rabbis to refer to the end of time and the coming of the Messiah.[5] This messianic hope was kept alive during the centuries; for Rabbi Nathan, who died approximately 160 A.D., and later Rabbis Jonathan and Samuel, still applied the text in Hab. 2:3 to the Messiah by

---

[1] *Septuagint Version*, (ed. S. Bagster and Sons). "Nicht alle Oden des Morgenofficiums kommen aus der Ostervigil. Manche waren gewiss von Anfang an als Morgen- oder Abendgebet ausgewählt, vor allem die Ode des Isaias, Is. 26,9–20," Schneider, *Bibl.* 30(1949), p. 47.

[2] Eph. 5:14, "Awake, thou that sleepest, and arise from the dead...." Isa. 26:19, LXX, "The dead shall rise, and they that are in the tombs shall be raised...." Bagster, *Septuagint Version*. Cf. Schneider, *Bibl.* 30(1949), p. 35.

[3] Arist. *Vesp.* 213 and Leon. Tarent. LXX 4 as referred to by Westcott, *Comm.*, p. 337.

[4] It is interesting to note that Clement of Rome joins Isa. 13:22, which is almost considered as a parallel passage of Hab. 2:3b, to Mal. 3:1, thus giving the combined quotation a messianic aspect.

[5] "Les paroles d'Habakuk sont devenues, selon toute probabilité, une formule en quelque sorte stéréotypée des espérance messianiques. C'est par elle qu'on a exprimé une, et non la moindre, des 'Promesses' messianiques qui circulaient dès avant le premier siècle de notre ère." Padva, *Les Citations*, p. 91. The same thought is expressed by Dodd from the point of view of the early Christian. "... The short oracle 2:1–4 announcing the certainty of deliverance, ... in the coming of the Deliverer, and in the salvation of those who put their faith in Christ." *Acc. to the Scr.*, pp. 87f.

declaring that the day of his coming, though the date be uncertain, must be awaited without discouragement.[1]

Except for the elimination of the causal ὅτι, the addition of the definite article ὁ, the omission of the negative particle μή, and the shift of tense and mood in the verb χρονίσει, the phraseology of the first part of the Habakkuk quotation in Hebrews does not differ much from the LXX version. The participle ἐρχόμενος receives the definite article so that the phrase may be recognized as the accepted appellation referring to the Messiah. In the Gospels (Mt. 11:3; Lk. 7:20) and in the Apocalypse of John (Rev. 1:4,8; 4:8), the term ὁ ἐρχόμενος has become the descriptive title of Christ. The change from the aorist subjunctive χρονίσει is rather insignificant, since both verbs ultimately refer to the future.

The reversal of the two clauses of Hab. 2:4 in the Epistle to the Hebrews has been brought about for reasons of specifying the proper subject and indicating the right proportion of emphasis. It is not the phrase ὁ ἐρχόμενος that is to be taken with the verb ὑποστείληται, but rather the substantive δίκαιος, which is preceded by the words ὁ δέ, indicative of change of subject. It is natural that this shift of clauses called for a conjunction καί to join the two parts of the sentence.

"But (my) righteous (one) shall live by faith," is a clause recorded twice in the Pauline Epistles (Rom. 1:17 and Gal. 3:11) and once in the Epistle to the Hebrews (10:38). Apart from the fact that the text is applied and understood differently in these Apostolic letters, it is clear that the words were not unfamiliar to the early Christians. Yet there seems to have been some marginal fluctuation in the exact wording of the clause. When in fact the Hebrew באמונתו is translated in the LXX by ἐκ πίστεως μου, it is this very pronoun μου which causes all the fluctuation. While Aquila correctly renders the Hebrew equivalent by αὐτοῦ, the author to the Hebrews places μου in front of ἐκ πίστεως, and Paul omits the pronoun altogether. In the

---

[1] Str.-Bill., IV, 2, p. 1011. Spicq. II, *Comm.*, p. 332. "... And the remaining period will be the Messianic era.... Rabbi Nathan said : This verse pierces and descends to the very abyss : For the vision is yet for an appointed time, but at the end it shall speak, and not lie ; though he tarry, wait for him; because it will surely come, it will not tarry," Sanhedrin 97b. *BT*, p. 658.

opinion of Jerome, the Greek translators may have been somewhat responsible for the textual changes: *Et ubi LXX posuerunt, "Justus autem ex fide mea vivet," omnes aequaliter transtulerunt, "ex fide sua vivet."* [1]

The last clause "if he shrinks back, my soul hath no pleasure in him," is made coordinate to the preceding ὁ δὲ δίκαιος by the insertion of καί. This last sentence is drawn, in its exact form, from the LXX version.

Genesis 21:12 (Heb. 11:18)

"The Jewish New Year constantly stresses the ideas of birth and moral rebirth. It is then that the passages Gen. 21 (Isaac's birth) and I Sam. 1–2 (Samuel's birth and Hannah's praise) are read." [2] This fact is reverberated in the NT, for the 21st chapter of Genesis plays a role in Rom. 9 and Gal. 4. The culminating point in this dramatic account of Sarah's envy is God's promise to a displeased Abraham: "Let it not be grievous in thy sight

---

[1] *Patrologiae Lat.*, XXV, (J. P. Migne), Operum Hieronymi, VI, col. 1280. It may be possible that the MSS used by the LXX translators were written in the early form of the square character, in which the ו and י are remarkably alike and subject to interchange (cf. S. R. Driver, *Books of Samuel*², pp. lxiv – lxvi). Also in the scrolls discovered near the Dead Sea the feature of interchanging characters is a fact. If we assume that Heb. 10:38 supports the LXX in the use of μου, then these two witnesses stand alone. The Targum, Symmachus, and the Vulgate support the reading of the NT. It is rather disappointing that the Habakkuk commentary of Qumran has been broken off in the midst of this particular verse. However, the interpretation of this verse, which has been saved fortunately, supports the MT. In addition to these two groups of textual witnesses, there are Rom. 1:17; Gal. 3:11; and the Peshitta on Hab. 2:4 (which in all probability was influenced by the reading in Rom. and Gal.). These three additional witnesses omit the pronoun entirely. Since the MT has all the support for the 3rd person singular suffix, it is more than likely that the reading of the LXX has originated through the interchange of the two Hebrew characters. In reaction to the Jewish doctrine of reward and retribution, the NT steered away from the use of the pronoun. In the case of Heb. 10:38 the pronoun μου may have been placed in the margin or above the line under influence of the LXX version. In the process of copying, the extra word was taken up in the text itself, but was incorporated in the wrong place. In later days the mistake was discovered and consequently corrected, as is shown by the translation of the Peshitta on Heb. 10:38, which reads: "The righteous, however, shall live, by faith in me."

[2] Werner, *Sacred Bridge*, p. 89.

because of the lad, and because of thy handmaid; in all that Sarah saith unto thee, hearken unto her voice; for in Isaac shall thy seed be called" (Gen. 21:12).

These words appeal to the heart of the Jew; hence Paul quotes the text in Rom. 9:7, the author to the Hebrews in 11:18, and Justin Martyr in his dialogue with the Jew Trypho (Dial. 56). All these writers in their respective arguments approach the Jew on his own terms.

The text of the LXX, which is literally identical to the quotation in Romans, Hebrews, and Justin's Dialogue, is an accurate translation of the MT. However, Paul and also the author to the Hebrews omit the causal ὅτι at the beginning of the quotation. In Heb. 11:18 the words are introduced by a recitative ὅτι, and in Rom. 9:7, by the adversative particle ἀλλ'. The omission of the conjunction ὅτι does not alter the meaning in the least, for the causal idea is found in the immediate context of the respective places.

Proverbs 3:11–12 (Heb. 12:5–6)

In the early Synagogue the idea of being chastised out of love was very prominent.[1] When the author to the Hebrews says, "and ye have forgotten the exhortation which reasoneth with you as with sons," it is evident that this is part of a cultural background. According to the *Index Locorum* in Nestle, Prov. 3 is quoted and alluded to more than any other chapter of this book. And again, of all the references to chapter 3, most of them touch upon the verses 1–12. In other words, Prov. 3:1–12 seems to have been a basic pericope in the moral training of the faithful in the Early Church. Also Clement of Rome quotes verse 12 in combination with passages drawn from Ps. 118:18 and Ps. 141:5.

The quotation would almost leave the impression that the author of this Epistle was acquainted with the Hebrew language. The Hebrew בני, translated in the LXX version by the vocative υἱέ, is correctly rendered by υἱέ μου in Heb. 12:5. But if this is

---

[1] Str.-Bill., III, p. 747. Mekh. Ex. 20,23 (79b) "R. Eliezer b. Jaᶜaqob (II, um 150) sagte : Siehe es heisst : Die Zucht Jahves, mein Sohn, verschmähe nicht Spr. 3,11. Weshalb? Denn wen Jahve liebt, den straft er Spr. 3,12. Komm und sieh : was verursacht (ermöglicht) es einem Sohne den Vater zu versöhnen? Sage : Die Züchtigungen." Transl. Str.-Bill.

considered as a correction of the writer, then it remains to be asked why he did not correct the LXX throughout this passage. It is not only the different translation of the Hebrew כאב, brought about by varying vowel pointing (read in the MT, "as a father"; and in the LXX, "he was pained")[1] but also by the LXX addition of the word πάντα, and the Greek παραδέχεται, which is a somewhat inadequate rendition of the Hebrew רצה. The author's source for this quotation must have been a LXX version, yet the addition of μου, corresponding to the MT and correcting the Greek translation, cannot serve as convincing proof for possible knowledge of the Hebrew tongue on the part of the author.

Exodus 19:13 (Heb. 12:20)

In chapter 12 of Hebrews the author introduces the Lawgiving scene with all its attending circumstances. By tracing the various details he appeals directly to the Jewish mind, which was entrenched in the stream of tradition and fully informed of the event at Mount Sinai. This event must have stood out distinctly in Jewish thinking, so that any one making a mere reference to the occurrence at Horeb might be clearly understood.

The author appears to cite Ex. 19:13 — but only the phrase "it shall be stoned" agrees with the LXX version. On the whole the text in Heb. 12:20 is closer to the MT than to the LXX; yet we cannot speak of a precise rendition. Scripture itself is not quoted word-for-word, but rather the general purport of the passage is given. Even though the present form of the quotation found in the Epistle to the Hebrews may have circulated in an oral tradition, this can never be verified; yet we may assume that the meaning and intent of the text was clear to all the recipients of this letter.

Deuteronomy 9:19 (Heb. 12:21)

Although the words ἔκφοβός εἰμι may be found in Deut. 9:19, they do not refer to Moses' fear at the time of the Lawgiving ceremony as the author to the Hebrews implies but rather to the

---

[1] Cf. Grosheide, *Comm.*, p. 288 n. 16; Riggenbach, *Comm.*, p. 394 n. 29; Delitzsch, *Comm.*, p. 613. The spelling of the Hebrew words in question presented by Grosheide is typographically wrong.

anger of the Lord, kindled by the Israelietes who built the golden calf, and which caused Moses to exclaim, "For I was afraid of the anger and hot displeasure, wherewith Jehovah was wroth against you to destroy you" (9:19). However, to say that the author "forgets that Moses uttered this cry of horror, not over the spectacle of Sinai but at a later stage, over the worship of the golden calf," [1] is doing gross injustice to the writer's knowledge of the Sinai incident and to the whole Jewish tradition concerning this event.

It is very well possible that reference is made to an oral tradition which in later times was written down. In Acts 7:32 Luke records the words of Stephen concerning Moses when he met God at the burning bush. While Luke expresses Moses' trembling with the adjective ἔντρομος, the LXX version at Ex. 3:6 describes his state of mind with the verb εὐλαβεῖτο. Whenever there is a meeting between God and man, the former causes either quaking and/or fire and smoke, while the latter's condition may best be described with the words "fear and trembling." Apparently, as the Talmud reflects,[2] the concept "fear and trembling," expressed by various verbs, nouns, and adjectives, was attributed to Moses when he ascended Mount Sinai.

Haggai 2:6 (Heb. 12:26)

It is interesting to note that all the citations found in chapter 12 of the Epistle to the Hebrews have a rather decidedly Jewish background. Not only are the quotations applied to illustrate thought motifs rooted in the religious culture of Judaism, but they are even peculiar to Jewish literature. Apart from the passage

---

[1] Moffatt, *Comm.*, p. 216.

[2] According to Bab. Shabbath 88b, *BT*, p. 422, Moses ascends Mount Sinai, fearing the consuming breath of the angels. "Sovereign of the Universe" replied he, "I fear lest they consume me with the [fiery] breath of their mouths." Michel comments, "Es ist wahrscheinlich, dass *rabbinische* Traditionen von dieser Furcht des Moses beim Besteigen des Berges wussten." *Comm.*, p. 315. Cf. also Enoch 89,30 and I Macc. 13:2 where haggadic formulations similar to Heb. 12:21 are found; and see Ps. 11. "Moses habe den 11. Psalm gesprochen aus Furcht vor den bösen Geistern, als er den Berg der Gesetzgebung bestieg. Offenbar hat das Spatjüdentum zu Ex. 19,19 irgendwie ergänzt, was Moses geredet hat. An dieser Auslegung nimmt auch Hebr. teil." Harder, "Septuagintazitate," *Theologia Viatorum*, p. 50.

out of Prov. 3, the NT and the Early Church Fathers do not mention any of the direct quotations found in Heb. 12. The NT world is utterly silent in this respect regarding the specific elements adduced by the writer to the Hebrews.

In the whole NT the prophecy of Haggai is quoted only once (Heb. 12:26). Yet in Rabbinic literature it is especially chapter 2:6 which is considered messianic, for it is reported that Rabbi Aqibah, who died approximately 135 A.D., applied this text to affirm the coming of the Messiah at the end of the second Temple.[1] In the light of the preceding, Harders contention [2] (the author to the Hebrews only quoted Hag. 2:6 for the sake of the word מעט) is not only partial to his specific hypothesis, but even ascribes to the writer a knowledge of the Hebrew tongue without offering any substantial proof for this assumption. It is admitted that the Greek translators have not rendered a verbal translation of the passage; nevertheless, the meaning of this text has been preserved. For stylistic reasons to effect greater emphasis, the author has added the words οὐ μόνον ... ἀλλά, which necessitated the shift of the nouns "heaven" and "earth."

Deuteronomy 31:6 (Heb. 13:5)

According to the author to the Hebrews the quotation, introduced by the words αὐτὸς γὰρ εἴρηκεν, is spoken by God. Though to

---

[1] In respect to the Messianic era Rabbi Nathan said, "... nor as R. Akibah who expounded, Yet once, it is a little while, and I will shake the heavens and the earth." Sanhedrin 97b,*BT*, p. 659; cf. Str.-Bill., III, p. 749. Also see Padva, *Les Citations*, pp. 95f., "C'était une des prophéties messianiques les plus connues; elle devait être présente à l'esprit de tous les fidèles, c'est aussi pourquoi l'auteur de l'épître aux Hébreux se permet de faire une paraphrase de ce passage et d'accentuer la gravité du bouleversement, 'non seulement la terre mais aussi le ciel,' convaincu que ses lecteurs ou ses auditeurs connaissent très bien le contenu du texte auquel il fait allusion."

[2] Harder, in his endeavor to prove the hypothesis that the author cited purposely those LXX quotations which depart from the MT, illustrates this by means of the LXX translation of Haggai 2:6. "Gerade das ἅπαξ, die Wiedergabe von מעט, veranlasst den Hebr., das Wort aus Haggai zu zitieren." *Theol. Viat.*, pp. 38f. However, this last sentence is not too accurately expressed, for in the words of Riggenbach, "Indem die LXX מעט היא unübersetzt lässt und אחת durch ἅπαξ wiedergibt, drückt sie den Gedanken aus, er werde nochmals (wie schon früher) und zwar noch ein einziges Mal eine die ganze Welt umfassende Erschütterung erfolgen." *Comm.*, p. 423. See also Delitzsch, *Comm.*, p. 658; Westcott, *Comm.*, p. 420.

a great extent identical to the LXX version, it is neither in the Old nor in the New Testament ascribed to God. In Deut. 31:6 Moses, in addressing the children of Israel, uses words which, on the basis of the LXX, approach the text quoted in Heb. 13:5. In spite of the fact that the expression "I will not fail thee, nor forsake thee" is spoken by God and strengthened by the agreement of the MT, the LXX shows a different phraseology at this place. A brief table will provide the necessary information.

Deut. 31:6 (LXX)	Deut. 31:6 (MT)	Josh. 1:5 (MT)	Josh. 1:5 (LXX)	Heb. 13:5
οὐ μή σε ἀνῇ οὔτε μή σε ἐγκαταλίπῃ	לֹא יַרְפְּךָ וְלֹא יַעַזְבֶךָּ	לֹא אַרְפְּךָ וְלֹא אֶעֶזְבֶךָּ	οὐκ ἐνκαταλείψω σε οὐδὲ ὑπερόψομαί σε	οὐ μή σε ἀνῶ οὐδ' οὐ μή σε ἐγκαταλίπω

It is rather simple to conclude that the author must have had a different translation of Josh. 1:5, from which he drew this quotation. Seeing that such a translation has not yet been discovered, we must leave it for the time being to the realm of assumptions.[1] However, the text in Heb. 13:5 is also recorded by Philo in exactly the same form.[2] Since Philo died approximately 40 A.D., it is tempting to infer that the author to the Hebrews borrowed the quotation from him.[3] But this would move the problem one step further back, and no answer is given to the question why Philo's version differs from the LXX. Apart from this question it should be noticed that there is one area of similarity between the writings of these two literary scholars. Both of them have God speaking as the direct subject of the utterance. Whereas the author to the Hebrews has the introduction "for himself hath said," Philo presents the quotation as "an oracle of the merciful God."

---

[1] Cf. Deut. 32:35a, p. 46 n.1.
[2] Philo, *Conf. Ling.* (xxxii)166, LCL, IV, pp. 100f.
[3] "The quotation ... is a popular paraphrase of Jos. 1:5 or Gen. 28:15 ... which the author owes to Philo." Moffatt, *Comm.*, p. 229.

The text itself is found at various places throughout the OT. Whenever it occurs the situation lends itself for divine sustenance and guidance. Jacob fleeing from his brother Esau hears in his dream the encouraging words of God, "And, behold, I am with thee ... for I will not leave thee ...." (Gen. 28:15). Moses, in one of his last speeches addressing the Israelites, delivers to them the words of God, which were given in the form of a source of encouragement (Deut. 31:6). Joshua receives a similar blessing from the Lord when he begins his tremendous task as leader of God's people (Josh. 1:5). Once again this adage occurs when David instructs his son Solomon to build the Temple for the Lord (I Chron. 28:20). Thus we may say that the quotation *"est igitur instar adagii divini."* [1]

We come to the conclusion that the words of the quotation were far from unknown to the people of the OT era, and that in all probability the quotation played a role in the liturgy of the Synagogue.[2] The early Christians who had only recently left the precincts of the Synagogue were quite familiar with the quotation. It may have been in use in the worship services of the Early Church.

Psalm 118:6 (Heb. 13:6)

The last quotation is taken out of a Hallel psalm and is separated from the preceding adage by the words, "So that with good courage we say." While the expression in Heb. 13:5 is, liturgically speaking, the *pars dei*, the verse out of Ps. 118 is the response of the people and thus the *pars populi*.

The word βοηθός is a hapax legomenon in the NT, yet Clement of Rome reveals in his writings that the word was firmly rooted in the liturgy of the Early Church.[3]

This Hallel psalm was known to Jews and Christians alike; "... it is both the Easter and the Passover psalm *par excellence* and was always so understood. It is sung during the entire week

---

[1] J. A. Bengel, *Gnomon*, Vol. II, p. 481.
[2] In the words of Delitzsch, *Comm.*, p. 669, "... dass Deut. 31:6 im liturgischen oder homiletischen Gebrauch der hellenistischen Synagoge diese Fassung annahm." Also see Grosheide, *Comm.*, p. 309 n. 7.
[3] Michel, *Comm.*, p. 333, refers to I Clem. 36,1; 59,3 and speaks of the word as a "feststehende liturgische Verwendung."

following Easter Sunday, being the last remnant of the seven-day long Jewish celebration of Passover."[1]

It is not in the least surprising that the NT Scriptures testify repeatedly to the constant use, to the Christological overtones, and to the source of joy and gladness of Ps. 118.

3. Conclusions

Having examined all the quotations, we do well to glean the results of our investigation. Perhaps the observations made on the basis of our research may contribute to a better understanding of the text.

It is clear that the author to the Hebrews does not rely on memory while citing from the OT, for his quotations are too much in harmony with a written text. His method of manipulating citations stands in sharp contrast to that of Paul, who knew a large number of passages by heart and showed skillful dexterity in constructing a beautiful mosaic of related texts.[2] The context quotations of Jer. 31:33,34 and Ps. 40:6-8 in Heb. 10:16,17 and Heb. 10:8-10 respectively, would willingly lend themselves to the supposition that the author quoted from memory, were it not for the sake of a twofold objection. First, it would be rather disparaging of the literary abilities of the author to expect that after having quoted a passage at length, his memory would fail when he tried to reproduce parts again, while, so to speak, his own written work was lying before him. Second, the author applies the context quotations in a slightly modified form in order to substantiate his arguments better.[3]

---

[1] Werner, *Sacred Bridge*, p. 159.

[2] N. J. Hommes, *Het Testimoniaboek*, p. 351.

[3] "Il ne semble pas en effect que les divergences avec le texte grec de l'A.T. des citations faites dans l'épître aux Hébreux puissent être attribuées à des erreurs de mémoire, ... et l'on doit admettre comme probable que le rédacteur avait sous les yeux le texte des LXX. Les quelques divergences qu'on remarque doivent donc être intentionnelles, visant à mieux adapter le texte cité au contexte dans lequel il doit prendre place ou à faciliter l'application qu'on en veut faire." Venard, "Psaumes," *Mélanges*, p. 255. Thomas, *Use of the Septuagint*, p. 14, intimates that in his dissertation the view will be maintained "that the variations are due to intentional changes made by the author of Hebrews." But throughout our study it is shown that at times variations may have been brought about by the liturgical use of the quotations in places of worship.

Also, a few quotations appear in a slightly different form effected by the replacing of words, the substitution by the use of synonyms, and the addition of a preposition or a pronoun. In spite of all these minor deviations the essential meaning of the text remains the same.

Although the source of the quotations in the Epistle to the Hebrews is found in a Greek version of the OT Scriptures, it agrees with the MT in a few instances, in contrast to the LXX known to us.

We may see the literary scholar at work when he balances constructions, when he adds a conjunction, or when he repeats a phrase for the sake of completeness.[1] At all times the author has recourse to the living language spoken in that day.[2]

Since all the quotations the writer has adduced are quite familiar to the recipients of his Epistle, it may summarily be said that the author in the application of the texts and in his choice of words is most effective in his approach to the Christian living at the beginning of our era.

It is not so much the constant usage of certain Scripture portions, as the influence of the psalm and hymn which seems to have made a direct impact on the Early Church. This is shown already in the NT Scriptures (Col. 3:16 and at various places in the Apocalypse).

> Whatever ancient description of psalmody we read, be it from the Gentile Christian, the Jewish, or even the pagan side, we cannot escape the thought that the invasion of psalmody into the ancient world must have been felt as an elemental, and often revolutionary force, that eventually broke all the conventions with which Hellas had surrounded her own musical tradition. From the historic point of view, psalmody was the greatest legacy of the Synagogue to Jewish Christianity, and thence to the Gentile Church.[3]

The Christian who attended the worship services in the Early Church undoubtedly became acquainted with the liturgical formulas spoken and the psalms and the hymns which were sung. "In the assemblies of Early Christianity, the faithful sang hymns

---

[1] Heb. 1:11f.; Heb. 1:8, 10:38; Heb. 10:16f., respectively.
[2] Ellis, *Paul's Use of the Old Testament*, p. 107.
[3] Werner, *Sacrid Bridge*, p. 145.

individually or in groups. Since many of the attendants were illiterate, they learned their song by heart, that means by ear."[1]

Most of the citations used find their origin in the liturgy of the Church and Synagogue. Although there may be occasion to point out that some quotations were chosen due to phraseology or sentence structure,[2] it is equally true that those quotations belonged to the ritual of the worship services[3] — for some of them may be traced to usage in the Temple and, after its destruction, to the Synagogue and Early Church.[4]

If we accept the Epistle to the Hebrews as one single literary unit,[5] we may infer that the author probably lived among the recipients of his letter prior to its composition.[6] But in all

---

[1] *Ibid.*, p. 213.

[2] Cf. Harder, *Theologia Viatorum*, pp. 38ff.

[3] Although Michel does not venture to offer a concrete solution for the presence of the OT citations in the Epistle to the Hebrews, he suffices by saying, "dass sich die verwandten at.lichen Zitate auch am besten aus dem Gebrauch der Gemeindeliturgie erklären lassen." *Comm.*, p. 7. But this suggestion has been furnished by E. Käsemann, who joins the thought with the conception that the Epistle to the Hebrews must have been originally a homily. "*Das wandernde Gottesvolk*," p. 109.

[4] Padva already indicates that a few of the citations find their origin in the ritual of prayers. In spite of his conclusion, "L'influence de la Grande Synagogue sur les idées de l'auteur est incontestable," he fails to come to more positive results simply because Padva is concerned with the worship services in the Temple and not with those in the Synagogue and the Early Church. *Les Citations*, p. 100.

[5] The verses 22–25 of Heb. 13 are considered by several scholars as a later addition to the Epistle. W. Slot has taken this assumption as the pillar for his hypothesis that the letter must have been a homily in its original state. That Slot has become a slave to his own system becomes apparent when he discusses the OT citations in the Epistle to the Hebrews. All the quotations are forced into the pattern of the Scripture portion (Pss. 94 to 110) which was read prior to the homily proper. In a rather artificial manner the quotations are made subservient to Pss. 94 to 110. According to Michel, *Comm.*, p. 6, it is Windisch who has pointed out that only Pss. 95 and 110 do justice to Slot's hypothesis. All the other passages are of no support. Slot, *De Letterkundige Vorm van den Brief aan de Hebreeën*, esp. pp. 94–103.

[6] Riggenbach observes, in summary form, that the author "hat eine Zeitlang in ihrer Mitte geweihlt und eine leitende Stellung in ihr eingenommen, wie er auch beabsichtigt, baldmöglichst zu ihr zurückzukehren (13,17–19. 23)." *Comm.*, p. XXXIV.

certainty we may gather that he was thoroughly familiar with their mode of worship, so that as a natural course of events he borrowed various elements from the ritual of the Early Church and employed these in his Epistle, in order to be most effective in his approach.

Chapter II

THE HERMENEUTICAL METHODS

1. Principles

The subject of the first chapter included 32 direct citations of the OT. The present chapter is concerned with the 11 psalm citations found in the Epistle to the Hebrews. We shall study them in the light of the hermeneutical principles prevalent in the age in which the Epistle was written.

The word *hermeneutics* is derived from the Greek verb ἑρμηνεύειν, which means *to explain, interpret; to translate*.[1] These three meanings comprise the conveyance of the right interpretation of a thought or word expressed. Possibly the word has been derived from the name of the Greek god Hermes. One [2] of the functions of Hermes was to be a messenger, to convey messages. His was the task to interpret these messages correctly to man living upon earth. In short the verb denotes the conveyance of the correct meaning of a word or thought. The adjective ἑρμηνευτική — to which our adjective *hermeneutic* corresponds — is to be taken with the substantive ἐπιστήμη (science) or τέχνη (art).[3]

In the study of hermeneutics concerning Scripture we necessarily turn to those men who are known to have begun with the practice of interpreting the Holy Books to the people. The time of Ezra provides the first indication of a thorough explication of "the law of God" (Neh. 8:8). When in fact the priests had explained the Scriptures to the people in the days subsequent to the Exile,

---

[1] Arndt & Gingrich, *Lexicon*, pp. 309f.; Liddell and Scott, *Lexicon*, Vol. I, p. 690.

[2] J. Behm, *TWNT*, II, p. 661, directs attention to Philo, who considered the prophets, *e.g.* Moses, as God's interpreters. "Auch andere Propheten sind in ähnlicher Weise Offenbarungsmittler gewesen zB Bileam . . . , sogar die griechische Götterbode Hermes."

[3] Cf. S. Greydanus, *Schriftbeginselen*, p. 5; F. W. Grosheide, *Hermeneutiek*, p. 1. It is admitted that a secondary meaning of ἐξηγεῖσθαι coincides with the verb in question; see Liddell and Scott, *Lexicon*, Vol. I, p. 593.

a few centuries later this task was assumed by the Scribes.¹ After the Scribes had established schools of learning, the study of hermeneutics was pursued with ardent fervor, was designated by the word מִדְרָשׁ (Midrash), derived from the verb דָרַשׁ (to expound), and was subdivided in Halakhic Midrash and Haggadic Midrash. The Halakhic trend in the interpretation of Scripture relates to conduct; the Haggadic, to edification, comfort, and admonition.² Although the two trends are found interwoven in Rabbinic literature, it is an understandable fact that with the coming of Christ and the fulfilment of the law, the emphasis in NT literature shifted from the Halakhic to the Haggadic Midrash. Hence our study will be concerned primarily with the latter type of interpretation, with its form and expression. "Haggadic statements are independent entities, containing ideas or describing situations that are complete in themselves." ³ These statements may be characterized as being of a homiletical nature. They may be "described as collections of sermonic material for ends of religious and moral instruction and edification." ⁴

The study of the interpretation of the Holy Books gave rise to a number of rules (מִדּוֹת) which were deduced from existing exegetical material and which were employed in the further exposition of Scripture. The collecting of a few of these conventional middoth is ascribed to Rabbi Hillel (died *c.* 20 A.D.), who formulated them in seven rules:

1. *a minori ad maius* (קל וחומר);
2. analogy of expressions (גזירה שוה);
3. and 4. generalization (בניו אב מכתוב אחד);
5. general and particular (כלל ופרט);
6. analogy of a similar passage (כיוצא בו ממקום אחר);
7. contextual explanation (דבר הלמד מעניינו).⁵

The *kal wahomer* expresses the idea of an inference from minor to major; *i.e.*, particulars which are applicable in the case of

---

¹ E. Schürer, *Geschichte*⁴, Vol. II, pp. 373ff.
² H. L. Strack, *Einleitung in Talmud und Midrasch*, pp. 4ff; and cf. J. W. Doeve, *Jewish Hermeneutics*, pp. 55f.; I. Elbogen, *Gottesdienst*, p. 195; G. F. Moore, *Judaism*, Vol. I, p. 319.
³ M. Kadushin, *The Rabbinic Mind*, p. 60.
⁴ Moore, *Judaism*, Vol. I, p. 133.
⁵ E. E. Ellis, *Paul's Use of the OT*, p. 41; and cf. Strack, *Einleitung in Talmud und Midrasch*, pp. 97ff.

minor things certainly hold for the major things. "And Jehovah said to Moses, If her (Miriam's) father had but spit in her face, should she not be ashamed seven days?" (Num. 12:14). The inference from the minor to the major is that now in the presence of Yahweh she should be ashamed for the period of fourteen days. [1] An example of analogy of expressions may be found in Ex. 20. In the 29th verse the word "midnight" is used, hence the demonstrative expression "that night" in the 12th verse must also refer to midnight. Likewise verse 8 is to be interpreted that "they may eat the flesh" until midnight.[2] The text "he shall pour out the blood thereof, and cover it with dust" (Lev. 17:13) is interpreted as a generalization; for with whatever member of his body he pours out the blood, he must also cover it, *i.e.*, he may not use his foot.[3] The particular is stated in Lev. 1:2, ,,When any man *of you* offereth an oblation unto Jehovah"; and the general in Lev. 13:2, "When a man shall have in the skin of his flesh a rising." [4] "And it came to pass, when Moses held up his hand, that Moses prevailed" (Ex. 17:11), signifies that as long as Israel lifted up their thoughts to God they would prevail. The same idea is expressed in the lifting up of the serpent on a pole (Num. 21:8), thus indicating that by analogy of a similar passage the Israelite who turned his thoughts to God would be saved.[5] "Ye shall not steal" in Lev. 19:11 refers to money theft, because the whole context (19:10–15) speaks of money matters.[6]

In the collecting and formulating of rules Hillel was followed by Rabbi Ishmael (died in the first half of the 2nd century) who expanded the existing seven rules to 13; and Rabbi Eliezer ben Jose ha-Galili, between the years 130 and 160, extended and supplemented these to the total number of 32. "It must be borne in mind, however, that neither Hillel, Ishmael nor Eliezer ben Jose ha-Galili sought to give a complete enumeration of the rules of interpretation current in his day, but that they omitted from their collection many rules which were then followed." [7] In

---

[1] Baba Bathra 111a, *BT*, p. 459.
[2] Pesachim 120b, *BT*, pp. 620f.
[3] Shabbath 22a, *BT*, p. 94.
[4] *Midrash Rabbah*, Leviticus, II,6, p. 24.
[5] Rosh Hashanah 29a, *BT*, pp. 133f.
[6] Sanhedrin 86a, *BT*, p. 569.
[7] J. Z. Lauterbach, "Talmud Hermeneutics," *JE*, p. 30.

Talmud hermeneutics various rules exist which relate to grammar and exegesis, prefixes and suffixes, as well as the interpretation of certain letters.[1]

This would have been the end of our historical survey [2] of hermeneutical principles which have direct bearing on the study of NT exegesis, had it not been for the discovery of the Dead Sea Scrolls (DSS) [3] and the subsequent results published in recent years.

> The importance of Biblical interpretation to ancient Judaism is one of the facts which is limelighted by the study of the Dead Sea Scrolls. ... [They] bear witness, not merely to the great importance attached to the study of the Scriptures, but also to the technique of Biblical interpretation among the ancient Jews. This information is all the more enriching and illuminating since it comes to us not from the Pharisees, but from a sect bitterly opposed to them.[4]

Although the Zadokite Document (CDC) mentions the word *pesher* once (iv. 13ff.), it was not until the discovery and study of the Habakkuk Commentary (1QpH), and fragments of Isaiah, Nahum, Hosea, Micah, Zephaniah, and Psalms, that this word

---

[1] *Ibid.*, p. 30.

[2] Of course, the writings of Philo, Josephus, and the Early Church Fathers are left to be investigated, but they do not contribute substantially in any way to the development in hermeneutics. Out of a mixture of rules and principles derived from *Midrashim* and Stoic literature Philo formulated his own hermeneutical maxims. While Josephus conservatively abides by the hermeneutical principles laid down by his contemporaries, the Early Church Fathers were guided by the fundamental idea of fulfilment, on the basis of which they considered the Holy Books of the OT amenable to a Christological interpretation. For further reference consult first, C. Siegfried *Philo von Alexandria*, p. 165; second, J. L. Koole, *Overname van het OT*. pp. 134–251; third, K. Grube, "Die hermeneutischen Grundsätze Justins des Martyrers," *Katholik*, 66(1880), I, pp. 21–34; fourth, J. Hoh, *Die Lehre des Hl. Irenäus über das Neue Testament*, p. 110.

[3] Throughout our study the following abbreviations will be used :
    DSS   Dead Sea Scrolls
    CDC   Zadokite Document
    1QpH   Habakkuk Commentary
    4QpM   Micah Commentary

[4] W. H. Brownlee, "Biblical Interpretation," *BA*, 14(1951), p. 54.

started to gain in significance. These writings reveal the régular manner of quoting a Biblical verse usually followed by the phrase פִּשְׁרוֹ עַל (its interpretation concerns) and the announced explanation. The root פשר is Aramaic, and is found in the book of Daniel more than 30 times either as noun or verb. The noun פשר is also used in Eccl. 8:1.

> Pesher as we chiefly know it from the sect in the wilderness of Judaea is either an interpretation of a consecutive text, DSH [1QpH] and DS Micah [4QpMicah], or it arises out of different fixed passages of text, CDC. It is always a question of a textual exposition, however. The word actually means "exposition," "interpretation." Furthermore, what is typical to pesher is that in the exposition certain words and sentences from the text are repeated.[1]

Yet the methodology of interpretation found in 1QpH and in the Rabbinic *Midrashim* differs in that the former quotes the whole Biblical text to be explained, thereby giving the interpretation with repeated references to words in the cited passage, while the latter adduces only single phrases, sometimes only words, followed immediately by the explanation. Characteristic of the Rabbinic *Midrashim* is the traditional question-and-answer method by which a Scripture passage is interpreted and surrounded by the names of all kinds of prominent Rabbinical authorities on the Holy Books. In the 1QpH we find none of this, but rather meet with a concrete exposition set forth in black and white.[2] For example the expounding of Hab. 2:17 in 1QpH is as follows:

> *For the violence done to Lebanon will overwhelm you; the destruction of the beasts will terrify you, for the blood of men and violence to a land, to a city and all who dwell in it.* This saying means the wicked priest, that to him may be paid his recompense, as he recompensed the poor; for Lebanon is the council of the community, and the beasts are the simple ones of Judah, the doers of the law. God will execute judgment upon him, and destroy him, as he plotted to destroy the poor. And as for what it says, *for the blood of a city and violence to a land,* this means the city, that is Jerusalem, in which the wicked priest wrought abominable works and defiled God's sanctuary; *and violence*

---

[1] B. Gärtner, "Habakkuk Comm. (DSH) and Matthew," *ST*, 8(1954), p. 12. Also see C. Roth, "Qumran Exegesis," *VT*, 10(1960), p. 51.

[2] Cf. Brownlee, *BA*, 14(1951), p. 75.

to a land, these are the cities of Judah, because he plundered the wealth of the poor.¹

A considerable degree of freedom in citing Scripture texts is displayed in those compositions of the DSS which exhibit the *pesher* type of interpretation. In respect to textual variants the commentator may take that reading which suits his purpose best, even though in the course of the explanation he may give evidence that he knows about an alternative reading. "He has been suspected of deliberately altering the text here and there in order to make the application more pointed, but the suspicion does not amount to proof." ²

It is rather difficult to deduce some concrete principles from the methodology prevalent in the days when the DSS were written. Brownlee has attempted to formulate some hermeneutical rules which he derived from a study on the 1QpH.

1. Everything the ancient prophet wrote has a *veiled, eschatological meaning*.
2. Since the ancient prophet wrote cryptically, his meaning is often to be ascertained through a *forced, or abnormal* construction of the Biblical text.
3. The prophet's meaning may be detected through the study of the *textual or orthographic peculiarities* in the transmitted text. Thus the interpretation frequently turns upon the special reading of the text cited.
4. A *textual variant,* i.e. a different reading from the one cited, may also assist interpretation.
5. The application of the features of a verse may be determined by *analogous circumstance,* or by
6. *Allegorical propriety*.
7. For the full meaning of the prophet, *more than one meaning* may be attached to words.
8. In some cases the original prophet so completely veiled his meaning that he can be understood only by an *equation of synonyms,* attaching to the original word a secondary meaning of one of its synonyms.
9. Sometimes the prophet veiled his message by writing one word instead of another, the interpreter being able to recover the prophet's meaning by a *rearrangement of the letters in a word, or by*
10. *The substitution of similar letters* for one or more of the letters in the word of the Biblical text.

---

¹ M. Burrows, *Dead Sea Scrolls,* p. 370.
² F. F. Bruce, *Biblical Exegesis,* p. 12.

11. Sometimes the prophet's meaning is to be derived by the *division of one word into two or more parts*, and by expounding the parts.
12. At times the original prophet concealed his message beneath abbreviations, so that the cryptic meaning of a word is to be evolved through *interpretation of words, or parts of words, as abbreviations.*
13. *Other passages of scripture* may illumine the meaning of the original prophet.[1]

Many of the proposed rules are easily recognized as principles pertaining to the ancient Jewish *Midrashim*. These early *Midrashim*, in the application of Scripture passages, reveal a more or less creative freedom in the manipulation of the scriptural text. There seems to be reason to suppose that it was not so much a fixed and recognized text which was used for interpretative purposes, as that it was a text which still circulated in a state of flux, so that it presented far more opportunities to the art and method of hermeneutics.[2] In addition, attention has been called to the fact that whenever one whose mother tongue is the Hebrew language, uses a word which is ambiguous, he is immediately conscious of the double meaning it conveys.[3]

Although the document entitled CDC has been discovered prior to the documents of the DSS, both corpora belong to the sectarian people adhering to the teachings of this literature. The question whether these sectarians had only one abode, Judaea, or whether they had moved to Damascus, remains debatable;[4]

---

[1] Brownlee, *BA*, 14(1951), pp. 60ff. The objections raised by K. Elliger, *Studien zum Habakuk-Kommentar vom Toten Meer*, to these principles are ably refuted by Brownlee himself in a review on Elliger's book; see *JBL*, 73(1954), pp. 255f.

[2] Cf. I. L. Seeligmann, "Midraschexegese," *Congress Volume, Copenhagen*, p. 150.

[3] D. Yellin, "Doppeldeutung in der Bibel," *Tarbiz*, 5(1934), pp. 1ff., (Hebrew), as referred to by Seeligmann, *Congress Volume*, p. 158.

[4] M. Burrows, "The Discipline Manual," *Oudtest. Stud.*, 8(1950), p. 150, has put forth the hypothesis that the DSS and the CDC reflect two phases in the history of the sectarian people. The DSS refer more or less to the days when these sectarians had their dwelling in Judaea, while the CDC had bearing on the period spent in Damascus. However, K. G. Kuhn, "Der gegenwärtige Stand," *ThLZ* 85(1960), col. 653, questions the sectarian sojourn in Damascus. "Strittig bleibt die Frage, ob die mehrmalige Erwähnung des Exils 'im Lande Damaskus' einen realen Aufenthalt der

but the question whether there are certain changes, modifications, and similarities reflected in the two bodies of literature mentioned is to be answered directly: "Moreover, it might be said that, after all, the Zadokite work is not a *pesher*, and that accordingly we need not expect to find its application of Scripture following *pesher* principles. It is doubtful, however, if we should take this consideration too seriously; it may be that the Zadokite writer did think of his exegesis as being in the true *pesher* style." [1] It is evident that the frequent use of the phrase "its interpretation concerns" in 1QpH is found only once in CDC. On the other hand, in the Zadokite work the Hebrew demonstrative זה (this is) is found occasionally, and it is considered synonymous to the word *pesher*.[2]

Perhaps a certain trend of development in CDC may be noticed in respect to the choice of citations taken from Scripture. Whereas the 1QpH is somewhat of a running commentary on the text of Habakkuk, CDC presents a great variety of quotations taken from the Pentateuch, the Psalms, and the Prophets. Certain key-words are followed up in the Zadokite work, which result at times in the combination of several Biblical quotations. Similarities with 1QpH are seen not only in the freedom of citing Scripture, and in the use of part of a citation merely to prove the point at stake, but also in the changing of suffixes and tenses of some verbs and nouns so that they are adaptable to context quotations.[3]

It will be apparent that the literary principles and practices brought to light in the DSS and CDC find response in the NT Scriptures. Hence the results of the recent studies in the literature pertaining to the sectarians are of great importance to a better understanding of the NT. Also, in addition to the principles and practices, it is equally important to be aware of the application of the exegetical contents of sectarian literature. Thus we may observe similarity of thought between DSS, CDC, and the NT. There is *e.g.* the tendency to succumb to the motif of adaptation

---

Gemeinde in diesem Land bezeichnet, oder ob Damaskus hier 'apokalyptischer Deckname' für Qumrän ist, und das dann wohl auf Grund von Amos 5,26f."

[1] Bruce, *Biblical Exegesis*, p. 28.
[2] B. J. Roberts, "Damascus Document," *BJRL*, 34(1951-54), p. 375.
[3] Gärtner, *ST*, 8(1954), pp. 14f.

which was coupled in the entire post-exilic era with the expectation of the Messiah.[1]

There was the hope that the Messiah would not only come in the form of king, but would also come as a prophet, such as Moses had predicted in Deut. 18:15ff. This expectation lived among the people at the time John the Baptist and Jesus began their public ministries. In John 1:19ff. we read that a delegation from Jerusalem came to John, and one of the questions they asked is, "Art thou the prophet?" By using the definite article this delegation of priests and Levites pointed to a well-known concept, for John did not ask, "Which prophet?" He knew immediately that they referred to the national hope embodied in the prophecy recorded in Deut. 18:15ff. When Jesus broke the bread for the 5000, the people marvelled at the miracle and said, "This is of a truth the prophet that cometh into the world" (John 6:14). Again, when Jesus stood in the Temple on the last day of the feast and spoke of living water, some in the crowd said, "This is of a truth the prophet" (John 7:40). Also, the Samaritan woman at Jacob's well said to Jesus, "I know that Messiah cometh (he that is called Christ): when he is come he will declare us all things" (John 4:25).[2]

According to the Scriptures (II Sam. 7:12ff.) and as testified by the people (John 7:42), the Messiah must come forth out of the seed of David. This belief, present with the Jewish people of Jesus' day, is also reflected in the Qumran document provisionally entitled 4 Q Florilegium. This document is made up of some 21 fragments representing most of one column of 19 lines; it "is mainly concerned with the re-establishment of the House of David in the last days."[3] The fragmentary document, which may be called an anthology of Scripture passages referring to the rebuilding of the Davidic House, is a combination of II Sam. 7:12ff. and Pss. 1 and 2. "It will be seen that the scroll was apparently devoted to a collection of *midrashim* on certain biblical

---

[1] Seeligmann, *Congress Volume*, pp. 172f.
[2] Cf. Bruce, *Biblical Exegesis*, pp. 44f. Also cf. John 7:52 where P66 offers the definite article: "*the* prophet." And see O. Cullmann, *Christologie*, pp. 35f. on his interpretation of John 6:14, and his discussion on Jesus, the prophet.
[3] J. M. Allegro, "Messianic References," *JBL*, 75(1956), pp. 176f.

texts, compiled perhaps for their common eschatological interest."[1] Thus the document does not consist of a series of proof texts after the fashion of a *Testimony Book*, but rather of texts which are provided with interpretations in the *pesher* style.

A certain measure of similarity is found between 1QpH, CDC, and 4 Q Florilegium, in the display of a remarkable freedom in quoting the text of Scripture. Be this as it may, greater affinity is shown between CDC and the last mentioned fragmentary document in interpreting certain Biblical passages. On the exposition of II Sam. 7:14, 4 Q Florilegium speaks of an eschatological personality in the form of the "interpreter of the law," who is mentioned in the same breath as the Davidic Messiah. Behind this exposition lies a Jewish tradition based on Num. 24:17, "There shall come forth a star out of Jacob, and a sceptre shall rise out of Israel." According to this tradition the text refers to two eschatological personalities, the star and the sceptre: the interpreter of the law and the Davidic ruler. Now also CDC (vii. 18–20) gives a similar explanation of Num. 24:17: ". . . the star is the interpreter of the law who came (or: shall come) to Damascus, as it is written: 'There shall come a star out of Jacob and a scepter shall rise out of Israel' — the scepter is the prince of all the congregation, and when he arises he shall strike violently all the sons of Seth."[2] The "prince of all the congregation" is to be identified with the Davidic ruler, and the "star out of Jacob" with the Messiah from Aaron, the eschatological high priest, thus the "interpreter of the law."

The Qumran literature and CDC have been of great influence in providing a better understanding of the hermeneutical principles relative to the NT; and it is a matter of fact that some of these same principles should be found in the writings of the Apostolic Fathers, *e.g.*, in the Epistle of Barnabas (6,10 and 10,2.9). Something of the same spirit is reflected in patristic exegesis in which attempts are made to find a deeper meaning than the one presented in the literal interpretation.[3]

---

[1] Allegro, "Fragments of a Qumran Scroll," *JBL*, 77(1958), p. 350.
[2] Rabin, *Zadokite Documents*, p. 30; also see D. Flusser, "Two Notes on the Midrash on 2 Sam. vii," *IEJ*, 9(1959), pp. 104f.
[3] E. Osswald, "Zur Hermeneutik des Habakuk-Kommentars," *ZAW*, 68, NF 27(1956), p. 255.

2. Application

Jesus in defending himself against the Jews concerning his Sonship says, "For if ye believed Moses, ye would believe me. But if ye believe not his writings, how shall ye believe my words?" (John 5:46f.). These words of Jesus characterize the introduction of a new period in the interpretation of the OT Scriptures. The proclamation of the Kingdom of Heaven has called for a revision in exegesis, has demanded a new Christian midrash.

In Mt. 13:52 and 23:34 the word *scribe* is used, meaning unequivocally, according to the context, Christian scribes. In the parallel passage of Mt. 23:34 Luke does not use the word *scribes* but, rather, *apostles* (Lk. 11:49). "Matthew's version, as compared to that of Luke, already seems to indicate that in some circles of the very earliest Christians apostles were regarded as Christian scribes." [1] Hence the Gospels provide indirect evidence that the interpretation of Scripture is continued in the very early stages of the Christian Church according to the methodology prevalent in that day, but due to a different point of departure the resulting midrash deviates in content from its Rabbinic counterpart.

Rabbinic hermeneutical principles are not hard to find in the Gospels. The *kal wahomer* is to be located every time something of minor significance is compared to that of major importance and the customary comparative phrase "how much more" is used.[2] In Mt. 12:3-6, which represents two typically Jewish principles, we find a *gezerah shewah* (analogy of expressions) in the verses 3 and 4, and a *kal wahomer* in 5 and 6. The verses 2 and 4, representing the conventional question-and-answer of the midrash, show the analogous expression "it is not lawful"; again, verse 6, which is also given in the form of the traditional question-and-answer, gives evidence of the *a minori ad maius* with the use of the phrase "one greater than." [3]

In his *The School of St. Matthew*, Stendahl has attempted to show that the *pesher* type of interpretation is also expressed in the Gospel according to Matthew.[4] It is rather misleading to

---

[1] Doeve, *Jewish Hermeneutics*, pp. 103f.
[2] E.g., Mt. 7:11 (Lk. 11:13); Mt. 10:25; Lk. 12:28.
[3] Cf. Doeve, *Jewish Hermeneutics*, pp. 106f.
[4] K. Stendahl, pp. 194-206.

speak of this type of interpretation with reference to Matthew, since the Biblical citation with repetition of words and phrases and its accompanying explanation is lacking in this Gospel.[1] One aspect characteristic of the *pesher* is the textual exposition within a certain quotation. "In *pesher* quotation or Midrash the interpretation or exposition is incorporated into the body of the text itself, thereby determining its textual form."[2] Since *pesher* is much more than exposition by means of a textual variation, it is a misrepresenting of the case to apply this type of interpretation to the Gospel according to Matthew without further explanation.

If there should be any one of the NT authors who betrayed Rabbinic schooling in his writings, then it would be the apostle Paul. "Reading habits, methodology, and hermeneutical norms were firmly implanted by his parents, his synagogue and, most of all, his teacher in rabbinics — Gamaliel."[3] Although it is a well-known fact that Paul's use of OT quotations differs from the Rabbinic in emphasis and application, it is still profitable to detect various hermeneutical principles which both parties have in common.

A typical Jewish haggadic midrash with a Christian modulation is recorded in I Cor. 10:1ff. The haggada relating the baptism in the Red Sea belonged to the Synagogue, where it was taught.[4] Likewise the rock which accompanied the Israelites on their journey through the wilderness is a midrash taught in the Synagogue.[5] Although Paul gives a Christian interpretation to the text, "for they drank of the spiritual rock that followed them: and the rock was Christ," he nevertheless makes use of a synagogal midrash. According to the tradition in Ex. 17:3ff. Moses strikes a rock, and calls the place where the water comes forth Massah and Meribah (17:7); in Num. 20:2ff. Moses in an almost identical situation, produces water out of a rock, and Yahweh says, "These are the waters of Meribah" (20:13). In spite of the fact that the one incident took place at Rephidim and the other at Kadesh,

---

[1] Gärtner, *ST*, 8(1954), p. 12.
[2] Ellis, *Paul's Use of the OT*, p. 141.
[3] *Ibid.*, p. 38.
[4] Str.-B., III, p. 405.
[5] Str.-B., III, p. 406.

the ultimate conclusion in the eyes of the Rabbis was: the rock followed Israel on its journey.[1]

The Epistles of Paul do not not only give evidence of hermeneutical principles practised in the schools of the Rabbis, but even show some similarities to DSS and CDC, especially in the matter of the *pesher* type of explanation. An example may be found in Rom. 9:7f. where Paul quotes the text out of Gen. 21:12, "In Isaac shall thy seed be called." Instead of the phrase "its interpretation concerns" he used the equivalent expression τοῦτ' ἔστιν (that is), followed by an interpretation applicable to the discourse. But a more pronounced example of the *Midrash pesher* is recorded in Rom. 10:5–9. Here passages of the OT Scriptures are quoted, adapted, and interpreted. Several times the expression "that is" is employed in order to bring out the interpretation of the quoted Scripture verse;[2] and according to true *pesher* style phrases of the citation are repeated in the accompanying explanation (10:9).

The Epistle to the Hebrews and also the Epistle to the Romans exhibit Hillel's *kal wahomer* principle by comparing the minor to the major. Obvious instances are given by the author to the Hebrews, *e.g.* 9:13f., "For if the blood of goats and bulls, and the ashes of a heifer ... sanctify unto cleanness of the flesh, how much more shall the blood of Christ." Also Heb. 10:28f., "A man that hath set at nought Moses' law dieth without compassion ... of how much sorer punishment ...." In Rom. 11 there are two outspoken examples of this hermeneutical rule, *i.e.*, verses 12 and 24, with the phrase "how much more." Granted that we cannot speak of clear-cut instances of the *kal wahomer* principle, it is undeniable that the author to the Hebrews employs the concept of comparison, exemplified in contrasting the Son to the angels (1:4), Jesus to Moses (3:3), and the old to the new covenant (8:6).

Perhaps traces showing affinity to characteristics in Jewish

---

[1] Tos. Sukkah III, 11ff. Str.-B., III, pp. 405f. Doeve, *Jewish Hermeneutics*, pp. 110f.

[2] Cf. CDC vii, 18ff. Rabin, *Zadokite Documents*, p. 30. See also Gärtner, *ST*, 8(1954), p. 14.

midrashim may be found in the quotations which are stated in interrogatory form in the first chapter of Hebrews.[1] Yet of far greater significance is the manner in which Scripture is explained in this Epistle according to the *pesher* style of interpretation so common in DSS and CDC. Nearly every chapter of Hebrews reveals the peculiar features of the *Midrash pesher.*

One feature typical of *pesher* is the substitution of words. This substitution may be due at times to textual variants, at other times to a choice of synonyms. Most likely the author has chosen his words in order to be able to explain the point at issue in such a way that the essential meaning of Scripture is brought to light. The author's choice of the word "angels" (1:6), which supports the proposition of the superiority of the Son over the angels, may have been a variant reading.[2] The word "sons" at this place would have been a source of confusion, especially in the light of the next chapter in Hebrews. Interpretative molding of the OT citation is displayed in Heb. 10:37f., where the meaning of the text is placed within an apocalyptic framework, so that the quotation itself has become a quotation-exposition, a *Midrash pesher.*[3] It is rash to conclude that the author changes the text of the citation without regard for the correct translation rendered in the Greek version. In Heb. 7:2 he uses the *ad hoc* rendering "divided," instead of the LXX form "gave"; yet in 7:4 he gives the reading which had been expected in the 2nd verse. In addition, it is superfluous to mention that the use of the LXX version presented far more hermeneutical possibilities than the MT could provide.

A second feature characteristic of the *Midrash pesher* is the length of the Biblical passage quoted, immediately followed by its interpretation. It is not difficult to locate examples illustrative of this tendency in the Epistle to the Hebrews. In 2:6–8 a few verses from Ps. 8 are given with their subsequent interpretation. A rather lengthy OT quotation is recorded in 3:7–11 where half of Ps. 95 is quoted. The commentary on this psalm takes up all

---

[1] Heb. 1:5,13.

[2] Cf. P. Winter, "Söhne Gottes," *ZAW*, 67, NF 26(1955), p. 48; A. Bakker, "Christ an Angel," *ZNW*, 32(1933), p. 261.

[3] Cf. E. E. Ellis, "A Note on Pauline Hermeneutics," *NTS*, 2(1955–56), pp. 127–133.

of the third and most of the fourth chapter of Hebrews. Similar instances may be found in Heb. 10:5–10 and 12:5–8.

The third feature is the repetition of words, phrases, and sentences of the quotation, provided with an applicable interpretation in the ensuing commentary. Examples are not only limited to the passages referred to already; they are also to be found throughout the Epistle.

Psalm 2:7

When we direct our attention to the individual psalm quotations in the Epistle to the Hebrews, we are confronted with a citation taken from Ps. 2:7: "Thou art my Son, this day have I begotten thee." The author already referred to the word *Son* in his introduction (1:2). It is interesting to note the analogy between Rom. 1:2–4a and Heb. 1:1,2, and 5. Both introductions speak of prophets, Son, Son of God, and seed of David — although Hebrews does so in the form of a quotation out of II Sam. 7:14a. While much is taken for granted in the first few verses of Rom. 1, the author to the Hebrews searches the Scriptures and quotes the OT verbally.

The combination of the first two quotations in Heb. 1 may lead to the question whether Ps. 2:7 could not stand alone — why does it need the confirmation of II Sam. 7:14a? This question cannot be answered before we know what the associations were which the recipients of the Epistle attached to Ps. 2:7.

In Rabbinic literature the text was interpreted to refer to the children of Israel, or to the Messiah who occupied himself with the Torah.[1] The stumbling-block in ascribing the verse in Ps. 2:7 to the Davidic Messiah is presented in the word *Son*. Only when the OT Scriptures necessitate the application of the title *Son of God* to the Messiah, will Rabbinic Judaism consent to this interpretation.[2] In all probability the Rabbis purposely avoided

---

[1] Cf. W. G. Braude, *Midrash on Psalms*, Vol. I, pp. 40f.

[2] "...als selbständige, von einer Schriftstelle unabhängige Messiasbezeichnung findet sich 'Sohn' Gottes... nicht in der rabbinischen Literatur." Str.-B., III, p. 20. Also see A. S. van der Woude, *Mess. Vorstellungen*, pp. 173f. "Judaism energetically objected to the title 'Son of God' being given to the Messiah. It was the stumbling-block for Israel, and brought Jesus to the Cross," D. Plooy, "Baptism of Jesus," *Amicitiae Corolla*, p. 247.

the messianic interpretation of this appellation because of their opposition to Christianity. This supposition is based on several well-founded reasons. *1.* In the Jewish pseudepigrapha the term *Son of God* is used.[1] *2.* In the Gospels this title played a major role : the Temptation account centers around the title *Son of God*; in the trial before the high priest the expression is decisive in Jesus' verdict.[2] *3.* In the conception of the Early Church Jesus was called *Son of God* at the time of his baptism. *4.* The Targum on Ps. 2:7 has not only weakened the meaning of Sonship, but also on II Sam. 7:14 it has taken the force out of the Biblical passage.[3] *5.* The fragmentary document 4 Q Florilegium, by quoting II Sam. 7:14 which adds "He is the shoot of David," definitely refers to the Qumran Davidic Messiah, just as the NT applies this thought to Jesus.[4]

It may be submitted as relatively certain that the recipients of the Epistle to the Hebrews understood the term *Son of God* to refer to Christ. Yet the question remains why the author of this Epistle adds the quotation of II Sam. 7:14 to Ps. 2:7. We would be tempted to suppose that he is applying one of Hillel's hermeneutical rules, *e.g.*, *gezerah shewah* (analogy of expressions). Perhaps this is true; but there is a greater possibility that this combination stems from a common tradition.

Acts 13:33 also renders the quotation from Ps. 2:7. The verses 17-23 of Acts 13 call for an OT passage which may supply the details that are mentioned. The source of information is found in the words of II Sam. 7:6–16, for this passage speaks of the Exodus, the Judges, and Saul (cf. vv. 6,11,15), and above all refers to the seed of David and the Son of Yahweh (vv. 12–14). With this OT Scripture passage as basis it was rather easy to make the transition from Acts 13:23 to 13:33.[5] It is not merely in this

---

[1] IV Esra 7:28f.; 13:32,37,52; 14:9; cf. I Enoch 105,2.

[2] Mt. 4:3,6 (par.); 26:63 (par.); 27:40,43,54 (par.).

[3] Cf. Str.-B., III, p. 16. "Merkwürdig ist jedenfalls dass II Sam. 7, 14 in der rabbinischen Literatur nirgends messianisch gedeutet worden ist (cf. Str.-B., III, p. 677). Die Stelle wurde von Salomo her erklärt," van der Woude, *Mess. Vorstellungen*, p. 174.

[4] Y. Yadin, "A Midrash on 2 Sam. vii and Ps. i – ii (4 Q Florilegium)," *IEJ*, 9(1959), p. 97. Also see Allegro, "Messianic References," *JBL*, 75(1956), pp. 176f.

[5] Doeve, *Jewish Hermeneutics*, pp. 172f.

recorded speech that the apostle Paul shows the intricate relationship between the passages out of Ps. 2 and II Sam. 7; also in his introductory words of the Epistle to the Romans this combination is manifested; "... concerning his Son, who was born of the seed of David ..." (Rom. 1:3).

Psalm 104:4

By means of the quotations in chapter 1 the author to the Hebrews is trying to substantiate his proposition that the Son has "become so much better than the angels." While in the introductory formula "for unto which of the angels said he at any time ...," (with its respective quotations), there is a contrast between Son and angels with emphasis on the word *Son*, the declarative statement "and of the angels he saith ...," (with its quotation), puts the weight of the argument on the words *angels* and *ministers*. The implied meaning of Ps. 104:4 in the context of Heb. 1 is that the angels are devoid of ruling power, since they are but servants.

Apparently the author to the Hebrews was motivated in his choice of Ps. 104:4 by at least three reasons. First, the LXX version employed by the writer of the Epistle afforded him the reading *angels* instead of *sons* in Deut. 32:43. In this verse the angels are exhorted to pay homage to the Son, the firstborn. The implication of the servility of these heavenly beings undoubtedly has induced the author to quote Ps. 104:4. Second, in this psalm passage the word *angels* occurs, which is needed in building up the contrast in chapter 1, as well as the word *servants* ($\lambda\epsilon\iota\tau o\nu\varrho\gamma o\iota$), which describes the quality and function of these heavenly beings. Third, the reading of the LXX in this OT Scripture passage with its hermeneutical trend lends itself much better to the author's purpose than a literal rendition of the MT. In the MT Yahweh is described as God "clothed with honor and majesty" (v. 2), to whom all the forces in nature are obedient, for it is he "who maketh winds his messengers, flames of fire his ministers." With the interchanging of the double objects in the Greek translation the conveyed meaning of the psalm verse has been altered, resulting in a shift of emphasis. It is most suitable in bearing out the author to the Hebrews' claim of Jesus' superiority over the angels. A literal translation of the MT would have been rather out of place in the context of Heb. 1. In the Greek version God is given absolute rule over the angels, for in his hand they are no more than winds; as his servants they are but a flame of fire.

Psalm 45:6,7

The author to the Hebrews continues working out the contrast between the Son and the angels. With the μέν ... δέ he balances the two introductory formulas with their respective quotations (1:7,8); also with the words "but of the Son he saith..." he returns once again to the proof that Jesus is worthy of the title *Son of God*. Superficially we might ask why the author tries to prove Jesus' superiority over the angels by using a quotation out of Ps. 45, which is only indirectly considered messianic.[1] Yet, by returning to the passage in II Sam. 7 we notice some indications which possibly led the author to the choice of this psalm citation. It is II Sam. 7:13 which reads, "He shall build a house for my name, and I will establish the throne of his kingdom for ever"; and v. 16, "And thy house and thy kingdom shall be made sure for ever before thee: thy throne shall be established for ever." It is not amiss to assert that there is a close affinity between II Sam. 7:13,16 and Ps. 45:6 (Heb. 1:8), for the same elements are stressed: *throne, kingdom, forever*. In passing, it should be remarked that in II Sam. 7:13 the reading *"his* kingdom" is comparable to the αὐτοῦ reading of Heb. 1:8.

It remains to be answered yet why the author to the Hebrews also added the seventh verse of Ps. 45. A simple solution would be to point to the verbal correspondence between the word *"anointed"* (ἔχρισεν) and the word *Christ* (Χριστός). This answer would be satisfactory, but not thorough. The quotation ends in the words παρὰ τοὺς μετόχους σου, which is best translated: *above thy partners*. The preposition παρά, taken in the comparative sense:

---

[1] N. H. Ridderbos, "Christus in de Psalmen," *GTT*, 44(1943), p. 144, says: "Alleen Ps. 110 is een direct-Messiaanse Psalm. De bedoeling van den term 'direct-Messiaans' zal duidelijk zijn. Direct-Messiaans is een Psalm als hij rechtstreeks op Christus slaat. Indirect-Messiaans, als hij in de eerste plaats van een mens zingt, maar pas in Christus zijn vervulling vindt. ... Beginnen we met Ps. 45, den bekenden bruilofts-psalm. Dat deze Psalm niet direct, maar indirect-Messiaans is, is moeilijk te loochenen."

"in comparison to, more than, beyond," corresponds to the emphasized contrast between the Son and the angels. The substantive μέτοχος means one who shares, who participates. It points to all those who with Christ have been assigned an official function. Christ has received a place far above them.

The contrast found in the quotations of Heb. 1:7,8–9 lies in the function which Christ and the angels perform. It is the contrast of ruling and of serving. "The angels are subject to constant change, He has dominion for ever and ever; they work through material powers, He — the Incarnate Son — fulfills a moral sovereignty and is crowned with unique joy."[1] The quotations serve the purpose of stressing the essential contrast between the Son and the angels.

Psalm 102:25–27

To complete the description of the function of the Son the author quotes the verses 25 to 27 of Ps. 102. Also this quotation stresses the superiority of the Son over the angels. It indicates, first, that the Son was present and active at the time of creation. Thus, while the Son is designated as Lord of creation, it follows that the angels are but mere creatures. Second, it stresses the unchangeableness of the Lord. The angels may be changed into winds, he remains the same. The length of the citation is dependent on the thought of eternity which is placed in between the phrases "in the beginning" and "thy years shall not fail." The concept of infinite duration has already been suggested by II Sam. 7:13,16 and Ps. 45:7.

Naturally the question may be posed why the author chose a quotation out of Ps. 102, which is a psalm devoid of messianic themes.[2] Although the rule that what originally applied to God

---

[1] B. F. Westcott, *Comm.*, p. 26.
[2] E. Böhl, *Die Alttestl. Citate*, p. 269, asserts that Ps. 102 has a Christological character and that through its combination with Pss. 2, 45, and 110 it is part of a messianic tradition. "Schon diese Verknüpfung mit lauter messianischen Psalmen führt uns auf die gleichfalls messianische Deutung *dieses* Psalms." F. Delitzsch, *Comm.*, p. 39, in milder tones, suggests that the author to the Hebrews had applied Ps. 102 to Christ. However, it is hazardous to read more into this psalm than the writer of Hebrews had intended in Heb. 1:10ff. The fact remains that Ps. 102 has at all times been understood of Yahweh. "We zullen uit Hebr. 1 niet hebben af te

is now brought to bear upon Christ, provides an answer to some extent, it does not do justice to the hermeneutics current in the author's day. The LXX version in this particular passage lends itself much more to a Christological exegesis than a literal translation of the MT could bring about. It is the LXX that has the addition of the emphatic pronoun σύ and the vocative κύριε. This is what the author to the Hebrews needed in order to apply the quotation to the Son. In short, the choice of this specific verse may be classified as that aspect of the *Midrash pesher* which concerns textual changes, whereby the interpretation of the quotation is adapted to the author's purpose.

Psalm 110:1

Once again the writer returns to the literary practice of asking a rhetorical question by making use of an introductory formula, which, apart from stylistic changes, is identical to the formula in Heb. 1:5. Hence this practice is a factor which binds the quotations out of Ps. 2:7 and Ps. 110:1 together and places them on an equal level — one at the beginning and one at the end of this series of seven OT passages. However, Heb. 1:5,13 is not the first time that reference is made to these two psalms. In the first three introductory verses of Heb. 1 there is an allusion to Ps. 2:8 as well as an indirect use of a phrase out of Ps. 110:1. Besides the fact that both psalms have messianic themes, there is some correspondence between the Hebrew form חק of Ps. 2:7a and the introductory words נאם יהוה of Ps. 110:1. This utterance of Yahweh may in turn be compared to the somewhat synonymous expression *vision* in II Sam. 7:17 : "According to all these words, and according to all this *vision*, so did Nathan speak unto David." [1] This text from Ps. 110:1 is not only basic to the Epistle to the Hebrews — it is referred to and quoted in 1:3,13; 8:1; 10:12; and 12:2 — but it is found throughout the NT Scriptures. "It seems clear, therefore, that this particular verse was one of the fundamental texts of the *kerugma*, underlying almost all the

---

leiden, dat de bedoelde uitspraak van Ps. 102 speciaal den Zoon geldt, maar omdat de Zoon ook God is, geldt deze uitspraak ook van den Zoon," N. H. Ridderbos, *GTT*, 44(1943), p. 136.

[1] Cf. E. G. Briggs, *Book of Psalms*, Vol. I, p. 13; Vol. II, p. 376.

various developments of it, and cited independently in Mark, Acts, Paul, Hebrews and I Peter." [1]

Psalm 8:4–6

Still the author to the Hebrews is not finished working out the contrast between Christ and the angels, for he continues the discourse into the second chapter of his Epistle. Since Paul in I Cor. 15:25,27 and Eph. 1:20,22 and the writer of Hebrews in 1:13 and 2:8 show the succession of the quotations out of Ps. 110:1 and Ps. 8:6, it is tempting to assert that the two authors have depended on each other; or that they have relied on a *Testimony Book*; or that both have followed the same hermeneutical principle, thereby arriving at the same order and choice of quotations.

> ... What the evidence points to is a high degree of interdependence of the various Epistles on a common stock of teaching and of hymnody current in the Church which is their background. When to this are added the solid core of the Apostle's own witness to the historical facts of the Gospel: the common problems of ecclesiastical policy, both in the Church's inner life and in its relation to the outside world, which had to be faced and solved; the pervasive influence of the chief leaders, notably St. Paul; ... — when these facts are considered, they provide all the explanations we need for the many parallels which the Epistles present.[2]

While Paul in the two mentioned Scripture places only quotes the sixth verse of Ps. 8, the author to the Hebrews cites the verses 4 to 6 of this psalm. He cites these for two reasons. First, in the structure of Ps. 8 the psalmist who is speaking in the first person singular exclaims, "What is man...?" Hence within the psalm itself there is direct quotation of the thought of the poet, which requires the supplementation of a verb of thinking.[3] Second, Jesus, when led before the council, testified saying, "But from henceforth shall the Son of man be seated at the right hand of the power of God" (Lk. 22:69 par.). This utterance is a combination of Dan. 7:13 and Ps. 110:1. Apparently the synthesis of the concept "Son of man" and "sitting at the right hand of

---

[1] C. H. Dodd, *Acc. to the Scr.*, p. 35.
[2] E. G. Selwyn, *The First Epistle of St. Peter*, pp. 19f.
[3] R. Gordis, "Quotations as a Literary Usage," *HUCA*, 22(1949), p.81.

God" became tradition, for Stephen's last words created vehement reaction, "Behold, I see the heavens opened, and the Son of man standing on the right hand of God" (Acts 7:56). Thus the logical train of thought has moved from Ps. 110:1 via Dan. 7:13 to Ps. 8:4. In the discourse of the author to the Hebrews the Daniel passage happens to be the missing link. The expression υἱὸς ἀνθρώπου occurs in Dan. 7:13 and Ps. 8:5 (LXX) without the definite articles.[1]

If we may refer to a case in point in which all three features of the *Midrash pesher* are exhibited, then it is the Ps. 8 quotation in the second chapter of Hebrews. First, there is the tendentious changing of the text which, though in this case due to the LXX version, gives ample opportunity for possible interpretation applicable to the context of the exposition. The Hebrew verb חסר in the Piel state means: *to cause to want*, followed by מִן of the thing.[2] There is a comparison between the lower and the higher. The Greek verb ἐλαττόω means: *to make someone lower, inferior*, followed by the preposition παρά which "shows the person or thing in comparison with whom, or with what, the subject is made inferior."[3] There is a comparison between the higher and the lower. The Hebrew adverb מְעַט, which may be taken in the temporal or spatial sense, is in Ps. 8:6 (LXX) to be taken in the latter sense, thus referring to degree.[4] The Greek equivalent βραχύ τι, also denoting time or space,[5] may refer to either one in the quotation; but in the context it is to be understood as denoting time. The twofold meaning of words presented in the quotation

---

[1] It is rather interesting to note that in the midrash on Ps. 2:7 not only Ps. 110:1 is quoted in a catena of explanatory Scripture verses, but that immediately following this quotation Dan. 7:13,14 is cited. These two passages (Ps. 110:1 and Dan. 7:13,14) seem to belong together in the exposition of Ps. 2:7. See Braude, *Midrash on Psalms*, Vol. I, p. 40; and cf. F. W. Grosheide, *Zoon des Menschen*, (1921), p. 15.

[2] Gesenius, *Lexicon*, p. 295, "that he should not be much lower than God." See Brown, Driver, Briggs, *Lexicon*, p. 341; cf. Eccl. 4:8.

[3] Arndt & Gingrich, *Lexicon*, p. 247; and see Böhl, *Die Alttestl. Citate*, p. 273.

[4] Brown, Driver, Briggs, *Lexicon*, p. 590, lists the word as an adverbial accusative denoting place, II Sam. 16:1; time, Job 10:20b; degree, Ex. 23:30; Deut. 7:22; II Kings 10:18; Ezk. 11:16; Zech. 1:15. See Gesenius, *Lexicon*, p. 493.

[5] Arndt & Gingrich, *Lexicon*, p. 146; Liddell and Scott, *Lexicon*, pp. 328ff.

terminates with the word אלהים (*gods* or *deities*),[1] which in Ps. 8 is translated by the word "angels." Of course this fits admirably well into the author's discourse on the contrast between Christ and the angels.[2]

Second, an entire passage of Scripture is quoted, which becomes the object of a more or less lengthy exposition. The author to the Hebrews is not interested in giving an explanation of Ps. 8:4; apparently in accordance with tradition the concept *Son of man* was in need of no further comment. He devotes his time to the interpretation of the verses 5 and 6 of Ps. 8. There is no point in citing the rest of this psalm due to the word πάντα (8:7b – LXX) which capitulates all the details that follow.

The third feature of *Midrash pesher* is found in the repetition and exposition of various words and phrases out of the quotation. The verses 8 and 9 of Heb. 2 are exemplary of this aspect, since words such as βραχύ τι and ἐλαττόω in their application expose the meaning of the passage in question.

Psalm 22:23

The verses 10 and 11 in the second chapter of Hebrews reveal new aspects leading to introductory and preliminary remarks about the high priestly calling of the Son. The ninth verse already introduces the phase of Jesus' "suffering of death," thereby leaving the precincts of Ps. 8 and pointing to the theme of the agony of Christ. The next verse, by referring to the work of the Son, once again repeats the thought of suffering. It is this theme which in all probability led the author to the Hebrews to think

---

[1] Gesenius, *Lexicon*, p. 49, interprets the word in the plural sense, "of *gods* or *deities* in general, whether true or false," but adds in a note that "Hebrews, chaps. 1:6 and 2:7,9 shew plainly that this word sometimes means *angels*, and the authority of the N.T. decides the matter."

[2] The Dutch translation (*Nieuwe Vertaling*, N.B.G.) renders Ps. 8:5, (8:6 in N.B.G.) "Toch hebt Gij hem bijna goddelijk gemaakt"; and Heb. 2:7, "Gij hebt hem voor een korte tijd beneden de engelen gesteld."

of Jesus' death on the cross when Christ fulfilled the prophecies of Ps. 22.¹

However, the author did not take his quotation from the first part of the psalm, which deals with suffering and affliction, but from the second half which speaks of praise and glorification. The quotation represents an introduction of an expression of joyous thanksgiving offered by the psalmist. In other words, verse 23 may be regarded as a prelude to the actual song of glorification.² It is the motif of glory and honor which has been the bridge between the last half of Ps. 8 and the second part of Ps. 22.

Yet, the first part of the 22nd Psalm is not entirely lost out of sight. Once again the author seems to reach back to the agony of Christ on the cross, when he heard his scoffers say, "He trusteth on God" ($\pi \acute{\epsilon} \pi o \iota \theta \epsilon \nu \ \dot{\epsilon} \pi \acute{\iota}$);³ for the author quotes a verse found in Isa. 8:17 and II Sam. 22:3, "I will put my trust in him" ($\pi \epsilon \pi o \iota \theta \dot{\omega} \varsigma \ \dot{\epsilon} \pi'$).⁴ The addition of this citation serves the purpose of affirming the intermediary work of the high priest in the person of Christ. This quotation, as well as the next (Isa. 8:18), is connected with the formula "and again" — which is also the mark of division between the second and third OT passage. Purposely the author separated verses 17 and 18 of Isa. 8 by means of this phrase.

Now all three citations contribute to the clarification of Heb. 2:11a; and this fact has given rise to the accumulation of the

---

¹ References and allusions to the first part of Ps. 22 are almost exclusively located in the Passion narrative as recorded in the four Gospels.
Ps. 22:2 — Mt. 27:46; Mk. 15:34.
Ps. 22:6 — Rom. 5:5.
Ps. 22:8 — Mt. 27:39; Mk. 15:29; Lk. 23:35.
Ps. 22:9 — Mt. 27:43.
Ps. 22:16 — John 19:28.
Ps. 22:19 — Mt. 27:35; Mk. 15:24; Lk. 23:34; John 19:24.
See the *Index Locorum*, pp. 662f., in E. Nestle, *Novum Testamentum* ²³.
² Cf. Gordis, *HUCA*, 22(1949), p. 188.
³ Mt. 27:43.
⁴ The concept "to trust in God" is manifested by a variety of expressions in both Hebrew and Greek. When Mt. 27:43 makes use of the verbal form $\pi \acute{\epsilon} \pi o \iota \theta \epsilon \nu$ instead of the LXX form $\ddot{\eta} \lambda \pi \iota \sigma \epsilon \nu$ (Ps. 22:9), the hermeneutical rule is demonstrated that it is not so much the letter as much as the meaning of Scripture which must be explained.

passages concerned. It is Christ who is able to do justice to the words of Ps. 22:23; for he had revealed the Father's name to all those doing the will of God, becoming thereby brethren of Christ. It is Christ, in all his suffering and agony, who trusted in his Father's sending him. It is Christ, who after his "it is finished," could truly point to the fruits of his mission, *i.e.*, the children whom God had given him. All three quotations contribute to a better understanding of the work of Christ in the capacity of high priest.

Psalm 95:7–11

In an interlude of nearly two chapters the author to the Hebrews deviates from the introductory remarks on the high priesthood of Christ, by exhorting the "holy brethren, partakers of a heavenly calling" to guard against "falling away from the living God." Perhaps the discourse on the house of God, together with the association of being the people of God's pasture, induced the author to employ the last half of the 95th Psalm for the prompting of the believers. Whereas all the other citations from the OT thus far supported the argument in question and were directed to the preceding discourse, the lengthy quotation out of Ps. 95 stands separate from the foregoing and is quoted for the sake of exposition and application. The most natural explanation for the introductory word διό (3:7) is to connect it with βλέπετε (3:12) and to consider the verses 7 to 11 as a parenthetical thought.[1]

Nevertheless, the writer of the Epistle does not seem to follow the LXX version at his disposal, but appears to provide an interpretation within the text itself. Although he displays some differences in punctuation, he does not depart from any scribal rules of his contemporaries.

> One of the oldest functions of the scribes was to settle the proper division between sentences, portions of sentences and words. This was no easy work, since the ancient texts were without much visible punctuation. ... But even when a

---

[1] The commentators Moffatt, Windisch, Bonsirven, Michel, and Spicq do not advocate taking the psalm quotation as a parenthesis, thereby disagreeing with Bleek, Bisping, Weiss, Westcott, Callan, Seeberg, and Grosheide. However, the decisive element in speaking in favor of the parenthesis explanation is the inherent meaning of the word "wherefore."

measure of agreement as to periods, clauses and words had been reached, there remained a good many problems concerning the exact way in which they were related. ... Actually, under Rabbinic law, a scroll with clauses or sentences marked off from one another was — and still is — invalid for official, liturgical purposes (*Sopherim* 3, 7).[1]

Yet with this arrangement of phrases the author is able to insert the word διό at the beginning of the citation — most likely through the influence of the same inferential conjunction. However, in verse 10 διό answers fully to its expectation. On the basis of the preceding it makes the succeeding clause conclusive.

The citation, as well as its exposition, provides a most splendid exhibition of all three aspects of *Midrash pesher*. With a single glance at chapters 3 and 4 no one will doubt the presence of this type of midrash. Repetition and explanation accompanied with the necessary application is found throughout.

Psalm 110:4

After this digression the author to the Hebrews returns once more to the theme of the high priesthood of Christ. Whereas Ps. 2:7 (Heb. 1) in combination with Ps. 110:1 serves to point out Christ's kingly office and his ruling powers, Ps. 2:7 (Heb. 5) is applied with Ps. 110:4 to set forth the high priesthood of Christ, becoming "unto all them that obey him the author of eternal salvation; named of God a high priest after the order of Melchizedek" (Heb. 5:9,10).

In view of the Maccabean period and the recent studies resulting from the discoveries of the DSS, some attention should be devoted to the phenomenon in Hebrews of presenting Jesus as the kingly and the priestly Messiah. In the Maccabean era there were such personalities who were both king and high priest at the same time. The thought that the author was influenced by such historical figures while he composed his Epistle, is, however, highly unlikely. For the Maccabean princes were not of the seed of David; they were from the line of Aaron — Levitical priests — before they attained the status of royalty.[2] Could it be that the doctrine of the two Messiahs held by the DSS Sect may indirectly have had

---

[1] D. Daube, "Alexandrian Methods," *Festschrift Hans Lewald*, pp. 37f.
[2] Cf. Briggs, *Book of Psalms*, Vol. II, p. 374.

some bearing on the author's thinking? Whatever the case, the basic difference between the Sect's conception of the offices of the Messiah and the author to the Hebrews' conception, is and remains that the former expected two Messiahs from Aaron and Israel, while the writer of the Epistle combined the kingly and priestly office in the Person of the one Messiah.[1]

Psalm 40:6–8

"Now in the things which we are saying the chief point is this: We have such a high priest, who sat down on the right hand of the throne of the Majesty in the heavens" (Heb. 8:1). "But he, when he had offered one sacrifice for sins for ever, sat down on the right hand of God" (Heb. 10:12). Between these two texts — with the exception of the repetition of Jer. 31:33,34 in 10:16,17 — the author to the Hebrews presents his last didactic discourse. In this discussion of the old and the new, exemplified by a lengthy citation out of Jer. 31, the cardinal point is that Christ, in the capacity of high priest, could terminate the old dispensation by offering himself once and for all. Throughout the ninth chapter the theme of the complete efficacy of Christ's sacrifice is stressed; thus this chapter prepares the way for a quotation out of the first part of Ps. 40. The introductory $διό$ (10:5) answers fully to its expectation, for the succeeding OT passage is a statement corresponding to the foregoing disquisition. Only Christ could fulfill the words of this citation to the fullest extent.

"Just as the Qumran commentators at times chose that form of the biblical text which lent itself best to their interpretation, so in the NT we note the same sort of thing time after time."[2] The MT "mine ears hast thou opened" is not as suitable for the argument as "but a body didst thou prepare for me." It is the word *body* ($σῶμα$), not *ears* ($ὠτία$), which the author to the Hebrews is able to use beneficially. Hence he has employed his LXX text which offered him not only the reading $σῶμα$, but also the adversative particle $δέ$, providing him the opportunity to apply this reading to the sacrificial work of Christ. "By which

---

[1] See Y. Yadin, "The Dead Sea Scrolls," *Scripta Hierosolymitana*, Vol. IV, pp. 36–55.
[2] Bruce, *Biblical Exegesis*, p. 70.

will we have been sanctified through the offering of the *body of Jesus Christ once and for all"* (10:10).

It is quite apparent that the author is working according to the methodology characteristic of *Midrash pesher*. He presents the reading which lends itself best to the discourse; he quotes a few verses of the OT with accompanying interpretation; he expounds those parts of the quoted passages which have bearing on the matter, indicating this by the repetition of phrases and clauses. All three aspects of the *pesher* are clearly demonstrated in the verses 5 to 10 of the 10th chapter of Hebrews.

Psalm 118:6

The last psalm quotation in the Epistle to the Hebrews is void of any interpretative qualities which may serve as earmarks of certain hermeneutical principles. Ps. 118, in a threefold invocation (vv. 5-7), gives thanks unto Yahweh by showing the help of the Almighty in past, present, and future. It is verse 5 which speaks of the past in which Yahweh answered to distress; the next verse has reference to the present, for Yahweh is near; the seventh verse looks towards the future during which the aid of Yahweh is needed.[1] It is this sixth verse, speaking of Yahweh's nearness in the present, which the author has decided to quote. Although it does not provide any textual changes or accompanying interpretative verses, it nevertheless is a worthy conclusion to all the psalm quotations in the Epistle, for it stresses the dependence on — and trust in — the Almighty.

3. Conclusions

Now that we have gained a better understanding of the author's methodology in hermeneutics, the hypothesis that certain citations were chosen due to phraseology and sentence structure [2] causes

---

[1] T. Torrance, "The Last of the Hallel Psalms," *EvQ*, 28(1956), pp. 102f.

[2] G. Harder, "Septuagintazitate," *Theologia Viatorum*, pp. 38ff., constructs the hypothesis — suggested to some extent by F. Delitzsch, *Comm.*, p. 37, already — that the author to the Hebrews purposely chose those LXX passages which deviated from the MT, *e.g.*, Ps. 104 (103, LXX):4; Ps 45:6 (44:7, LXX); Ps. 102:25(101:26, LXX); Ps. 8:5(8:6, LXX); Ps. 95 (94, LXX):11; Ps. 40:6 (39:7, LXX); Hab. 2:3-4; Hagg. 2:6. However, this hypothesis is fallacious in that it presupposes knowledge of the Hebrew language on the part of the author to the Hebrews.

us to reflect upon the choice of psalm quotations in the Epistle to the Hebrews. The unknown writer of the Epistle to the Hebrews reveals his thorough acquaintance with the Greek text of the OT by exploiting those psalm citations which are most suitable in support of his argument. Of course it has been the LXX version which has extended to the author the opportunity of constructing his discourse on the basis of the OT Scriptures.[1]

Granted that the author, influenced by the methodology of his contempories, displays characteristics akin to the hermeneutics of the DSS Sect, we must direct our attention toward the apostolic Church and to Christ himself, if we want to come to a complete understanding of the emphases and applications of the OT quotations in Hebrews.[2] The coming of Jesus Christ into the world was *the* important factor in the interpretation of the OT. Several passages which had never enjoyed any messianic recognition were now without question applied to Christ.

The rise of Christian exegesis, marked by its emphasis on fulfilment, was not in the least out of place within the setting of first century A.D. hermeneutics. Fully persuaded that with the coming of Jesus Christ the OT prophecies concerning Christ had become reality, and guided by this basic idea of fulfilment, the authors of the NT Scriptures searched the OT for passages pertaining to the Messiah (cf. Lk. 24:27). They displayed thereby a creativity in their searching in and application of Scripture which finds its justification in the employment of hermeneutical principles current in their day.[3] This creativity did not result

---

[1] Ps. 104:4 in the LXX reveals the subordination of the angels. Ps. 102:25 has the additional words *Thou* and *Lord* which are lacking in the MT. Ps. 8:5 presents several opportunities for a Christological interpretation of the passage. Ps. 40:6, with the Greek translation *body*, provides the applicability of the citation to the sacrificial work of Christ.

[2] "Il est remaquable en effet que, dans la prédication apostolique, de caractère apologétique, telle que la révèle la littérature épistolaire du Nouveau Testament, les déclarations concernant la personne du Christ et son rôle sont appuyées moins sur les affirmations mêmes de Jésus que sur les textes de l'Ancien Testament considérés comme prophétiques," L.Venard, "Psaumes," *Mélanges*, p. 260.

[3] In contrast to the NT authors the present day writer is bound in his writing and thinking by profane motifs, by grammatico-historical principles, which characterize him as a child of his time. Hence our motifs and principles may never be foisted upon the writers and literature of the first century of our era.

in arbitrariness, but was always bound by the fundamental principle of fulfilment, and was limited by the prerequisite of harmonizing prophecy with fulfilment. It is not so much the tenacious clinging to the individual letter, but rather the sense of Scripture, which is normative in the exegesis of the OT prophecies. The author to the Hebrews interpreted the Scripture passages only in the light of the fulfilment of the OT. Therefore, it was not the letter that counted, but rather the interpretation which was directed to Jesus Christ, who fulfilled Scripture.[1]

The early exegete looked upon the OT writings as an ever-present reality. These writings spoke to him not with reference to the hoary past in which they were written, but with direct application to the exegete's day. Peter, brought before the Sanhedrin on the charge of healing a lame beggar, speaks of Jesus Christ in terms of the stone which, though rejected by the builders, became the head of the corner (Ps. 118:22).

However, in the quoting of this Scripture verse he does not abide by the text, but he applies it with the necessary changes to the rulers, elders, and scribes. Peter is saying, "He is the stone which was set at nought *of you the builders*" (Acts 4:11). Whereas the Greek version has the words οἱ οἰκοδομοῦντες, in Acts it has become ὑφ' ὑμῶν τῶν οἰκοδόμων. The Targum to this psalm passage indicates that the term "master builders" was understood to mean *the learned, the scribes*. In citing the words of Ps. 118 Peter showed that Scripture was fulfilled in Christ, and that it was to be considered as a present reality. This, therefore, justifies the free handling of the Scriptures and the direct application to the situation at hand.[2]

Characteristic in the quoting of OT Scripture passages is the fact that historicity which played a role in times past has now been relegated to an insignificant rank, as exemplified by the use of the clause, "one hath somewhere testified" (Heb. 2:6; cf. 4:4).[3]

---

[1] P. Bläser, "Schriftverwertung und Schrifterklärung," *ThQ*, 132(1952), pp. 152–169, in discussing Pauline exegetical methods, says, "Aus diesem vom Christus herkommenden Verständnis des Hl. Schrift erklärt sich wohl auch die grössere Freiheit des Apostles dem Schrifttext gegenüber; nicht mehr der einzelne Buchstabe, sondern der Sinn der Schrift allein ist massgebend," p. 169.

[2] Gärtner, *ST*, 8(1954), p. 24.

[3] Cf. L. Diestel, *Geschichte*, p. 11.

It is the Word of God spoken by the Holy Spirit or laid in the mouth of Christ, which is all-significant. Whether this word is taken out of the Pentateuch, out of the Writings, or is an utterance of one of the Prophets, the reality remains that Scripture with all its variety is regarded as one.

Nevertheless, during the first century A.D. a radical difference between the Jewish use of the OT Scripture and that of the early Christians was manifested. The distinction came to light in the shift of emphasis. No longer was the law the nucleus in Christian exegesis, but prophecy — in which the Early Church saw fulfilment in the coming of Jesus Christ. The Jews, on the contrary, used prophecy to strengthen the Torah, so that the place which the Early Church ascribed to Christ was occupied in Judaism by the five books of Moses.[1] Hence the author to the Hebrews, finding his point of departure not in the Torah but in the Psalms and Prophets which speak of Christ, applies passages out of Moses to supplement prophecies about the Messiah.

The abundance of OT quotations in the Epistle to the Hebrews tempts one to accuse the author of having resorted to a *Testimony Book*,[2] especially when certain textual combinations are also employed in other NT Epistles, *e.g.*, the succession in the quoting of Ps. 110:1 and Ps. 8:7. However, there are two basic reasons directly opposed to the supposition of borrowing from such a possible *Testimony Book*. 1) Since Ps. 110:1 is cited in Matthew, Mark, Luke, Acts, and Hebrews, we would expect identical wording of the quotation if all had drawn from the same source.[3]

---

[1] Cf. Bläser, ThQ, 132(1952), p. 164; Diestel, *Geschichte*, p. 13. Koole, *Overname van het OT*, pp. 230f., and especially p. 236, concludes that "de plaats welke Christus naar de mening der Kerk in het OT inneemt, in het Jodendom dikwijls door de Thora bekleed wordt."

[2] F. C. Synge, *Hebrews*, p. 54, is adamant in his belief that the author to the Hebrews depended solely on a *Testimony Book*. "The author has not got the Scriptures in front of him at all. What he has in front of him is a catena of passages, a Testimony Book.... Hebrews expounds them as they stand in the Testimony Book, not as they stand in the Bible." Synge's conclusion would lead to the supposition that the author's knowledge of the Scriptures must be a bare minimum, whereas in fact the contrary is true.

[3] Since we are reasoning within the realm of possibilities, it is rather simple to suggest that there were two *Testimony Books* in circulation. If this were true, the baptism scene of Jesus (Mt. 3:17, par.) would have been derived out of two different *Testimony Books*.

But while Matthew and Mark have the reading ὑποκάτω, the others give the form ὑποπόδιον.[1] 2) It is not the quotation as such that proves something, but it is the passage in its context that bears weight; e.g., it was not the mere citation of II Sam. 7:14a that was all important, rather it was the Scripture portion in its context, which provided all the links with the other quotations in the first chapter of Hebrews.

Harris' hypothesis[2] that the OT passages in Hebrews must have been gathered from a *Testimony Book*, due to their agreement with parallel quotations found in certain anti-Judaic writers, is rather loose. In the words of C. H. Dodd, "his theory outruns the evidence, which is not sufficient to prove so formidable a literary enterprise at so early a date."[3] Yet this very hypothesis may not be dismissed without further notice, for from the Qumran literature and from Jewish *Midrashim* it appears that certain quotations were brought together by means of a common motif. The 4 Q Florilegium seems to be a collection of OT passages which have reference to the restoration of David's house. Perhaps the difference between this collection and a *Testimony Book* is that the former provides a commentary along with the quoted text, while the latter apparently[4] consisted merely of assembled Scripture passages.

The Epistle to the Hebrews stands far removed from any dependence on a *Testimony Book*, for the author does not put together isolated passages, and out of this mosaic construct his argument. Behind the mere quoting of a text stands Scripture itself. "Words lifted from their Scriptural context can never be a testimonium to the Jewish mind. The word becomes a testimonium for something or other after one has brought out its meaning with the aid of other parts of Scripture."[5]

Throughout his Epistle the author features characteristics of the midrash in his interpretation of Scripture. This is nothing

---

[1] Stendahl, *The School of St. Matthew*, p. 211.
[2] R. Harris, *Testimonies*, Vol. II, pp. 43–50.
[3] Dodd, *Acc. to the Scr.*, p. 26.
[4] In the realm of suppositions and possibilities shrouding the *Testimony Book* hypothesis the word *apparently* is perhaps too strong.
[5] Doeve, *Jewish Hermeneutics*, p. 116.

new: for the midrashic method of interpreting the OT is indeed very old. Ezra and the Levites, in the time when the Jews returned from exile, interpreted Scripture for their compatriots who did not understand the Hebrew tongue anymore. "And they read in the book, in the law of God, distinctly (*i.e.*, with an interpretation); and they gave the sense, so that they understood the reading" (Neh. 8:8). The practice of expounding Scripture is marked in later years by the hairsplitting work of the Scribes and Pharisees, the composition of Targums in the vernacular, and the *Midrashim* of the Rabbis. "Midrash Haggadah arose primarily as a mode of public instruction, and constituted the sermons preached by the Rabbis. The sermons contained midrashim as the latter were employed in the course of public instruction; the sermon itself had necessarily some form of coherence of unity."[1]

It is quite understandable that this type of sermon delivery was transferred from the Synagogue to the Early Church. Many of the characteristics in the Jewish manner of expounding a portion of Scripture in respect to method, were directly passed on to the sermons preached by the apostles and evangelists. There are still a few of these early Christian *Midrashim* extant. The Second Epistle of Clement, usually considered a homily, is in fact an early midrash.[2] It may be said conclusively that the recipients of the Epistle to the Hebrews were addressed in accordance with the literary methods prevalent in that day.

Perhaps we may look upon the early Christians as a group which, on account of its relationship to Jesus Christ, stands apart and separate from the main stream of Judaism; yet "Paul, like the other NT writers, regards the Christian *ecclesia* as the faithful remnant of Israel, the true people of God."[3] The Church is the true continuation of the children of Israel who became unfaithful through unbelief at the time of the coming of the Messiah.

Recent studies resulting from the literature and customs of the DSS Sect have led some scholars to the formulation of the hypothesis which envisions a possible link between the recipients

---

[1] Kadushin, *The Rabbinic Mind*, p. 62.
[2] Cf. C. W. Dugmore, *Influence of the Synagogue*, p. 74.
[3] Ellis, *Paul's Use of the OT*, p. 136.

of the Epistle to the Hebrews and a movement stemming from the Qumran habitation.[1] Of course, the possibility is not excluded that a certain "group of Jews originally belonging to the DSS Sect were converted to Christianity carrying with them some of their previous beliefs."[2] This hypothesis would supply an answer to such questions as the superscription of the Epistle, the marked emphasis on the priestly office of Christ, and the reference to OT rituals. On the other hand, the hypothesis is not entirely free from difficulties pertaining to such matters as the salutation (Heb. 13:24), Clement of Rome's thorough acquaintance with the Epistle, and the recipients' knowledge of the Greek language.

---

[1] Cf. Yadin, "The DSS and the Epistle to the Heb.," *Scripta Hierosolymitana* Vol. IV, pp. 36–55. H. Kosmala, *Hebräer-Essener-Christen*. Also see C. Spicq, "L'Épitre aux Hébreux," *RevQ*, 1(1959), p. 389.

[2] Yadin, "The DSS and the Epistle to the Heb.," *Scripta Hierosolymitana*, Vol. IV, p. 38.

Chapter III

THE EXEGETICAL METHODS

Any author writing about the Epistle to the Hebrews attempts to point out the permanent contribution to Christian theology laid down in this NT Bible book. Whatever the theological solutions attained may be, it is a fact that the exegesis of OT passages in this Epistle does not receive great attention. The exegetical methods employed have been labeled obsolete, and they are of no interest to many modern theologians. Many "would be prepared to add that the abiding value of his (the author's) message is actually obscured by the scriptural argument in which it is embedded." [1] Charges are made that "to a modern reader the argument of Hebrews is obscure and unconvincing," and that the author employs "a method of proof which appears to us artificial." [2]

The truth of the matter is that the writer composed his Epistle independent of exegetical methods which guide "a modern reader." In his use of the Scriptures and in the formulation of his thoughts the author was dependent upon the tradition of his time. If he wanted to be effective in his approach, he had to resort to the use of methods and thoughts with which the recipients of his Epistle were familiar. Since his methodology was taken out of his time and directed towards his immediate audience, there will be much that appears strange and out-of-date to later generations. This strangeness is not located in the content of Hebrews, but rather in the formulation of the ideas expressed. [3]

Instead of passing rash and ill-founded judgments on the working methods of the author to the Hebrews, it is a judicious approach to detect his main thesis throughout his exposition of OT passages and to follow him in his reasonings in order to determine the plan and perspectives of his composition.

---

[1] G. B. Caird, "Exegetical Method," *CanJTh*, 5(1959), p. 44.
[2] E. F. Scott, *Hebrews*, p. 69.
[3] E. Riggenbach, *Brief an die Hebräer*, (Bibl. Z. und Strf.), p. 34.

1. Plan and Perspectives

In our study of the author's exegetical methods we will be concerned primarily with the didactic part of the Epistle, which extends from 1:1 to 10:18. From 10:19 to the end of Hebrews the writer enforces the practical consequences derived from his conclusions established in the doctrinal discussions.

One of the key-words found several times in nearly every chapter of the didactic part is the word *Son*, with reference to Jesus.[1] In the first chapter the appellation *Son* occurs four times (1:2,5a,5b,8): its reference is to Jesus, who has spoken the final word of God and whose relation to the Father is confirmed. The four references definitely testify to the superiority of the Son of God, who excels far above prophets and angels. In the second chapter the word *son* is used twice (2:6, the son of man; 2:10, many sons), introducing other aspects of this designation with its incumbent implications.

The words of Ps. 8:4–6 were understood generally to refer to man; and the author to the Hebrews does not intend to alter this interpretation. But realizing the incapability of sinful man, he considers the quotation fulfilled in the sinless humanity of the Son of God. Thus the exegesis of the psalm citation is applied to Jesus, and in him it is directed to man (2:9). It shows the humanity of Christ, *i.e.* his humiliation for the sake of his brethren (2:11), the "many sons" (2:10). There is a close relationship between the Son and the sons, for these two belong together and cannot be considered separate from one another.[2] Every state of the Son — suffering, sanctification, perfection, glory — is of immediate importance to the sons. Whatever is significant for the one, is equally significant for the other.[3]

Again the two parties are mentioned, but now in different

---

[1] See also J. Kögel, *Theol. Stud.*, p. 63. The passages in Heb. are: 1:2,5,8; 3:6; 4:14; 5:5,8; 6:6; 7:3,28; also 10:29.
  Cf. G. Vos, *Teaching*, pp. 73ff. Vos understands the title *Son of God* in the functional (messianic) as well as in the ontological sense (designating *nature or origin*).

[2] Cf. Rom. 8:14,17.

[3] J. Kögel, *Sohn*, p. 22, "Beide sind nicht ohne einander zu denken, und was von dem einem gilt, hat nicht weniger seine Bedeutung für die anderen; in dem Geschick des einen hat sich das der anderen verwirklicht."

wording and setting. Christ, being compared to Moses who was faithful as a servant in the house, is said to be faithful "as a son over his house, whose house are we (the sons)" (3:6). Also 4:14 reveals the two parties, "having then a great high priest..., Jesus the Son of God, let us (the sons) hold fast our confession." In this verse Jesus is pictured as our high priest. This implies his task of leading "many sons unto glory" (2:10). "In 4:14 the author's conception of Sonship is a very high one. He gives exceptionally high value to the high priesthood of Christ, and derives its eminence from the Sonship."[1] The combination of Sonship and priesthood in one person is confirmed by the use of two psalm citations in 5:5,6 (Ps. 2:7 and Ps. 110:4).

These verses emphasize the exalted position of the Son of God; yet the author does not neglect to call attention to Christ's state of humiliation. There is e.g. 5:8 which speaks of the obedience of the Son.[2] It is he who sets the example for all those who are to be called *sons*. They must realize that the virtue of faith and faithfulness is fundamental to sonship.

"In 7:3 we read that Melchizedek was made like unto the Son of God, which is a reversal of the usual statement, that Christ was made a priest after the order of Melchizedek."[3] Chapter 7, which refers twice to the Son (7:3,28), establishes the eminence of Christ as high priest and Son. Christ, in comparison to the sons of Levi (7:5), is appointed high priest as a Son, perfected for evermore.

Just as the Son of God had to endure suffering, was chastised, learned to be obedient, so his brethren must experience the same thing in order to become true sons (12:5–11). "Chastisement in the severest form is thus strong evidence of one's sonship."[4] Throughout the Epistle the author has indicated the importance and implications of Son and sons. The one does not exist and operate apart from the other.

[1] Vos, *Teaching*, p. 77.
[2] O. Michel, "Vollkommenheit," *TSK*, 106(1935), p. 348, remarks, "Wer Sohn ist, gehorcht — oder er ist nicht Sohn; aber Jesus lernt, obwohl er Sohn ist, Gehorsam auch im Leiden. Nicht aber Sohn und Gehorsam, wohl aber Sohn und Leiden scheinen Gegensätze zu sein."
[3] Vos, *Teaching*, p. 78.
[4] R. C. H. Lenski, *Comm.*, p. 434. See M. Dibelius, "Kultus," *ThBl*, 21(1942), col. 2, "Züchtigung ist ein Zeichen, dass ihr wirklich Gottes 'Söhne' seid."

Besides the word *Son* in the Epistle to the Hebrews, the word *priest* is of equal, if not greater, significance. It is striking that none of the other NT books ever refers to Christ as priest, and that the author to the Hebrews makes the words *priest* and *high priest* (with reference to Christ) key-words in his Epistle. The heart of the didactic part lies in the discussion of the high priesthood of Christ (chapter 7). Everything preceding this chapter is introductory and leads up to the full import of this high priesthood.[1]

Heb. 1, attesting the exalted position of the Son, is in fact nothing more than the preface to the didactic sections which the author discusses in Heb. 2–10. By means of the OT quotations chapter 1 reveals the exalted position of Christ. The names *Son*, *God*, and *Lord* (Pss. 2:7; 45:6; and 101:26LXX respectively) are attributed to him. It is also said of him that he occupies the place of honor: to sit at the right hand of God (Ps. 110:1). But before he is to occupy the seat at God's right hand, he is to experience the state of humiliation. After he has completed the task assigned to him in this state, he is raised to the state of exaltation. In preliminary form Heb. 1:3 provides the first indication of the task and office of Christ: "when he had made purification of sins, (he) sat down on the right hand of the Majesty on high."[2] The task of Christ is antecedent to his exaltation. First he is to fulfill his priestly task, before he may occupy the seat which entitles him to glory and honor. The motif of humiliation and exaltation is also found in the author's exegesis of Ps. 8:5 (Heb. 2:9): "... for a little while lower than the angels, even Jesus, because of the suffering of death crowned with glory and honor."

---

[1] Scott, *Hebrews*, p. 70 states that "the earlier chapters are little more than introductory to the central theme of the great High Priest." Also see Vos, *Teaching*, p. 91.

[2] F. W. Grosheide, *Opmerkingen*, p. 45 explains that the remainder of the Epistle works out the concept and the *modus quo* of the "purification of sins." Also see his *Comm.*, p. 65 n. 11, where he adds: "Het komt vaak voor in Hebr., dat een onderwerp eerst wordt genoemd, later breed uitgewerkt ...." P. Feine, *Theologie*, p. 382, commenting on Heb. 1:3 does not so much refer to the preliminary statement of this verse, but rather to the fact that humiliation is antecedent to exaltation. "Also schon hier [1:3] ist die Grundlage seiner Erhöhung sein heilsmittlerisches Tun als Mensch." And see F. Büchsel, *Christologie*, p. 15.

It is interesting that the author commences his series of direct and indirect references to the OT Scriptures with an oblique citation from Ps. 110:1 in Heb. 1:3, and in this same chapter (1:13) he has a direct quotation from this psalm passage. In the oblique citation he presents summarily the priestly function of Christ, which entails humiliation. In the direct quotation he presents the glory and honor of Christ. The motif that Christ's humiliation is prior and basic to his exaltation, is introduced by Heb. 1:3; elaborated in Heb. 2:9; proven at the close of the didactic discourse (Heb. 10:12); and in its application is indicative of the lasting significance of Christ's exaltation (Heb. 12:2). Except for Heb. 2:9, this motif has been expressed in terms of Ps. 110:1.

Also the thought of remission of sin (Heb. 1:3), for those who are faithful, is worked out step by step until it reaches the climax in 10:18. Jesus became one of us (2:14,17; 9:26; 10:5), in order that God might perfect our sanctifier (2:10,11,17; 5:9) through suffering and temptation (2:9,10,18; 4:15; 9:26; 12:2,3; 13:12) on the basis of his faithfulness.[1]

After citing that part of Ps. 8 which considers the littleness of man, the author gives his interpretation of the psalm quotation. However, this is not the end of the explanation which concerns the suffering and exaltation of Jesus. The thought of suffering in his human state as well as the thought of exaltation after his task has been completed (7:28) are taken up in summary fashion in chapter 2. The author appears to follow the exegetical method of stating something summarily, thereby revealing all the necessary perspectives which are elaborated in the succeeding chapters. One of the aspects of Christ's humiliation is the suffering he had to experience for the sake of his brethren. Whenever the author to the Hebrews speaks of the death of Jesus, he never uses the verb ἀποθνῄσκειν, although it occurs seven times in his Epistle (7:8; 9:27; 10:28; 11:4,13,21,37), but always the verb πάσχειν and its derivatives.[2] Since πάσχειν with respect to Jesus' death receives the meaning, *to die*,[3] it is interesting to trace the word, so that its implications may be determined. In 2:9 the word

---

[1] Cf. J. Th. Ubbink, *NThSt*, 22(1939), p. 172.
[2] W. Michaelis, *TWNT*, V, p. 916.
[3] *Ibid.*, p. 934. Arndt & Gingrich, *Lexicon*, p. 639, interpret the word also in an unfavorable sense: "*suffer death, be killed, [have to] die.*"

πάθημα clearly implies the death of Jesus on the cross. It refers to the suffering which is experienced in dying. The singular form found only here in the whole NT may be compared with the singular θάνατος.¹ The plural form (2:10) must be taken in the collective sense of the word. When in 2:18 the author mentions the temptation of Jesus, he is not referring to the temptation of Jesus prior to his passion, but rather to the death of Jesus (see 2:9; 5:7,8).² Also 5:7 and 9:26 are further explication of the death of Jesus, which culminates in our sanctification "through the offering of the body of Jesus Christ once and for all" (10:10).³

Heb. 2:10, yielding far-reaching perspectives, ascribes great importance to the verb τελειοῦν. The word "is usually understood to mean *completion* and *perfection* of Jesus by the overcoming of earthly limitations"⁴ (see 2:10; 5:9; 7:28). Jesus' completion consists in a twofold objective attained : *1*) he kept his Sonship, and *2*) he claimed the worthiness of high priest. His perfection concerns as much his person as his work.⁵ In addition to this it should be noted that only the Epistle to the Hebrews of all NT books directs attention to the fact that the verb τελειωθῆναι involves not only the ἁγιαζόμενοι — the sons — but also the ἁγιάζων — the Son.⁶ This aspect is also found in 5:9, "and having been made perfect, he became unto all them that obey him the author of eternal salvation." The Son, perfected for evermore (7:28), "by one offering hath perfected forever them that are sanctified" (10:14).

Another meaningful perspective is opened by the verb ἁγιάζειν. Christ himself had to be ἅγιος in order to be able to function as the ἁγιάωζν,⁷ for in this state he could bring the offer of reconciliation thereby effecting sanctification (10:10,14).⁸

The verse which proves to be the acme of summarization filled

---

[1] Michaelis, *TWNT*, V, p. 934.
[2] H. Windisch, *Comm.*, p. 38, says, "Abgesehen von den synoptischen Evangelien, ist Hebr die einzige Schrift im NT, die von den Versuchungen Jesu redet."
[3] Michaelis, *TWNT*, V, p. 917.
[4] Arndt & Gingrich, *Lexicon*, p. 817. See also Windisch, *Comm.*, pp. 44ff.
[5] Michel, *TSK*, 106(1935), p. 348.
[6] Cf. Ubbink, *NThSt*, 22(1939), p. 174; Kögel, *Theol. Stud.* pp. 60ff.
[7] O. Procksch and K. G. Kuhn, *TWNT*, I, p. 104.
[8] *Ibid.*, p. 113.

with major issues is 2:17. In this verse we meet for the first time the significant word ἀρχιερεύς. The noun is not introduced by phrases referring to Christ's exaltation; rather, the introductory clauses reveal his state of humiliation, so that his solidarity with fallen humanity might be established.[1] The same thing holds true for 4:15. This text gives ample indication that Christ's high priesthood is in the first place one of humiliation. In this state he is fully equipped to serve as a human being, like unto his brethren, sin excepted.[2] Jesus' work as high priest culminates in the bringing of his offer once for all in the form of his own body (7:27; 9:24–28; 10:10; also see 10:14).

Heb. 2:17 offers in a nutshell all the perspectives necessary for the entire Epistle. The first clause, "wherefore it behooved him in all things to be made like unto his brethren," sums up the main issue of chapter 2, i.e. Jesus' humanity. The next clause, "that he might become a merciful and faithful highpriest in things pertaining to God," reveals those aspects which are treated in chapters 3, 4 and 5:1–10. The virtue of faithfulness is discussed in chapters 3 and 4, where in the first place the faithfulness of Jesus, the Son, is mentioned, followed by a summons to obedience on the part of believers, the sons. The description of a merciful high priest in things pertaining to God is worked out in the pericope 4:14–5:10. The purpose clause "to make propitiation for the sins of the people," is elaborated in the passage 9:1–10:18.[3]

Therefore, in short, it may be asserted that the author's argument in the Epistle falls into four parts, each having a psalm citation as basis; and that all other scriptural references are supplementary to the four psalm citations out of Pss. 8, 95, 110 and 40. The passages out of these psalms control the drift of the argument in the Epistle to the Hebrews.

---

[1] G. Schrenk, *TWNT*, III, p. 279.
[2] J. Schneider, *TWNT*, V, p. 189.
[3] Cf. J. Herrmann and F. Büchsel, *TWNT*, III, pp. 310ff. To some extent Grosheide, *Comm.*, pp. 45ff., refers to the leading thoughts of the Epistle to the Hebrews. He takes his point of departure in the quotation and exegesis of Ps. 95, and couples to this the discourse on the high priesthood of Christ, expressed in Christ's faithfulness and in the bringing of his sacrifice. Also in a few words he mentions the humanity of Christ. However, Grosheide does not refer to the major psalm citations which are basic to the development of the Epistle.

2. Psalm 8:4-6

In discussing the author's exegesis of the psalm citations, we shall concern ourselves mainly with those parts of the citation which are exegeted. They are decisive in the development of the argument. Hence the emphasis in the quotation from Ps. 8 is placed on the second half of the passage (2:7,8). The writer shows no interest in explicating the first part of the citation, which apparently serves the purpose of calling attention to man, the created human being.

The conjunction γάρ (2:8) resumes the thought which 2:5 began, and at the same time it introduces a commentary on the citation from Ps. 8. It is important in the discourse that the conjunction γάρ is used and not the inferential conjunction οὖν, otherwise 2:8b would have taken on a form of conclusion. Now, however, on the basis of the psalm quotation and common knowledge of human experience, the author constructs an exegetical syllogism. For in that God subjected all things to man, he left nothing of that which is created unsubjected to him — this is the *propositio major*. But now at the present time all created things are not yet subjected to man — this is the *propositio minor*. Man in his present state does not function as lord over all that is created; thus the psalm citation is given a prophetic character. However, it is Jesus, who has fulfilled this prophecy. He as human being has subjected all things to himself — this is the *conclusio*.[1] "For not unto angels did he subject the world to come" (2:5), but to Jesus in his human state. And in him the world to come is subjected to redeemed mankind (2:8b,9).

But in this present world the subjection of Christ's enemies (1:13) has not come to an end as yet.[2] "As Christ carries on war continually with various enemies, it is doubtless evident that He has no quiet possession of his kingdom. He is not, however, under the necessity of waging war; but it happens through His will that His enemies are not to be subdued till the last day, in order that we may be tried and proved by fresh exercises."[3]

The sentence "for in that he subjected all things unto him,

---

[1] F. Delitzsch, *Comm.*, p. 59.
[2] Windisch, *Comm.*, p. 20.
[3] Calvin, *Comm.*, p. 60.

he left nothing that is not subject to him," is an absolute statement of fact referring to time. God subjected everything created upon earth to man at the time of creation (Gen. 1:28). Though this is an understandable fact, it is a probing question to ask whether the human author of Ps. 8 could ever write the verses 6–9 in view of Gen. 3.[1] In answer to this inquiry we may notice that in the general tone of Ps. 8 the concept of guilt is absent, and that in this respect the content of the psalm harmonizes with that of the first chapter of Genesis. These two OT passages direct attention to the absolute valid and insoluble ordinance of God: man is part of the world created by God, from whom he has received the inalienable right to rule, and by whom he has been crowned with glory and honor.[2]

Although this is true, the author to the Hebrews has given content to the verb *to subject* by using it in a prior context (2:5). The eschatological aspect of man's ruling function puts the citation of Ps. 8 in a different light. Thus some commentators have ascribed the positive statement of Heb. 2:8b to Jesus — only he could fulfil the words of the text. But if he alone could fulfil Ps. 8, the writer of the Epistle would have been more specific in his immediate application of the psalm. Also it might be expected that the first recipients would not have taken Ps. 8 to refer to man in general. Therefore it is the author himself who makes it plain that the psalm finds its fulfilment for man in the work of Jesus (2:9).[3]

It is evident that 2:8b refers to man who is to rule over all things. In view of the eschatological realm in which man shall find all things subjected to him, the expression $\tau\grave{\alpha}$ $\pi\acute{\alpha}\nu\tau\alpha$ might conceivably be applied to both the present and the future world. However this may only be understood in such a manner that the two worlds are the $\tau\grave{\alpha}$ $\pi\acute{\alpha}\nu\tau\alpha$ itself in two successive appearances.[4] All that has been created and that had been subjected to man at the time of creation will be subjected to him in the world to come. It is remarkable that the author to the Hebrews devotes the major

---

[1] F. Delitzsch, *Psalmen*, I, p. 115.
[2] H. J. Kraus, *Psalmen*, I, p. 72.
[3] Cf. Grosheide, *Comm.*, p. 82; E. Riggenbach, *Comm.*, p. 39; J. Th. Ubbink, *NThSt* 24(1941), p. 184.
[4] Delitzsch, *Comm.*, p. 61.

part of the text (2:8a) to the concept of subjection, and expresses this rather emphatically by using two negatives. The negative substantive οὐδέν supplemented by the verbal adjective ἀνυπότακτον takes up the concept of collectivity once more already expressed in *all things*. Whereas 2:8b by referring to Ps. 8 reaffirms the truth of the mandate recorded in Gen. 1:28, the words of 2:8 actually point beyond this psalm passage. This is due to the all inclusive and collective use of the definite article τά which is followed by two negatives. Even though the author to the Hebrews fails to specify, he nevertheless makes it clear that nothing belonging to the collective *all things* (the entire created universe) shall be free from the rule of man.[1]

The transition from the major to the minor proposition is facilitated by the particle δέ. "When there is a direct and sharp opposition, ἀλλά follows the negative *not . . . but*. When the negative marks a sentence which is complete in itself, and another sentence is added as a fresh thought, this, though it does in fact oppose the former, is introduced by δέ."[2]

The adverb of time *now* is not to be taken logically but rather temporally. It directs attention to the world of here and now. However, the words *not yet* are a clear indication that the author to the Hebrews considered 2:7, 8a a prophecy of things that would come to pass.[3] The *not yet* calls to mind Gen. 1:28 as well as the fulfilment of 2:8b in the world to come. At present "we see" — the author includes himself — the unfulfilled state of affairs. We notice, recognize, and understand [4] the unfulfilled character of this prophecy day by day.

The writer is constantly emphasizing the importance of the verb *to subject*. In the *propositio minor* he places the verb form, a perfect participle, at the end of the sentence, thereby creating a chiasm in word order with respect to the preceding sentence.

---

[1] C. Büchel, *TSK*, 1906, p. 565, correctly points out that *all things* refers to the whole created universe. Hence the universe comprises all that is created "mit Einschluss der Engel." Also see Windisch, *Comm.*, p. 20.

[2] B. F. Westcott, *Comm.*, p. 43.

[3] Cf. Grosheide, *Comm.*, p. 83. Michel, *Comm.*, p. 71, comments: "Die urchristliche Spannung zwischen Jetzt und Einst verbirgt sich in diesem 'Noch nicht'. Die Gegenwart liegt zwischen der noch nicht erfüllten Weltherrschaft und der schon geschehenen Erniedrigung und Erhöhung."

[4] Arndt & Gingrich, *Lexicon*, p. 582.

The perfect tense of the participle is indicative of a process involving time. There is a beginning at which time the subjection began.[1] At present there is the continuing, lasting, action until the end will have come in which the subjection is complete. Thus the text does not say that there is nothing subjected to man.

In order to understand the import of Heb. 2:9 correctly, it is advisable to take note of the fact that the author was not thinking along the same lines as the psalmist who composed Ps. 8. "He starts from Christ and from the Christian experience of salvation which he shares with his readers. He goes back to the OT with his ears already attuned to the voice of him who spoke from heaven."[2]

The *conclusio* is introduced by τὸν δέ, which at all times denotes a change of subject. In this case the introduction unmistakably proves that 2:8 refers to man *eo ipso*. Whereas verse 8 is devoted to man as such, the following text is interpreted of Jesus. The verbal form βλέπομεν — the author again includes himself — takes the accusative "him who hath been made lower" with the participle "crowned." This leaves the proper noun *Jesus* appositional. The phrase "because of the suffering of death" can either be taken with the preceding accusative or with the following participle. Because of word order it is perhaps better to take the phrase with the participle,[3] so that Jesus' exaltation is based upon his suffering of death.

It appears that by the change in word order in the repetition of 2:7a the author intends to place βραχύ τι (2:9) in a brighter light. Arguments based on the Hebrew text or on the LXX in the interpretation of these two words are rather out of place.[4] The author looks upon the psalm citation as a Christian and exegetes the passage as such. The Greek could understand βραχύ τι either in the gradual, the qualitative, sense (like the Hebrew מעט) or

---

[1] Grosheide, *Comm.*, p. 83, speaks of an act of God which has not yet taken place.

[2] Caird, *CanJTh*, 5(1959), p. 51. C. Spicq, II, *Comm.*, p. 31, aptly remarks: "L'auteur interprète les textes de l'A.T., non d'après le sens compris par leur auteur humain, mais tels que la révélation chrétienne les éclaire." See also J. Van der Ploeg, *RB*, 1947, p. 209.

[3] Windisch, *Comm.*, p. 20, thinks of "Lohn für das Leiden." Cf. Westcott, *Comm.*, p. 45; Delitzsch, *Comm.*, p. 62.

[4] Vs. E. König, *Psalmen*, p. 154. See Ubbink, *NThSt*, 24(1941), p. 182.

in the temporal sense. Due to the emphasis the author has placed upon the construction of 2:9, it is incontestably clear that he wishes to explicate the *status exinanitionis* and the *status exaltationis* of Jesus. The Son of God, who took upon himself humiliation in order to bring many sons to glory, has passed from the former to the latter state.[1] It was but a short time that he experienced his "being made lower than the angels." The state of humiliation was necessary only to execute his mission. Of course, "the human nature which Christ assumed He still retains."[2] It is the tense of the perfect participle ἠλαττωμένον which "fixes attention upon the permanent effect and not on the historic fact."[3] The perfect participle is expressed in the passive voice, which indirectly reveals that God has been the agent in this action.

In Heb. 2:9 the author employs the word *Jesus* for the first time in his Epistle, without the use of a definite article and placed characteristically at the end of a clause.[4] So far he had designated the person of Jesus with the appellation *Son*. Now in availing himself of the personal name *Jesus*, he wishes to draw attention to the historical setting of Jesus in his suffering and death.[5] It may be assumed that this name is also vivid in the minds of the recipients of the Epistle, due to the preaching of the Gospel. In view of this historical setting the temporal meaning of βραχύ τι appears to gain in importance.

The author turns from Jesus' state of humiliation to the state of exaltation by means of the epithet "glory and honor" and the perfect participle "having been crowned." This epithet in Hebrews appears to point in the direction of Jesus' position (cf. 3:3; 5:4,5), which is one of exaltation to the right hand of God (1:3,13; see also Lk. 24:26; John 17:5; I Tim. 3:16; I Pet. 1:11,21).[6] The concept "glory and honor" reflects somewhat the honorable

---

[1] Delitzsch, *Comm.*, p. 63. Also see Windisch, *Comm.*, p. 20; Ubbink, *NThSt*, 24(1941), p. 185.

[2] Westcott, *Comm.*, p. 45.

[3] Westcott, *Comm.*, pp. 58f.; and see Delitzsch, *Comm.*, p. 62.

[4] The name *Jesus* occurs frequently in the Epistle : 2:9; 3:1; 4:14; 6:20; 7:22; 10:19; 12:2,24; 13:12,20. See Westcott, *Comm.*, pp. 33ff.; Windisch, *Comm.*, p. 25; F. C. Synge, *Hebrews*, pp. 19f.

[5] H. Strathmann, *Comm.*, p. 85.

[6] The epithet *glory and honor* is also found in the LXX; see *e.g.* II Chron. 32:33; Job 37:22; 40:5 (10 LXX); Ps. 8:5; Ps. 96 (95 LXX):7; Ps. 29 (28 LXX):1; Dan. 2:37; 4:27.

state of Jesus' high priesthood.[1] Jesus' task as high priest is re-echoed in the preceding phrase "because of the suffering of death", and in the succeeding purpose clause "that by the grace of God he should taste death for every man."

In retrospect we may well ask the question whether this interpretation of the psalm passage and the methodology involved would not be strange to the first recipients of the Epistle. The answer, though given in general terms, will be considered in the light of exegetical methods prevalent in the first century A.D. With the aid of the exposition of Ps. 8 given by Paul in I Cor. 15 a better insight may be gained in interpretation and methodology current in that day.

In I Cor. 15:21 Paul says: "for since by man came death, by man came also the resurrection of the dead." A fact to be noted here is the omission of the definite article before the word *man* in either case. The next verse is explanatory of this sentence, for the noun refers to Adam in the one clause and to Christ in the other. These two verses are introductory to 15:25–28, which speaks of the rule of Christ. Christ has taken the place of Adam and in this capacity fulfills the psalm citation (Ps. 8:6) quoted in verse 27. This kind of introduction together with an explanation of the quotation corresponds closely to that of the author to the Hebrews. In the pericope I Cor. 15:20–28 as well as in the passage Heb. 2:5–10 a great similarity is found in the employment of like concepts. God acts, subjects, controls; man on account of inability — death — could not maintain his position. Christ took his place, fulfilled the prophecy of Ps. 8 and ruled over all that was subjected to him, even death (I Cor. 15:26; Heb. 2:14b). The verb *to subject* is a key-word in both passages. Whereas I Cor. 15:28 has "that God may be all in all," Heb. 2:10 reads "for whom (God) are all things and through whom (God) are all things." Since I Cor. uses the word *Son* only twice — 1:9 which is part of the introduction to the Epistle, and 15:28 — the designation *Son* seems to play a predominant role in the interpretation of Ps. 8:6. The same tenses are used of *to subject* in both pericopes; also the addition of the definite article to *all things* is found in the explication of Ps. 8:6 in the two passages.

Both Paul and the author to the Hebrews in a few sweeping

---

[1] Strathmann, *Comm.*, p. 84.

statements introduce the exegesis of the psalm citation (I Cor. 15:21f.; Heb. 2:5f.). The accent in the application of the exegesis may be somewhat different in the two epistles, yet the method of explication is practically the same. Out of the psalm citation which presents the verbal forms in the active voice, both NT authors, having transformed the verbs into the passive, deduce that God is the agent, that Christ has taken the place of the first man, and that a time element is involved before the work of Christ has been brought to completion.

3. Psalm 95:7-11

After alluding to the high priestly virtue of faithfulness exemplified in Jesus, the Son, the author exegetes a lengthy citation from Ps. 95, in Heb. 3:12-4:11. Similar fidelity is requested of the sons. In the first verse following the citation the author reveals the import of his discourse by means of the antithetical meaning of the Greek words πιστός (3:2,5) and ἀπιστία, translated into English by "faithful" and "unbelief" respectively.[1] These two words together with subsidiaries form the underlying concept prevalent in chapters 3 and 4. Having provided the key-thought *unbelief* in 3:12, the author continues his exegesis by introducing the word "today" in a rather general manner. This word is followed by the verb *to harden* (3:13), which, though written in the citation in the active, is given in the explication in the passive voice. Heb. 3:12,13 may not only be considered fundamental to chapters 3 and 4. These two verses also form a suitable introduction to the more detailed exegesis of the psalm quotation.

It is 3:15 which marks the actual beginning of the running commentary provided in 3:16-19. The introduction to the repetition of the first part of the quotation is given in the form of a verbal noun denoting time, "while it is said." Although the repetition is short, this does not imply that no more of the quotation is intended. On the contrary, the construction which almost could be considered an anacoluthon [2] seems to suggest

---

[1] Cf. the remark of Lenski, *Comm.*, p. 118, "The Greek makes this contrast more effectively than the English...." See Westcott, *Comm.*, p. 83.

[2] Cf. A. T. Robertson, *Grammar*, p. 439.

the remainder of the psalm citation. In addition, the author explains the most important features of the quotation in a few broad statements, even though the repetition reveals only the first two lines.[1]

In his use of the rhetorical questions the author does not stand alone among other NT writers. In Mt. 11:7ff. and Lk. 7:24ff.; 17:7ff. Jesus is pictured employing this very same method while teaching the crowds. This methodology appears to have been the accepted thing in convincing hearers and readers of an argument.[2] The object of the rhetorical questions in 3:16–18 is to point out briefly the significance of certain elements in the psalm citation. Because the word τίνες specifies in this lesson from church history those that provoked, sinned, died, and did not enter into the promised rest, the interrogative pronoun is of great importance in this pericope.[3]

Chapter 4 takes up the same theme, but in the exegesis it reveals a more eschatological trend. "It follows from the consideration of the history of Israel that the promise of God to his people was not fulfilled by the entrance into Canaan." [4] After comparing the children of Israel of the Exodus to the generation of the author to the Hebrews (4:3), thereby stressing the element of faith as a prerequisite, the writer of the Epistle boldly asserts, "for we who have believed do enter into that rest" (4:3). The author does not employ the future tense, nor does he say, "we are sure to enter." By placing εἰσερχόμεθα emphatically first in the sentence, he wishes to affirm that God's promise has become reality in accordance with his plan and purpose.[5]

Something characteristic in the methodology of the author's exegesis is the generality with which a new thought is introduced, and which for the sake of clarity is elaborated in detail in

---

[1] It is Grosheide, *Comm.*, p. 109, who observes that as in 3:13 the word *today* was sufficient to call the whole sentence to mind, so in 3:15 a few lines represent the entire quotation. "Al de hoofdmomenten van het citaat worden toegepast." See Delitzsch, *Comm.*, p. 129.

[2] Windisch, *Comm.*, p. 32.

[3] See also the use of the indefinite pronoun in 3:12; 4:1,6,11.

[4] Westcott, *Comm.*, p. 92.

[5] Spicq, II, *Comm.*, pp. 81f., "C'est l'affirmation d'une réalité actuelle envisagée d'une part en fonction du dessein de Dieu qui garantit à la foi l'accès au repos."

subsequent verses. Having repeated the last verse of the psalm quotation once again (4:3), he adds "although the works were finished from the foundation of the world." This statement has been placed there not merely purposely, in order to prevent an erroneous interpretation of the citation.[1] It also serves as an introduction to the detailed statement (4:4) which beyond doubt places the concept of rest within the realm of spiritual things. The author concerns himself with the deeper spiritual meaning of the psalm citation. With the aid of the Scriptures [2] he wishes to prove that the promise *to enter into God's rest* remains for those who believe.[3] "The words of the psalm, as used here (4:3), prove that there is a rest and that it has not been attained. It follows therefore, this the writer assumes, that Christ has brought this rest within the reach of His people." [4]

On the combined strength of two OT passages the author draws the conclusion that those who believe shall enter God's rest. Thus God's promise has become reality. Looking back to the beginning of the psalm citation, we may come to the realization that in spite of the stern warning and the terrible oath, the promise still remains. This promise is repeated time after time. It was offered to the children of Israel in the desert; in Ps. 95 it is repeated; and again in the author's day and age — so long as it is called *today* (3:13) — this promise is extended, so that "there remaineth therefore a sabbath rest for the people of God" (4:9).

Once more it is shown that not the earthly but the heavenly rest is meant. This is done by an appeal to history by which the rest of Canaan at the time of Joshua is compared to the sabbath rest of those who cease from working, in accordance with the example set by God. "This is the definition of that perpetual Sabbath in which there is the highest felicity, when there will be a likeness between men and God, to whom they will be united." [5]

---

[1] Cf. *Ibid.*, p. 82.

[2] Grosheide, *Comm.*, p. 113, cautiously remarks: "Onze brief bewijst alles uit het Oude Testament, dat blijkbaar voor de lezers het gezaghebbende boek was; op woorden van Jezus en de apostelen beroept hij zich niet."

[3] Cf. Spicq, II, *Comm.*, p. 83, "C'est un repos de satisfaction infinie, de parfait contentement d'esprit et de coeur."

[4] Westcott, *Comm.*, p. 95.

[5] Calvin, *Comm.*, p. 98.

The passage 3:12–4:11 is exemplary of the methodology employed by the author. He begins with a few sweeping statements in which he reveals the heart of the matter. This is followed by a detailed exegesis of several important concepts, succeeded by a conclusive remark which summarizes the matter as a whole. It is evident that this type of exegesis calls for considerable repetition.

Some of the main elements in the exegesis recur several times in the entire discourse. The word ἀπιστία occurs in 3:12, which is the opening verse, and in 3:19, which is the concluding verse in the first part of this exegetical discourse. The related words support this concept of faith and unbelief in 3:18 ("them that were disobedient"), 4:2 ("by faith with them that heard"),[1] 4:3 ("we who have believed"), 4:6 ("because of disobedience"), 4:11 ("example of disobedience").

It is this thought of belief and unbelief which is the basis of the exegetical discourse upon which the structure of the promise of God is built, entailing eternal rest. "This thought of 'unbelief,' 'unfaithfulness,' stands in contrast with the 'faithfulness' which was the glory of Moses and of Christ."[2] Unbelief is not a lack of faith, a lack of trust, but it is a refusal to believe.[3] "'Unbelief' is thus understood in the sense of once having believed in the living God and then having turned away from him."[4] It culminates in sin, the sin of open defiance to God, the sin of tempting God (3:8f. and 3:17). This sin is regarded as an agent — the verb *to harden* is in the passive voice (3:13) — "as the power that deceives men and leads them to destruction."[5] It is the sin of hardening the heart, of refusing to hear, of shutting the ear to the Word of God. It is absolutely contrary to everything classified under faith and faithfulness. This sin of unbelief put to action issues forth into disobedience. Hence disobedience should not be understood as a lack of obedience, but rather as a refusal to obey.

---

[1] *To hear* in 4:3 means *hearing in faith;* see Heb. 11:8 and cf. Delitzsch, *Psalmen*, II, p. 133.

[2] Westcott, *Comm.*, p. 83.

[3] Cf. R. Bultmann, *TWNT*, VI, p. 205; Michel, *Comm.*, p. 93; E. Riggenbach, *Comm.*, p. 93.

[4] Lenski, *Comm.*, p. 118.

[5] Arndt & Gingrich, *Lexicon*, p. 43.

Though it is true that there are cases in the NT which render the word *disobedience* synonymous to *unbelief* (cf. John 3:36; Acts 28:24), there are two instances in the NT and LXX which indicate that wherever the verbal form *to disobey* is used, it refers to an action against the Lord (cf. Deut. 9:23,24 LXX; Acts 14:1,2).[1] Also, in view of the quotation from Ps. 95, the Epistle to the Hebrews supports the interpretation that disobedience is an open action against the Lord (3:13,17). In 3:13 the word "sin" does not denote the sin of worldliness. It is the sin of refusing to obey.[2] It is 3:17, which by using the aorist participle of the verb *to sin*, shows that the sin committed against Yahweh received its just reward. This verbal form *sinned* refers directly to the rebellious acts of disobedience stemming from a refusal to believe (cf. Num. 14:9,11ff. and Deut. 9:23f.). In 3:17,18 the verbs *to sin* and *to disobey* are to be taken as synonyms; while the first verb represents the action followed by just punishment, the second verb reveals the root of the evil. "In this verse and in the next the reference is not to the general character of the people, but to the critical acts which revealed it."[3]

In chapter 4 the author applies the basic truth of faith and faithfulness to his own generation. He compares the believers to the children of Israel of the desert journey: "... we have had good tidings preached unto us; even as also they" (4:2). The writer, having stated the reason why "the word of hearing did not profit them," indicates that "we who have believed do enter into that rest" (4:3). The aorist participle employed is not to be understood as the historical but rather as the ingressive aorist.[4] "Moreover the efficacy of faith is regarded in its critical action and not, as might have been expected, in its continuous excercise."[5]

The believers of the NT era are partakers of Christ (3:14),

---

[1] R. Bultmann, *TWNT*, VI, p. 11, mentions I Pet. 2:7f. in support of his assertion that the verbs *to disobey* and *to believe* are used antithetically. Bultmann neglects to mention that the evidence in I Pet. 2:7f. is a variant reading. Also see the pointed comment of Riggenbach, *Comm.*, p. 93 n. 46.

[2] Cf. Michel, *Comm.*, p. 106; E. Käsemann, *Gottesvolk*, p. 25.

[3] Westcott, *Comm.*, p. 87.

[4] Cf. Grosheide, *Comm.*, p. 130; see also his *Grammar*, p. 149. Cf. A. T. Robertson, *Grammar*, p. 834.

[5] Westcott, *Comm.*, p. 95; see Delitzsch, *Comm.*, pp. 138ff.

and on that account, if they are obedient to his Word (4:2,3), will be participants in the promise of entering into God's rest. In the clause "today if ye shall hear his voice" the Christian should hear the voice of God spoken through Christ (1:1) in the period which is called *today*. For the *today* is not limited to the time of the psalmist, nor is it bound to the OT period, but it extends beyond this to the day of salvation which arrives when the glad gospel tidings are being heard.[1] Just as the word *today* is not to be limited to a specific period in history, so the promise of God — entering into rest — is not to be associated with entering into the Promised Land at the time of Joshua.

By combining the two verses referring to *rest* (Gen. 2:2 and Ps. 95:11), the author to the Hebrews employs the word "rest" *sensu pleniore*. This issues forth out of the consideration that if Joshua had provided the promised rest, the psalmist would not have repeated the promise. The rest promised to the believers will be similar to the rest of God himself (4:10).[2] Although the promise given by God to the Israelites of the desert generation referred to the rest in Canaan (Deut. 12:9f.), the psalmist specifies this rest by calling it God's rest (Ps. 95:11). The Israelites could attain this rest only by means of personal repentance and renewed dedication to obedience. With this representation the author to the Hebrews draws attention to the rest of God, which is "a sabbath rest for the people of God" (4:9). "The principle underlying the Sabbath is formulated in the Decalogue itself. It consists in this, that man must copy God in his course of life." [3]

It is one of the earmarks of Jewish learning and teaching to know the details of the history of the Israelites, as recorded in the OT. Scripture was authoritative for the author and recipients of the Epistle to the Hebrews. The author never appeals to words of Jesus and the apostles — although historical facts of Jesus' earthly life are not neglected — but everything is proven out of the OT.[4] It was not only the fancy of the Rabbis to quote a few

---

[1] G. Von Rad, *ZdZ*, 11(1933), p. 109, "Der Verfasser ... will die Worte des Psalms auf die Situation seiner Leser anwenden: Das 'Heute' jenes zweite Anerbieten, von dem Psalm 95 spricht, ist mit Christus angebrochen." See Michel, *Comm.*, p. 102.

[2] Cf. van der Ploeg, *RB* 1947, p. 213; O. Bauernfeind, *TWNT* III, p. 629.

[3] G. Vos, *Bibl. Theol.*, p. 156.

[4] Cf. Grosheide, *Comm.*, p. 113, already cited on p. 110 n. 2.

phrases of an OT book and apply these to a given situation: even the NT shows that reciting parts of the history of Israel was a favorite pastime. Often certain aspects were cited and applied by teachers who expected their audience to be thoroughly familiar with a particular historical situation. While accompanying the two men from Emmaus, Jesus rebuked them for their indolence in searching the Scriptures (Lk. 24:27). Stephen, standing before the council, began to recite the history of the Jews, beginning with Abraham and ending with Solomon (Acts 7). Also the author to the Hebrews displays his desire to trace the history from the day of creation to the time of the Former Prophets (11:1–32).

Recognizing the knowledge of sacred history present with the recipients of the Epistle, we may assume that as soon as the author alluded or referred directly to any part of the history recorded in the OT, it was understood and placed in the correct historical setting. This knowledge of sacred history was stimulated, kept alive, and augmented by the use of the psalms in Synagogue and Church. Several of the psalms are composed in the form of summarizations of Israel's history (see *e.g.* Pss. 78, 106). Also the second half of Ps. 95 calls to mind the journey through the desert.

Being assured of the recipients' knowledge of Israel's history, the author could bring together some allusions and citations out of the OT with a measure of ease. He could present a lesson to his readers which would offer no obstacles to the understanding of his teaching. Hence, after he has cited Ps. 95:7–11, he does not furnish a series of conclusions (3:16–19), but he unfolds history in order to draw a lesson from the past. In the use of the verb παραπικραίνειν the author calls attention to incidents which took place during the desert journey.[1] Since the word is used rather frequently in the LXX, he specifies the group he has in mind by posing another question: "nay, did not all they that came out of Egypt by Moses?" (3:16). The phrase "all they that came out of Egypt" points to the Exodus and to the whole

---

[1] In the words of Grosheide, *Comm.*, p. 105, "Doch, gelijk reeds gezegd werd, worden Massa en Meriba vermeld als voorbeelden, die heel Israëls gedrag voor den geest moeten roepen." Also see W. Michaelis, *TWNT*, VI, p. 127; E. Nestle, *ExpT*, 21(1910), p. 94.

generation that perished in the wilderness. The next question definitely directs attention to Num. 14, which describes God's displeasure with the children of Israel. It also records the subsequent punishment and oath of Yahweh. When in fact the first question in Heb. 3:16 could refer to a number of provocations, the first question in 3:17 is direct in its reference to one historical incident. This incident is clarified by the succeeding rhetorical question. When was God displeased for forty years, so that he pronounced an oath? After the children of Israel had tempted him 10 times (Num. 14:22).[1] Massah and Meribah were not solely responsible for the pronouncement of the oath. Yahweh waited 10 times, and then deprived them of the privilege to enter into rest.

It is the book of Deuteronomy which equates the promise *to rest* with the *inheritance of the Promised Land* (cf. Deut. 3:20; 12:9; 25:19). Nothing is said about spiritual rest in this book; the promise is *hic et nunc*. That the promise of receiving rest was fulfilled is testified at several places in the Former Prophets and the Writings.[2] While the oath of Yahweh pronounced in the desert spoke of not entering the land which he had promised (Num. 14:30), the words of the psalmist, "wherefore I sware in my wrath, that they should not enter into my rest" (Ps. 95:11), give an eschatological coloring to the idea of rest.[3] With the personalized "my rest" of Ps. 95, the author to the Hebrews combined the words of Genesis which speak of God's rest (Gen. 2:2). After showing the unreality of Joshua's leading the Israelites into rest, he fixes attention on the spiritual meaning of the word *rest*. This rest after the analogy of Gen. 2:2 is called "a sabbath rest for the people of God" (Heb. 4:9). The sabbath rest is given to the people (λαός) of God. They have a merciful and faithful high priest, who makes propitiation for their sins (2:17). They are the many sons brought unto glory — entering into God's rest.

By means of the phrase *people of God* the author permits his readers to catch a glimpse of the pattern he is weaving. If that

---

[1] The references in all probability are : Ex. 5:21; 14:11; 15:24; 16:2; 17:2,3; 32:1; Num. 11:1,4; 12:1; 14:2.
[2] Josh. 21:43ff.; 23:1; I Kings 8:56; I Chron. 23:25; II Chron. 6:41.
[3] Cf. Von Rad, *ZdZ*, 11(1933), pp. 104–110.

which is true for the Son, also holds true for the sons, then the latter should display faith and faithfulness. These virtues are prerequisites for entering the rest into which the Son has entered already. While Heb. 2 pictures the Son taking the place of the sons, that they may receive glory, it is the pericope Heb. 3:7–4:11 which depicts the children of Israel perishing in the wilderness due to unbelief and consequent disobedience. In order to be truly worthy of the epithet *sons of God*, the people of God must have the virtues of faith and faithfulnes as permanent characteristics.

The author to the Hebrews has skillfully constructed chapters 3 and 4, so that they fit in properly with the rest of the Epistle. The reference to "a merciful and faithful high priest" (2:17) is taken up in 3:1 and, after the exegetical discourse on Ps. 95, is resumed in 4:14ff. All this material has aptly prepared the way for the subject: the high priesthood of Christ after the order of Melchizedek.

4. Psalm 110:4

With the combination of two psalm citations (Ps. 2:7; Ps. 110:4), the author to the Hebrews depicts Christ as king and as priest in the pericope 5:1–10. The combination, which to some extent reflects a trend in the Synoptic Gospels,[1] is based upon the methodology of the author. When he cites Ps. 2:7 for the second time, he does not employ the text inadvertently, but rather purposely. By means of this quotation he calls the attention of his readers to the first chapter of his Epistle, in which he has established the kingship of the Son in a series of psalm citations (Pss. 2:7; 45:6f.; 102:25ff.; 110:1). The Messiah is not only king — a fact readily understandable to the Jewish mind which saw in him the deliverer from oppression — but also priest — a fact which seemed to have been neglected, although the prophet Zechariah mentioned the twofold office of the royal priest Messiah: "... and he shall be a priest upon his throne" (Zech. 6:13).

---

[1] "Gerade diese Verbundenheit mit den Evangelien, die doch nicht zur Abhängigkeit wird, steht im ganzen Abschnitt Hb. 5,1–10 zur Diskussion," Michel, *Comm.*, p. 132. Also see Delitzsch, *Psalmen*, II, p. 206.

"The Epistle to the Hebrews stands alone among the New Testament books in calling Christ priest."[1] The cause for this NT neglect to call Christ priest may perhaps be found in the history of the Jewish people. The prophet Jeremiah (30:21) had prophesied that their future leader might approach Yahweh in the capacity of priest. Also Zechariah had pictured a union of the kingly and priestly office in the person of the Messiah. But throughout the ages the Jews had fostered the conception of receiving a king out of David's house, who would deliver them. They were reminded of the union of offices in one person during the Maccabean period. However, the priestly was almost overshadowed by the ruling function.[2] This is exemplified to the fullest extent by the account of Jesus' earthly life as recorded in the four Gospels. At his birth the wise men call him the *king of the Jews*; especially in the passion week the name is commonplace.[3] Jesus was known as *king* and in some measure as *prophet*, but certainly not as *priest*.

Now that the author to the Hebrews has reminded his readers of Ps. 110:1 in the first chapter of his Epistle, he continues by applying Ps. 110:4 to Christ (5:6). In a few verses he describes the Son (5:8) in his priestly function and purpose — "named of God a high priest after the order of Melchizedek." Concerning this function and purpose *"there is much to be said, and it is hard to explain* Hb 5:11."[4] The recipients of the Epistle had lived, even though they had heard the Gospel, in the same spiritual lethargy as their fathers and forefathers (5:12). Their knowledge and insight of the OT Scriptures had not been stimulated and augmented by the preaching of the Gospel (6:1,2). They had failed to see in Jesus various aspects which he had fulfilled in OT prophecies. Although the Gospels related that Jesus had applied Ps. 110 to himself (Mt. 22:44 par.), they had never devoted any attention to the words recorded in the fourth verse of this particular psalm.

Entirely in harmony with his method of interpretation the author quotes the psalm citation in a setting amenable to the general

---

[1] Vos, *Teaching*, p. 91.
[2] Cf. Riggenbach, *Brief an die Hebräer*, (Bibl. Z. und Strf.), pp. 14ff.
[3] See *e.g.*, Mt. 27:11,37,42 par.
[4] Arndt & Gingrich, *Lexicon*, p. 208.

purpose of the Epistle. Having mentioned the priestly aspect of Christ's atoning work in 2:17 already, he repeats this aspect in the pericope 4:14–5:10. However, in the other two instances in which the psalm citations were interpreted, the exegesis followed the quotations almost immediately. In the case of Ps. 110:4, the writer wishes to exhort his readers before undertaking the exegesis of a text which, though contrary to Jewish thinking on the sacrificial system, referred directly to the priesthood of Christ.

After the exhortation, which in itself returns to its point of departure (5:10 and 6:20),[1] the exegesis of Ps. 110:4 is given. Stated in summary form the exegesis recorded in the pericope 7:1–25 in general terms may be classified in four divisions. This runs somewhat backwards from the normal order of Ps. 110:4, "Thou art priest for ever after the order of Melchizedek." The author takes hold of the last word "Melchizedek" and places it in a historical setting (7:1–3); in the next passage he discusses the word "priest" (7:4–11) and priestly "order" (7:11–13); two verses are devoted to the personal pronoun "thou" (7:13–14); and the remainder (7:15–25) elaborates the epithet "for ever."

Although these four divisions are outlined in a rather vague manner, characteristic of the author's style, there is a well-defined division between 7:1–12 and 7:13–25. The first part (1–12) refers to the words "priest after the order of Melchizedek," while the second half (13–25) exegetes the clause "thou art a priest for ever." The latter passage takes up again the thread of Christ's priesthood which was broken off at 5:10.[2] This thread picturing Christ's atoning work in the capacity of our high priest gradually comes more clearly into focus. It was stated in summary form (2:17); it was augmented by the qualifications for the high priestly task (4:14–5:10); and it was strengthened by just claims to the priesthood (7:13–25).

The pericope 7:13–25, devoted to the exegesis of Ps. 110:4, reveals four conclusive summarizations pertaining to the priesthood

---

[1] "Der Abschnitt 5,11 – 6,20 ist ein rhetorisches Meisterstück, eine geschickte Vorbereitung der Leser für die Aufnahme der nun folgenden schwierigen Belehrungen über die Hohepriesterwürde Christi," Windisch, *Comm.*, p. 59.

[2] Of course, the words *these things* (Heb. 7:13) refer to Ps. 110:4. Cf. Grosheide, *Comm.*, p. 136.

of Christ.[1] The first conclusion (13,14) is stated in terms acceptable to those readers whose minds were thinking only in terms of Mosaic law. The author agrees with those that object to Christ's priesthood by admitting that he comes forth out of the tribe of Judah. Still Christ is called priest, though not in accordance with Mosaic law, but, like Melchizedek, after the power of an endless life. The second conclusion (15–19) states the scriptural fact that if Christ is priest for ever — not after the order ordained by the law, but after the order of Melchizedek — then this implies superiority and a disannulling of the law. The author is not yet finished in his exegesis of Ps. 110:4. If someone should voice the objection that Christ had no right to take this priesthood to himself, the writer would merely point to Ps. 110:4a, "the Lord sware and will not repent himself." With these words he proves that Christ has been installed as priest by God himself on the strength of an oath. The recipients of the Epistle know what is meant by an oath of God. Twice already the author has referred to the divine oath which excludes all doubt, and which is a guarantee to the content of the promise given (3:11,18; 4:3; and 6:13ff.).[2] This is more than the Levitical priesthood could claim for itself. Not only that, but with the disannulling of the law Jesus has also become "surety of a better covenant" (7:22). This is the third conclusion (20–22). The last conclusive summary asserts that Christ's priesthood is for ever (23–25). It is inviolable and unchangeable, so that his task of saving *the sons* becomes meaningful, "seeing he ever liveth to make intercession for them" (7:25).

Before the author to the Hebrews could arrive at this fourfold conclusion, it was necessary for him to provide the historical background of Ps. 110:4b and to point out that the priesthood of Melchizedek was superior to that of the sons of Levi. Just as in his interpretation of Ps. 95:11 he turned to the very first scriptural instance in which the word *rest* is used (Gen. 2:2), so in his explanation of Ps. 110:4b he consulted that passage of Scripture in which the word *priest* is first mentioned (Gen. 14:18).

---

[1] Cf. Delitzsch, *Comm.*, pp. 291,299,304.
[2] See. J. Schneider, *TWNT*, V, p. 183, who comments: "Der göttliche Schwur ist die allen Zweifel ausschliessende, den Inhalt der Verheissung sichernde Garantie für den Glauben."

The appearance of Melchizedek in Genesis is unique, for it occurs only once. He is described as king and as priest, while nothing is said of his genealogy.[1] Abram received his blessing and, in recognition of Melchizedek's priesthood, gave him a tenth of all the booty. On the basis of these few facts the author to the Hebrews works out 1) the identification of Melchizedek with Christ, and 2) the comparison of the priesthood of Melchizedek to that of the sons of Levi. In Gen. 14:18ff. the author finds an allusion to Christ, which he understands as a messianic prophecy.[2]

The priesthood of Melchizedek is fundamental; it identifies him with Christ. This priesthood is not an extraordinary office which he filled beside his kingship. His being priest signified nothing more and nothing less than the normal relationship between God and man. When sin broke this relationship, there resulted an abnormal situation of hostility toward God. Some office, some service, had to be created by which the former relationship might again be attained. For this purpose the priesthood of Aaron was installed, so that through this extraordinary office the sons of Levi might restore the intimacy between God and man. In this respect the priesthood of the sons of Levi is a reflection of the offer which Christ brought for the atonement of his people. The result of Christ's atoning work is the return of the normal relationship between God and man, so that man may dedicate himself to God once again as priest.

Melchizedek was priest "like unto the Son of God" (Heb. 7:3). His

---

[1] All other persons playing a role in the history of salvation as recorded in Genesis are provided with a genealogy; and genealogies listing the ages of the persons concerned at their time of death are only given in the lineage of the people of God (Gen. 5; 11; 23:1; 25:7,17; 35:28; 47:28; 50:26). The genealogies of those not belonging to this lineage are devoid of any age reference (*e.g.* Gen. 4:17-22; 36:1-43). Now Melchizedek is called "priest of God Most High," and therefore he belonged to the lineage of those who served Yahweh.

[2] Schneider, *TWNT*, V, p. 189. Riggenbach, *Comm.*, p. 184, "In der Anfangs- und Endlosigkeit seines Lebens ist Melchisedek ein Gegenstück des Sohnes Gottes und stellt an seiner Person abbildlich dar, was dieser urbildlich besitzt." Also see Michel, *Comm.*, p. 164.

priesthood did not consist of works of atonement, but rather in the dedication of himself to God Most High.[1]

Though some of the NT authors refer indirectly to Christ's priesthood in their writings, they nevertheless present a priesthood which reflects the Aaronic type. It concerns itself only with the work of atonement, of intercession, and of comforting.[2] This indirect representation of Christ's priesthood, typified in the work of Aaron, is a fair indication of the traditional trend of thinking present with the apostles and their followers. They were rooted in the Jewish world, which had a Levitical priesthood ordained according to the law. Since theological thinking among the contemporaries of the author to the Hebrews was conditioned by this Levitical priesthood, it is not in the least surprising that he calls the priesthood of Christ, after the order of Melchizedek, something hard to explain.

On the basis of the pentateuchal law it became the *communis opinio* during the time of Ezra and Nehemiah that only the sons of Aaron were to serve as priests in the sacrificial system.[3] Hence the priests formed a close-knit community, which could not be violated. Its members could claim the right to priesthood only through descent. This close-knit community was the sole possessor

---

[1] Cf. J. H. Kroeze, *Gen. XIV*, pp. 102ff. The offering of bread and water to someone signifies willingness to help (see Isa. 21:14); to give wine instead of water implies honoring the recipient. *Ibid.*, p. 99. Hence J. Schildenberger, *BenMnts* 20(1938), p. 374, misinterprets Gen. 14:18 when he tries to find correspondence between the sacrifice of Christ's body and the bringing of bread and wine of Melchizedek. "Dieses eine Opfer erneuert er bis zur Vollendung der Zeiten unblutigerweise unter den Gestalten von Brot und Wein, der einstigen Opfergaben des Melchisedech (Gen. 14,18). So zeigt die Erfüllung eine neue Aehnlichkeit Christi mit Melchisedech."

[2] See Rom. 8:34; I Tim. 2:5,6; I Pet. 2:5; Rev. 1:6; 5:10; 20:6. Also see Vos, *Teaching*, pp. 93f. A. J. B. Higgins, "Aspects of NT Christology," *CanJTh*, 6(1960), p. 209, in an attempt to prove that the introduction of the high priesthood of Christ in the Epistle to the Hebrews is caused by early Christian thinking on "the intercessory activity of the Son of Man as priestly," says, "...that Ps. 110:4 did indeed encourage and support the belief in Jesus as a High Priest, but the idea itself arose from the teaching of Jesus about the Son of Man and his heavenly intercession, interpreted by the church as a priestly function." This may be true, but the question still remains why the author to the Hebrews called Ps. 110:4 something hard to explain.

[3] Cf. Ex. 28-29; Lev. 8-10; Num. 16-18; and see Ezra 2:61-63; Neh. 7:63-65.

of the greatest privilege imaginable, *i.e.*, the privilege of presenting the sacrifices of the people to God, and of serving as intermediary between man and God. "Thus a priest is one who brings men near to God, who leads them into the presence of God." [1] It is quite understandable, therefore, that the first prerequisite to the priesthood would be a proven genealogy. This was of the greatest importance to any priest.[2] It is Josephus, who assures his readers that he has found his genealogy recorded in "public registers." [3]

It appears that the author to the Hebrews asked himself the question what the words of Ps. 110:4b meant to the psalmist who wrote them. In order to find the answer the author ascertained his point of departure in the propositions *1*) that the particular psalm was a messianic prophecy, and *2*) that Melchizedek of the hoary past was a prototype of the priesthood of Christ. In the words "Thou art priest for ever after the order of Melchizedek" the writer of the Epistle found confirmation for the messianic application of the psalm. In the description of Melchizedek (Gen. 14:18ff.) the office of kingship precedes that of priesthood. His name is interpreted *king of righteousness*; he is also king of Salem, which is *king of peace*. This Melchizedek lacks a genealogy, for neither father nor mother is mentioned. Yet this man is priest of God Most High. Nothing is said about the age of this priest, although all the other personages prominent in the history of salvation are given some description in regard to age and time of death. The appearance of Melchizedek is unique; it is once for all.

All the things mentioned by the author to the Hebrews concerning Melchizedek apply directly to the Son of God. Thus in his identification of Christ with Melchizedek he is justified in using the words "like" and "likeness" (7:3,15); and in his comparison of Christ to the priesthood of Aaron and its entourage of the pentateuchal law he may speak of a "shadow" (8:5; 10:1). Christ, though fulfilling both the priesthood of Aaron and that of Melchizedek, has his prototype in the person and office of the latter.

---

[1] Vos, *Teaching*, p. 94.

[2] E. Schürer, *Geschichte*, pp. 279ff., adds the information, "Auf diesen wurde das grösste Gewicht gelegt. Wer ihn nicht aufzeigen konnte, hatte keinen Anspruch auf Anerkennung seiner priestlichen Rechte," *Ibid.*, p. 280.

[3] Josephus, *Life*, 6(1), *LCL*, Vol. I, p. 4.

However, for the author to the Hebrews this is the most difficult doctrine to explain. The recipients of his Epistle are rooted in the conception of an Aaronic priesthood on the basis of the pentateuchal law. Therefore, after his short historical sketch he continues, "Now consider how great this man was . . ." (7:4). Twice he compares the Aaronic priesthood to that of Melchizedek; both times he points out the superiority of the latter.

In the first instance (7:5,6) the constituents in the comparison are the sons of Levi, who receive the priest's office and who take tithes of their brethren — their equals — according to the commandment of the law; and Melchizedek without genealogy, taking tithes of Abram, and exercising his priestly function by blessing "him that has the promises." The comparison is complete in proving that the priesthood of Melchizedek is superior. The word *Levi* places the concept priesthood in sharper focus than e.g. the expression *the sons of Aaron*. The sons of Levi perform their function in accordance with the law. Melchizedek is pictured once again (see also 7:3) without genealogy; this was of the greatest importance to the sons of Levi in their claim to priesthood.[1] He takes tithes of Abram and blesses him. The sons of Levi were only entitled to take tithes of their equals and consequently were devoid of authority to bless their brethren.

In the second instance (7:8) the comparison between the sons of Levi and Melchizedek concerns death and life. In this comparison the element of time is predominant: to the Levites there was a termination, but to Melchizedek there was freedom from any temporal limitation. "To live often means to be perpetual; and to die intimates what is evanescent. The Levites were dying men, which shewed the character of their office: Melchizedek is represented as not dying, which betokens that his office as a priest is perpetual." [2]

The adverbs *here* and *there* (7:8) do not refer to time or locality, but probably to scriptural references, thus implying: in the one instance — in the other instance.[3] Although the first clause in the comparison is no clear allusion to a specific scriptural passage, it is the second part ("of whom it is witnessed that he liveth") which unmistakably refers to Ps. 110:4. It is Ps. 110:4

---

[1] G. Wuttke, *Melchisedech*, p. 6.
[2] Calvin, *Comm.*, p. 163 n. 1.
[3] Grosheide, *Comm.*, p. 167.

in combination with Gen. 14:18, which provides the testimony that the priesthood of Melchizedek is perpetual. The psalm quotation is outspoken in its concept of perpetuity. If the psalmist asserts that the king-priest is "priest for ever after the order of Melchizedek" (Ps. 110:4b), then it is equally valid that Melchizedek's priesthood has not been terminated by death.[1]

If then the psalmist writes that the priesthood of Melchizedek remains for ever, and if the recipients of the Epistle to the Hebrews regard Ps. 110 as messianic,[2] it is the author who combines these two concepts in his exegesis, in order to clarify an important aspect of one of the offices of Christ. If the recipients are able to understand the exegesis, they will look beyond the fact of Christ's fulfilling the Aaronic priesthood to the fact of Christ's fulfilling the priesthood of Melchizedek.

5. Psalm 40:6-8

The introduction to the last psalm quotation which the author exegetes is rather lengthy; it comprises chapters 8 and 9 of the Epistle. In these two chapters the author builds upon the exegesis of Ps. 110:4 offered in the seventh chapter. His main proposition in the lengthy introduction to the quotation and exegesis of Ps. 40:6ff. is to prove that Christ has fulfilled the Aaronic priesthood as well as the priesthood of Melchizedek, whereby the former has come to an end, while the latter remains for ever. The priesthood of Aaron effected atonement, whereas that of Melchizedek consists in dedication.

While Heb. 2:17f. in summary form makes reference to a high priest, it is the passage 4:14 to 5:10 which gives content to the

---

[1] *Ibid.*, p. 168.

[2] A. Vis, *Mess. Psalm Quotations*, p. 78, and *VoxTh*, 15(1944), p. 93, attributes the messianic interpretation of Ps. 110 chiefly to the Christians. But if the Jews had applied the psalm to David, they would have objected violently when Jesus applied the psalm to himself (Mt. 22:44ff. par.). It is N. H. Ridderbos, *VoxTh*, 15(1944), p. 99, who makes the sobering observation: "... want wanneer reeds David of een van zijn opvolgers priester naar de wijze van Melchizedek kon genoemd worden, kon moeilijk Christus' priesterschap naar de wijze van Melchizedek aangehaald worden als bewijs voor de afschaffing van het Levietisch priesterschap."

qualifications of a high priest. While chapter 7 establishes the valid claims of a high priest, it is the chapters 8 to 10 which elaborate upon the task of the high priest, Jesus Christ. His task is marked by fulfilment. The old covenant was characterized by one serious deficiency.[1] Though instituted for the sake of atonement, it was unable to take away the consciousness of sins (10:2). Christ in the capacity of high priest fulfilled this first covenant in order "to make propitiation for the sins of the people" (2:17). Just as Paul designated Christ as the "end of the law" (Rom. 10:4), so the author to the Hebrews could speak, as it were, of Christ as the $\tau\acute{\epsilon}\lambda o\varsigma\ \lambda a\tau\varrho\epsilon\acute{\iota}a\varsigma$.[2] The sacrifice of Christ was given once for all. By offering his own body he marked the end of the Aaronic priesthood with its sacrifices and offerings for sin, and terminated the validity of the first covenant. The sacrifice of Christ's body had to be offered, for "apart from shedding of blood there is no remission" (9:22). This is an old Jewish doctrine which is found quite often in the Mishna.[3] However, the shedding of Christ's blood signified not only the termination of the first covenant, but also the introduction of the new. Just as the first covenant had been dedicated by means of blood, so also the second (9:17,18).

If Christ had merely fulfilled the Aaronic priesthood — thereby effecting the atonement for his people — there would not have been a new covenant, and there would not have been a heavenly high priest. The chief point which the author to the Hebrews tries to make is stated clearly in 8:1 : "We have such a high priest, who sat down on the right hand of the throne of the Majesty in the heavens." This high priest "is also the mediator of a better covenant, which hath been enacted upon better promises" (8:6). After he had offered himself without blemish to God, Christ has become the mediator of the new covenant. He cleansed the consciences of the members of this covenant, so that they might truly serve the living God (9:14f.). This is the fulfilment of a higher priesthood, which is eternal. Its fulfilment results in dedication of Son and sons to the living God — the priesthood after the order of Melchizedek.

---

[1] Cf. J. Schniewindt and G. Friedrich, *TWNT*, II, p. 581.
[2] Ubbink, *NThSt*, 22(1939), p. 183; and see p. 179 n. 2.
[3] Cf. G. Schrenk, *TWNT*, III, p. 278.

The somewhat lengthy discussion on the bringing of sacrifices in 10:1–4 finds its explanation in the mechanization of the offerings, characteristic among the Jews belonging to the period prior and posterior to the Exile. The act of offering was no longer a matter of the personal relationship to God. A mechanical conception of the meaning of offering to God had taken hold of the thinking of the people. It seemed that the act of shedding blood in itself secured forgiveness of sins.[1] The fact is that man should offer his own life — were it not that God had deemed the shedding of the blood of bulls and goats sufficient as a substitutionary measure. Hence the concept of offering in Israel became known in terms of substitution.[2] But in the OT Scriptures the prophets voiced God's dissatisfaction with this sacrificial system, because of the inadequacy of the offerings. There are clear indications in several OT passages [3] which show that offering to God is not to be found in the thing (the sacrifice), but in the person (the heart). All these passages reveal that God is not satisfied with the mere bringing of the sacrifices. He desires service — the service of a true, genuine, and upright heart. He desires not only contrition of heart, whereby forgiveness of sins and reconciliation are obtained, but also obedience, whereby the will of God is done. He desires atonement according to the priesthood of Aaron as well as dedication according to the priesthood of Melchizedek.

The author to the Hebrews wishes to give scriptural proof for the genuine offer brought by Christ as a last, a once-for-all, sacrifice as propitiation for the sins of his people (7:27; 9:12; 10:10). Christ's offer is final in fulfilling the high priesthood of Aaron (9:25,26) and in ending all the offerings for sin (10:18). Man could not fulfil the offer as requested by God because the genuine sacrifice acceptable to God finds its fulfilment in the shedding of blood, and in the obedience to do God's will. Man is unable to bring this offer because 1) he is not free from the power of death (2:15; 9:27) and 2) he is totally incapable of showing perfect obedience. The Israelitic high priest had to offer for his

---

[1] Ubbink, NThSt, 22(1939), p. 182.
[2] W. Von Loewenich, ThBl, 12(1933), col. 169.
[3] See I Sam. 15:22; Ps. 40:6; Ps. 51:16,17; Ps. 50:8ff.; Isa. 1:10ff.; Jer. 7:21ff.; Hos. 6:6; Amos 5:21ff. Also see Westcott, Comm., p. 309.

own sins before he could bring the offer in behalf of the people (7:27; 9:7; see 5:3). Christ is not bound by these two limitations.[1]

Throughout chapters 7–10 the author asserts that although there, are two separate priesthoods to be found in the OT Scriptures, the order of Melchizedek is superior to the Levitical.

> But he uses this Levitical priesthood and ritual just as he uses books. It provides him with a starting-point and thus with a grammar and vocabulary, by means of which he will express quite other ideas of his own. For in this Epistle the Levitical priesthood is never treated as a symbol or sacrament. It is a starting-point, it provides an analogy.[2]

The burden of proof for the superiority of Christ's sacrifice is found primarily [3] in the pericope 10:1–18, which includes the quotation, explanation, and application of Ps. 40:6ff. It is the Greek text of the psalm which, due to its wording, is highly suitable to the author of the Epistle in offering him concrete proof. Through the addition of the word *but* (10:5) and the reconstruction of the clause "in the roll of the book it is written of me" into a parenthesis (10:7), the psalm quotation has resulted in parallelism.

The Greek text available to the author has been exploited to secure the greatest amount of proof possible. Besides the addition *but* and the formulation of the parenthesis, there are the word *body* and the plural *burnt offerings*. They serve their purpose well in the quotation and subsequent exegesis and application. The parallelism in the psalm citation has permitted the author to combine the first and the third line of the quotation into one text (10:8). With the words *sacrifices and offerings* (rendered plural in the exegesis) and the plural *burnt offerings* (singular in the Hebrew) *and sacrifices for sin* the author presents the totality of the Jewish sacrifices.

> The first pair describes them according to their material, the animal-offering and the meal-offering. The second pair give in the burnt-offering and the sin offering, representative

---

[1] Cf. 2:9,14,17; 4:15; 5:8; 7:3; 7:23f.,28; 9:12; 10:12; and see Von Loewenich, *ThBl*, 12(1933), col. 172.

[2] A. Nairne, *Epistle of Priesthood*, p. 140.

[3] Michel, *Comm.*, p. 218, in commenting says: "Kap. 10,1–18 ist also ein formal selbständiger, inhaltlich aber angehängter exegetischer Midrasch zur Verstärkung von Kap. 9." It is rather one-sided to say with Grosheide, *Comm.*, p. 224, that the passage 10:1–18 is merely a summary of chapter 9.

types of the great classes of offerings, eucharistic offerings, which belonged to the life of the Covenant and expiatory offerings, which were provided for the restoration of the life of the Covenant.[1]

God has no pleasure in all these offerings, although [2] they were offered according to the law (10:8).

By his coming into the world Christ has abolished [3] the old and has established the new. The author employs the terms *the first* and *the second*. The expression τό πρῶτον reminds the reader immediately of similar wording in 8:7,13; 9:1,2,8,15,18 and esp. 9:6, though it is given in 10:9 in the neuter. The neuter expresses the collective idea of totality. *The first* is abolished and *the second* is established by Christ.

This *the second* — also in the neuter to denote collectivity — is used in two clauses. The first clause, "but a body didst thou prepare for me," is clearly implying contrast to the preceding line, because of the particle δέ. Since this line describes the offerings according to their material, the word *body* fits quite well into the pattern. The second clause, "Then said I, Lo, I am come to do thy will, O God," by its first word *then* is separated from the preceding by the element of time. These two clauses describe the two phases of Christ's priesthood. In order to bring about "propitiation for the sins of the people" (2:17), "the offering of the body of Jesus Christ once for all" (10:10) was necessary. This signifies passive obedience; also Aaron's priesthood was typified in this work of atonement. The offering of Christ's body represents the one phase of his priesthood. The second phase is found in the last part of the psalm quotation: "Lo, I am come to do thy will." Doing God's will signifies active obedience, which in this respect typifies the priesthood of Melchizedek.[4]

The result of the combined import of the two phases has been that God according to his gracious will has sanctified the sons, the believers. With the words "for by one offering he hath perfected for ever them that are sanctified" (10:14) the author

---

[1] Westcott, *Comm.*, p. 309.
[2] See Lenski, *Comm.*, p. 329.
[3] Arndt & Gingrich, *Lexicon*, p. 54.
[4] Kroeze, *Gen. XIV*, p. 103.

to the Hebrews has returned to his initial summary statements in 2:10,11,17. The Son in the capacity of the "great priest over the house of God" (10:21; 3:5f.) teaches the sons also to offer in the capacity of priest, not in passive obedience like the priesthood of Aaron, but in active obedience like Melchizedek. God does not want a substitutionary offer from them. Instead he is claiming their whole being, for they are called to do God's will (10:7,36; 12:1; 13:21).[1]

Characteristic of the author's exegetical method of summarization is the integration of the primary truths found in the Jeremiah passage which was quoted in 8:8–12. At that place the entire citation was needed to prove that the establishing of the new covenant had made the old obsolete (8:13). In the context of chapter 8 the lengthy Jeremiah quotation did not contribute independently to the development of the discussion.[2] It is actually the pericope 10:1–18 with its quotation and application of Ps. 40:6–8 which integrates the basic thought of the Jeremiah citation.

The content of the new covenant is expressed in the words: "I will put my laws on their heart, and upon their mind also will I write them. And their sins and their iniquities will I remember no more" (10:16b,17). The relocation of the word *heart* and *mind* (see 8:10) is not to be ascribed to faulty memory or carelessness of the author, but rather to the importance of the word *law* and the word *heart* in the earlier part of the discourse. *Law* — singular Jer. 31 (MT):33; plural Jer. 38 (LXX):33 — signifies the inexorable pentateuchal law, which was given to the people on tables of stone. The law, though binding in every respect,[3] was an external entity to the people. Now the Lord will give the laws [4] on their heart, *i.e.*, the central organ of the human being (cf. 3:12), and they will be written upon their mind, *i.e.*, their moral understanding. If they who are sanctified have the laws put on their heart and written upon their mind, they are bent on doing God's will. They are manifesting active obedience, for the law (*i.e.* the will) of God has become an internal entity. The second part of the

---

[1] Ubbink, *NThSt*, 22(1939), p. 183.
[2] Von Loewenich, *ThBl*, 12(1933), col. 169.
[3] Cf. 7:5,12,16,19,28; 8:4; 9:19,22; 10:1,8,28.
[4] Heb. 8:10 and 10:16 are the only two places in the whole NT which have the word *law* in the plural.

new covenant ("and their sins and their iniquities will I remember no more") alludes to the passive obedience of Jesus Christ. Thus the fundamental truths of the Jeremiah citation serve the author's purpose of proving the significance of the two phases of Christ's priesthood.

6. Conclusions

In his exegetical method the author to the Hebrews has availed himself of four psalm citations, which have laid the foundation for the construction of his Epistle. These four (Pss. 8:4–6; 95:7–11; 110:4; 40:6–8) are of such universality that all other quotations of any importance are subservient to them. It is seen readily that the citations in Heb. 2:12,13 contribute to the unfolding of Christ's humanity introduced by the passage out of Ps. 8. However, Heb. 1 with a total of seven OT passages appears to have no connection with the first pivotal psalm citation (Heb. 2:6ff.).

> The psalm is quoted only at 2:6–8, but it controls the argument of the preceding chapter, for from the first mention of angels at 1:5 throughout the formidable catena of texts in ch. 1, the author's one aim is to illustrate the theme of the psalm that has been destined by God to a glory excelling that of the angels, and that this destiny has been achieved by Christ, both individually and representatively, as the pioneer of man's salvation who came to lead many sons into their destined glory.[1]

The subject of Christ's humanity and unity with his brethren is followed by that of faith and faithfulness, which finds its center in the second pivotal quotation from Ps. 95:7–11 (Heb. 3:7–11). This topic is introduced by a parallelism of the faithfulness of Moses and of Christ. The former, pictured as a servant *in* the house, represents the OT era. The latter in the person of the Son, who is *over* the house, *i.e.*, over the faithful sons, characterizes the NT period. Faith and faithfulness are the prerequisites of sonship for Christ (Heb. 3:2,6; 5:8) and for the believers (cf. Heb. 10:38; 12:5–8). The ultimate destiny resulting from the fulfilment of these prerequisites will be "a sabbath rest for the people

---

[1] Caird, "Exegetical Method," *CanJTh*, 5(1959), p. 49.

of God" (Heb. 4:9) which will be identical to the rest of God (Gen. 2:2).

The third pivotal quotation from Ps. 110:4 (Heb. 5:6) establishes the subject of the priesthood of Christ. In order to exegete the text properly the author had to consult the historical setting involved (Gen. 14:18-20). Though the sons of Levi "had been made priest without an oath," Christ's priesthood was confirmed with an oath of God (7:21). The import of an oath of God had been fully explained in the previous chapter, in which God swore by himself (6:13-18).

The matter of the office of Christ's priesthood is succeeded by the subject of his priestly task: the offering of his own body, and the performing of God's will. This phase of the author's discourse is centered in the fourth pivotal psalm quotation out of Ps. 40:6-8 (Heb. 10:5-7). Though the lengthy passage from Jer. 31:31-34 (Heb. 8:8-12) had been suggested indirectly in 7:22, it is Heb. 10:5-18 which fully integrates its basic truths within the framework of the exegesis and application of Ps. 40:6-8.

Proof for the fact that four psalm citations have been employed in the laying of the foundation for the Epistle to the Hebrews is given by the author himself. *1)* In comparison to all the other quotations the four psalm passages are exegeted and applied, so that they form the central core of each successive phase in the author's discourse.[1] *2)* The four subjects are mentioned consecutively in summary form in 2:17, and are elaborated consecutively in the didactic part of the Epistle. *3)* The element of unfulfilment in the four OT passages has been dissolved, and fulfilment has taken its place. This transformation took place through the author's exegetical approach of finding Christ in the Scriptures.

---

[1] In broad terms the practical part of the Epistle (10:19 to the end) may be classified under the second pivotal psalm citation (Ps. 95). The section 10:19-13:25 expresses the theme of faith and faithfulness. In fact the section is the practical application of the doctrines taught in chapters 3 and 4. The quotation from Prov. 3:11f. (Heb. 12:5f.) is actually an elaboration of the subject *faith and obedience* which are the prerequisites of sonship. Although the citation is exegeted by the author, it does not form a completely new subject comparable to the subjects founded upon the four pivotal psalm citations.

... The Old Testament is not only an incomplete book but an avowedly incomplete book, which taught and teaches men to live by faith in the good things that were to come. It had a doctrine of man which remained unfulfilled until the coming of Jesus, an offer of divine rest which remained outstanding because there was no way by which God's message of grace could be mixed with faith in those who heard it. It had a priesthood and looked for a better one to draw men near to God. It had sacrificial ordinances and knew them to be ineffective in dealing with sin.[1]

In the author's conception these psalm quotations were prophecies which have found their fulfilment in the coming of Jesus Christ. In his thinking the Scriptures are not confined with their message to the time in which they were written: their words in respect to validity are timeless. Ps. 8 reflects creation as well as re-creation; Ps. 95:11 speaks of a threefold rest: God's rest after creation, Israel's rest in Canaan, and the true rest for the people of God;[2] Ps. 110:4 mentions a personage of the hoary past who finds his likeness in the Son of God; and Ps. 40:7f. suggests the timeless priestly function of active obedience.

It is a fact that the author to the Hebrews understood the OT passages differently than their original composers had done. While the latter lived centuries before the coming of Christ and employed the Hebrew language for communication, the former belonged to the first century A.D. and expressed himself in the Greek language.[3] Since there is development in language and interpretation of the Scriptures in every period of history, the author does not write in complete conformity to the original

---

[1] Caird, *CanJTh*, 5(1959), p. 49. However, Caird bases the discourse in the Epistle to the Hebrews on four OT quotations, *i.e.* Pss. 8, 95, 110, and Jer. 31. In his choice of quotations he was guided by the motif of the unfulfilled condition (Heb. 4:8; 7:11; 8:7). This motif to a certain extent limited Caird in his research. Although in his summary statement (p. 49) he indirectly refers to Ps. 40, he fails to work out the significance of Jer. 31 in its context and consequently the relation of Jer. 31 to Ps. 40.

[2] Westcott, *Comm.*, p. 82.

[3] "Ein ähnliches Verhältnis zur Schrift liegt da vor, wo der Verfasser des Hebräerbriefs infolge der Weiterentwicklung der griechischen Sprache eine atliche Stelle nicht mehr so versteht, wie sie der Uebersetzer des hebräischen Textes gemeint hatte, sondern so, wie ein im ersten Jahrhundert nach Christus lebender Grieche sie nach dem Sprachgebrauch seiner Zeit verstehen musste," Riggenbach, *Brief an die Hebräer*, (Bibl. Z. und Strf.), p. 29.

meaning of the OT quotations, nor does he preach the simple apostolic *kerygma* of his immediate predecessors, but he presents a combination of the gospel of Jesus Christ intertwined with passages out of the OT. These passages, which in embryo form contained the grace promised and which were now placed in the light of fulfilment, could hardly embrace the riches of the NT revelation.[1]

In order to attain complete understanding on the part of the recipients of his Epistle, the author employs exegetical methods and concepts familiar to Jewish thinking. We have noted throughout our study of the author's exegesis that facts are stated in summary form at various places. These facts are worked out in detail when the discourse progresses and develops into its completely unfolded importance.

Reasoning from the silence of Scripture in a given instance is demonstrated in Heb. 7:2b,3. The OT passage (Gen. 14:18ff.) states only a few facts concerning Melchizedek. However, out of the facts which should have been given, but about which Scripture is silent, the author constructs his argument.[2] In that same chapter (Heb. 7:9,10) he applies Rabbinic logic and the Rabbinic exegetical method of generalization.[3] Levi and Melchizedek are inseparably bound to one another: as Abram offers tithes, so in him all the unborn descendants, the sons of Levi, paid tithes to Melchizedek, priest of God Most High.

The recurring unfulfilled condition (Heb. 4:8; 7:11; 8:7) forms a motif in the author's method of interpretation.[4] To him the OT had not lost its validity when NT revelation had completely overshadowed it. The OT was still the living word of God, "of old time spoken unto the fathers in the prophets by divers portions and in divers manners" (Heb. 1:1). But it was the coming of Christ and his revelation which brought fulfilment to promise and prophecy. It was this idea of fulfilment, which directed the author's pattern of thinking while he was exegeting the OT passages needed in the construction of his Epistle.

---

[1] *Ibid.*, p. 37.
[2] Wuttke, *Melchisedech*, pp. 11f., indicates that Philo resorted to this same method.
[3] Michel, *Comm.*, p. 168.
[4] Cf. Caird, *CanJTh*, 5(1959), pp. 47ff.

Chapter IV

THE THEOLOGICAL MOTIFS

Behind the author's exegesis towers the thinking mind of a first century A.D. theologian. This mind, guided by certain theological motifs and rooted in the OT Scriptures, selected those psalm citations which contributed most to the import of the Epistle. The citations were chosen because of theological predilections which the author to the Hebrews wished to express in a rather indirect manner. Some of the adduced OT passages are used to emphasize the contrast between the Son and the angels; others serve as steppingstones to certain historical personages; still others bear out the scriptural authority of words spoken by, or concerning, Christ.

1. Christ's Superiority

An important theological motif, controlling most of the first two chapters of Hebrews, is the outspoken stress on the concept *angels*, introduced succinctly by Heb. 1:4. In this verse the Son is contrasted to the angels, for "he hath inherited a more excellent name than they." This contrast is not expressed as a warning against angel-worship, but rather as an interpretation of the Son's superior status. Nevertheless, the danger of angel-worship was not in the least imaginary in those days. Paul warns against it (Col. 2:12), and the writer of the Apocalypse, falling down before the angel of revelation, is rebuked for worshipping the angel (Rev. 19:10; 22:8,9).[1] But in the Epistle to the Hebrews there is no such indication of angel-worship. Instead the humiliation and the unsurpassing glory and power of the Son are compared to the position and function of the angels.[2]

---
[1] See also 1 Clem. 56,1; Justin Martyr, Apol. 1,6.
[2] Cf. A. Bakker, "Christ an Angel?" *ZNW*, 32(1933), p. 258. G. Kittel, *TWNT*, I, p. 84, in respect to the relation between Christ and the angels says: "Der Messias ist nicht ein engelhaftes Wesen, auch nicht gehobener Art, sondern hat als 'Sohn' eine grundsätzlich andre Herkunft und Stellung: Mk 13,32 par; Heb. 1,4ff."

Perhaps indirectly there may have been occasion for the author to have had recourse to the angelology current among his contemporaries. In Jewish theology the angels fulfilled a significant role. As guardian angels and as companion angels they effected divine providence and interceded at the throne of God in behalf of the righteous.[1] Notably the archangel Michael occupied a major position in Jewish tradition. He is the heavenly high priest; he officiates at the heavenly altar; and with reference to Ps. 110 he is even called Melchizedek.[2] "It is not improbable that especially in contrast with this angel-High Priest the auctor ad Hebraeos has laid stress on the superiority of the High Priest Jesus."[3]

In addition to this tradition, the name Michael occurs also in the NT. In Jude 9 Michael, the archangel, is depicted as the contender with the devil. Rev. 12:7 speaks of Michael and his angels as warriors against the dragon. Among the early Christians Michael was one of the most beloved and honored angels.[4]

In Apostolic literature the *Pastor Hermae* attributes corresponding titles to the Son and to Michael. The Son is referred to as "the most reverend angel" (Vis. V,1,2), "the angel of the Lord" (Sim. VII,5), and "the glorious angel" (Sim. IX,1,3). Michael is called "the great and glorious angel" (Sim. VIII,3,3).[5]

---

[1] Kittel, *TWNT*, p. 81. Cf. Str.-Bill., I, pp. 781ff.; III, pp. 437ff.; IV, p. 1224; J. L. Koole, *Overname van het OT*, p. 236.

[2] For the Rabbinic references see W. Lueken, *Michael*, pp. 32ff. Cf. H. Windisch, *Comm.*, p. 71; G. Vos, *Teaching*, p. 91; F. Delitzsch, *Comm.*, p. 17.

[3] Bakker, *ZNW*, 32(1933), p. 260.

[4] Cf. J. Barbel, *Christos Angelos*, p. 36.

[5] K. Lake, *Apostolic Fathers*, II, *LCL*, p. 68; p. 186; p. 218; and p. 196 respectively. Cf. Barbel, *Christos Angelos*, p. 40. The oldest document concerning Christian angelology is the pseudo-Cyprian tract *De centisima sexagesima tricesima* edited by R. Reitzenstein, "Eine frühchristliche Schrift," *ZNW*, 15(1914), pp. 74–88. This document states that when the Lord created seven angels out of fire, he decided to make one of them his Son (*ex his unum in filium sibi constituere* line 216; p. 82). See also J. Daniélou, *Judéo-Christianisme*, p. 173. It is interesting to note that in *logion* 13 of the Coptic Thomas *evangelium*, Simon Peter says to Jesus: "You are like a righteous angel." R. Schippers, *Het Evangelie van Thomas*, p. 72, commenting about this saying, observes: "Wat de Koptische Thomas Petrus in de mond legt, kan alleen voortvloeien uit onkunde (of verwerping) van de brief aan de Hebreeën. In dit verband is interessant, dat in de oudste Syrische kerk Hebreeën niet tot de kanon behoorde."

"Both also have the special task of governing the people, that is, for Hermas, the Christians." [1] While Justin Martyr (Dial. 128,4) attempts to state the wide difference between *the angel* and the angels, Irenaeus (III,22) comments that Jesus is not merely man, nor an angel without a body, but that he is the Lord himself.

In his discourse the author to the Hebrews is not concerned about admonishing the recipients of his letter against the danger of angel-worship. Rather, he employs the theological motif of the position and task of the angels, in order to accentuate the superior status of Christ, for "he hath inherited a more excellent name than they" (Heb. 1:4). The names attributed to Christ in the first two chapters of the Epistle place him far above the angels. The name *Son* expresses the intimate relationship between God, the Father and Christ, the Son. Although the angels have their dwelling place with Jesus in the heavenly Jerusalem (Heb. 12:22), they do not have the same status and the same intimacy with God as Christ, the Son.

It is from a theological point of view that the author takes his first quotation from Ps. 2:7. This psalm passage reveals the word "Son." But in Jewish theology the title *Son* was never applied to the Messiah,[2] even though Ps. 2 was understood messianically. In the coming of Jesus the early Christians saw the fulfilment of this psalm. Whether the writer of the Epistle wished to give scriptural proof for the Sonship of Jesus Christ, in reaction to Jewish theology, is an open question. It is a fact that the title *Son* is used in opposition to the term *the angels of God*. In the OT the angels receive the title *sons of God* several times.[3] Since

---

[1] Bakker, *ZNW*, 32(1933), p. 257.

[2] J. Jeremias, *Gleichnisse Jesu*[4], p. 61, concludes that the term "'Sohn Gottes' im vorchristlichen palästinischen Judentum als Messiasprädikat nicht nachweisbar ist." See also E. Schweizer, *Erniedrigung*, p. 87. H. Herkenne, "Ps. 110(109)," *Bibl.* 11(1930), pp. 450ff., attempts to point out by means of the textual differences between MT and LXX, that the Greek text of Ps. 110:3 deviates considerably from its original, and for that reason has not been quoted by the NT authors. "Hatte der Verfasser des Hebr. textkritische Bedenken bei Ps 110,3?" (p. 453). This might have been possible if the author had had knowledge of the Hebrew language. Further, for his theological argument he could not use the Greek text of Ps. 110:3, even though it approaches the text of Ps. 2:7 to some extent in phraseology.

[3] Job 1:6; 2:1; 38:7 in the LXX version take the expression *the sons of God* to mean *the angels of God*. The words בר אלהין in Dan. 3:25 (MT)

the Messiah is designated as ἄγγελος in the LXX,[1] it is understandable that the author to the Hebrews wishes to rectify theological thinking in the Early Church. Not the angels — sometimes called *sons of God* — but Christ, the Son, will sit at God's right hand in glory and honor. It is precisely the contrast between Christ and the angels, which has given rise to the word "Son" in Heb. 1:2,5a,5b, and 8, and which has given occasion to the use of the reading "angels of God" in Deut. 32:43(LXX) (Heb. 1:6).[2]

The being and function of the angels is adequately expressed in Ps. 103(LXX):4, for nothing exalting is ascribed to them. "But of the Son he saith, Thy throne, O God, is forever and ever" (Heb. 1:8). When in fact the title *Son* (in the plural) could also refer to angels, the designation *God* places Christ in a category differing radically from the position and function of the angels. By attributing the title *God* to Christ, the author of the Epistle places him on equal level with Yahweh in regard to authority. Nowhere else does the writer assign such authority to Christ.[3] He is represented as God, who sits upon his throne and rules over his kingdom, and who is anointed above his partners (Heb. 1:9).

The exalted position of Christ is once more demonstrated in the succeeding psalm citation (Heb. 1:10), which refers to him with the name *Lord*. In spite of the fact that the angels were present at, and had part in creation, nonetheless they themselves are considered created beings.[4] Christ, on the contrary, is

---

are translated in Dan. 3:92 (LXX) by ἄγγελος θεοῦ and in Dan. 3:92 (Theod.) by υἱὸς θεοῦ. And see Gen. 6:2; Pss. 29:1; 89:6. Cf. C. Spicq, II, *Comm.*, p. 50.

[1] Isa. 9:5. Cf. Enoch 46,1, 61,10, Dan. 7:18,22,27. See Spicq, II, *Comm.*, pp. 51f.

[2] Cf. Bakker, *ZNW*, 32(1933), p. 261. Although the reading *the sons of God* is found in the Greek version of Ps. 29:1; Ps. 89:6; and Deut. 32:43 (Codd. B and A), the author is a partaker of the tradition which has the rendering *the angels of God*. This is also the translation which is most suitable to the construction of his theological motif.

[3] Whenever the name *God* is mentioned in other citations (Isa. 8:18; – Heb. 2:13; Ex. 24:8; – Heb. 9:20; Ps. 40:8; – Heb. 10:7), there is no identification with Christ.

[4] For the Rabbinic references see Kittel, *TWNT*, I, p. 81. Cf. Barbel, *Christos Angelos*, p. 24.

designated as the one who founded the earth, and who considers the heavens his handiwork. Thus he, as the uncreated, is represented as the Creator of heaven and earth. This implies that he exists from eternity to eternity. The appellations *Son, God,* and *Lord,* are used purposely to emphasize the difference between the position and function of Christ on the one hand, and the angels on the other.

Throughout the Epistle to the Hebrews there is the recurring reference (direct and indirect) to the exalted position of Christ, sitting at the right hand of God (1:3,13; 8:1; 10:12,13; 12:2). This position, which signifies the privilege of ruling, is given to Christ in the capacity of king. When the angels of God are exhorted to worship him (1:6), it is obvious that there is a wide difference between the two parties. God has appointed the Son "heir of all things, through whom also he made the worlds" (1:2), but he "maketh his angels winds, and his ministers a flame of fire" (1:7).

In resorting to the citation from Ps. 103(LXX):4 the author to the Hebrews places emphasis on the name πνεύματα. He employs the word again in 1:14. This name had already been given to angels by the Greek translators of the book Ezekiel, as recorded in the LXX version (3:12,14; 8:3; 11:24; 43:5).[1] While the author combines the parallelism of Ps. 103(LXX):4 in the term *ministering spirits* (Heb. 1:14), he uses the appellation πνεύματα for a special purpose: to connote that "a spirit hath not flesh and bones" (Lk. 24:39). Accordingly, the name indicates that an angel is devoid of a human body, and devoid of human needs.

The angels as spiritual beings are unable to contribute in any way to the salvation of man. Although it is true that they are "sent forth to do service for the sake of them that shall inherit salvation" (Heb. 1:14), they can in no wise restore the pristine position of man, nor bring about atonement for the sins man has committed. However, Christ during his earthly mission was human and divine; and he kept this dual nature even after his resurrection. He proves to his disciples that he is not a mere spirit (Lk. 24:41ff.). Thus if Christ had only been divine, he would not have been subject to death; but now in his human nature, he was able to sympathize with man, to take man's burden

---

[1] See also Enoch 15,4ff.

of guilt upon himself, and to die in order to attain atonement with God.

The reason why the contrast between Christ and the angels is stressed in Heb. 1 and 2, is found primarily in the humanity of Jesus. An angel could not have sympathized with the needs of human beings, could never have participated in the sufferings of men, cannot die,[1] and therefore cannot make atonement for the sins of men. It is Christ, who entered from his state of exaltation into his state of humiliation. In spite of the fact that this act placed him for a little while lower than the angels, he, by reason of his divine and human natures, was able to become "unto all them that obey him the author of eternal salvation" (Heb. 5:9). Not angels but Christ fulfilled God's plan of salvation "in bringing many sons unto glory" (Heb. 2:10).

In Heb. 2 it is the humanity of Christ which places him above the angels. They will not rule the world to come, but Jesus, and through him man, will be crowned with honor and glory.[2] Christ, being placed for a little while lower than the angels, has become one with his brethren. The OT Scripture passages (Ps. 8:4–6; Ps. 22:23; Isa. 8:18) bear proof of this oneness with the human race. With his brethren he shared flesh and blood, for "he also himself in like manner ($\pi\alpha\rho\alpha\pi\lambda\eta\sigma\acute{\iota}\omega\varsigma$)[3] partook of the same" (Heb. 2:14).

The author to the Hebrews comments once more on the position of the angels (Heb. 2:16). They have no part in humanity, and have no part in the aid of Christ. In the phrase "not to angels," the writer of the Epistle compares man and angels for the last time. Hence a parallelism may be found between 2:5 and 2:16.

---

[1] Jesus testifying before the Sadducees teaches that angels are not subject to death (Lk. 20:36). Cf. Bakker, *ZNW*, 32(1933), p. 262.

[2] F. W. Grosheide, *Comm.*, p. 83, remarks: "Onze brief denkt dan ook wel niet in de eerste plaats aan de engelen als dienende geesten, maar aan de engelen als hemelingen, d.w.z. aan de engelen, zoals ze waard waren gebruikt te worden om den Zoon met hen te vergelijken. Nu volgt de tegenstelling, God heeft den mens eer (het meer inwendige) en heerlijkheid (het meer uitstralende) als een krans om de slapen gelegd en alles aan hem onderworpen."

[3] Arndt & Gingrich, *Lexicon*, p. 627, offer the explanation: "The word does not show clearly just how far the similarity goes. But it is used in situations where no differentiation is intended, in the sense *in just the same way.*"

However, in verse 16 there is the implication of the incarnation, and the grace of God extended to the seed of Abraham.[1]

The theological motif brought about by the introduction of the word *angel* gathers impetus in chapter 2, where the *Midrash pesher* indicates that the superior status of Christ is rooted in his humanity. By means of the *Midrash pesher* on Ps. 8:4–6 the term *angels* reveals Christ's humiliation as well as his exaltation. When Jesus became man, he stood in rank below the angels; but in ability he stood above them. "The conclusion is that Jesus is Messiah, or Son of Man, in the sense that He has passed through death to glory and universal sovereignty as representative Head of a redeemed mankind." [2]

2. Historical Background

The Scripture portions explicated by the authors of the Qumran-commentaries on Habakkuk, Micah, Nahum, and Ps. 37, contained facts which lent themselves for application to contemporary events and persons of the time in which the *pesharim* were written. The Habakkuk-commentary applies the biblical passages to the Teacher of Righteousness, the Wicked Priest, and the Kittim. In the earlier part of the first century B.C. the personages of Simon ben Shetach, Alexander Jannaeus, and the Romans respectively, correspond in all probability to the people mentioned in the *pesher* on Habakkuk.[3]

Since the commentaries on Micah, Nahum, and Ps. 37 are applied to the same personages, it is assumed that the *pesharim* may be dated most likely from *c.* 100–75 B.C.[4] It may also be possible that the content of these commentaries circulated in an oral

---

[1] Grosheide, *Comm.*, p. 92.

[2] C. H. Dodd, *Acc. to the Scr.*, p. 20.

[3] See A. S. van der Woude, *Bijbelcomm.*, pp. 12,15; M. Burrows, *Dead Sea Scrolls*, p. 177.

[4] Van der Woude, *Bijbelcomm.*, p. 16, is of the opinion that the *pesher* on Habakkuk dates from 75 B.C., and the one on Nahum from a period prior to 63 B.C. (p. 20). Burrows, *Dead Sea Scrolls*, p. 186, says that the commentary on Habakkuk was "written, at the earliest, not very long before 63 B.C., and at the latest not long after that date."

tradition, at least until the end of the first century B.C. Perhaps at that time the commentaries were recorded on scrolls.[1]

Granted that the author to the Hebrews wrote approximately a century later, we nevertheless may detect the application of *Midrash pesher* rules in his Epistle. Seeing that he partakes of this same interpretative tradition, we must answer the question whether the author deals with historical facts and persons in the same manner as the composers of the *pesharim*. Before we try to seek an answer to this question, we must remember that the parties mentioned approached the Scriptures in different frames of mind : the writers of the *pesharim* were Jews who, living before the dawn of the Christian era, interpreted the scriptural text in terms of their own environment and history, in which the Teacher of Righteousness, the Wicked Priest, and the Kittim fulfilled the inspired prophecies; the writer of the Epistle — though he may have been a Jew — was a Christian who interpreted the quoted psalm citations with a view toward fulfilment in Jesus Christ.

Thus in the interpretation of Ps. 8:4–6 (Heb. 2:8,9) the author calls attention to the creation account in which man in pristine purity receives a mandate from God to subject the earth (Gen. 1:28). In the next sentence of his exegesis the writer considers man in his fallen state, limited by sin in fulfilling this mandate. With these historical perspectives he reminds his audience of more or less contemporary history. He mentions the name *Jesus*, because Christ fulfilled the words of Ps. 8 in his human state. Hence in the interpretation of this psalm citation the author reaches *through* the Psalms back to the first chapters in Genesis, and points forward to that period of history in which Jesus fulfilled the mandate which sinful man had failed to accomplish.

Any objection, that the rich historical background of the citations is incidental, is unfounded, for in two major psalm citations (Ps. 95:7–11 and Ps. 110:4) history plays a predominant role in the interpretation of the respective passages. In the first mentioned

---

[1] In a study on the present status of the research pursued in these newly discovered documents K. G. Kuhn, "Der gegenwärtige Stand," *ThLZ*, 85(1960), col. 653, writes : "Die jüngsten Qumränschriften sind zweifellos die pescharim, die Kommentare. Sie sind wohl frühestens gegen Ende des 1. Jahrhunderts v. Chr. niedergeschrieben. Das hindert aber nicht, setzt es vielmehr sogar voraus, dasz in ihnen älteres mündliches Traditionsgut an Schriftauslegungen seinen Niederschlag gefunden hat."

quotation all the historical details referring to the desert journey have been taken up in the author's exegesis (Heb. 3:16–18). Moreover, the name Joshua, the son of Nun, is connected with the entrance into the Promised Land. Since the name *Joshua* is written in the form *Jesus* in the Greek version of the OT, it is interesting to note that the author to the Hebrews has commenced chapter 3 with the name "Jesus," the Son of God, and in the exposition of Ps. 95 refers to Jesus, the son of Nun.[1] Joshua failed to provide rest for the children of Israel (Heb. 4:8), and could only lead them into the land of Canaan. Still he remains the foreshadowing and type of Jesus Christ, who leads "many sons unto glory" (Heb. 2:10). Jesus, the Son of God, represents the fulfilment of the promise which remained after Joshua's task was completed.

The second passage (Ps. 110:4) is another instance in which the author reaches *through* the Psalms to Genesis. Indeed, this citation is the most direct approach to a historical section in the first book of the Pentateuch. From a mere reference out of the Psalter he delves into the historical facts recorded in Genesis. With these facts concerning Melchizedek he is able to illustrate his exegesis of Ps. 110:4 to the fullest extent. Melchizedek has been "made like unto the Son of God" (Heb. 7:3), and therefore is to be considered the prototype of the person and office of Jesus Christ.

When the quotation from Ps. 110:4 is applied to Christ, who is consequently called *priest*, it is natural that this term in its context directs immediate attention to the historic personage Melchizedek, who was priest of God Most High. But Christ is given the titles *priest* and *high priest* in the Epistle to the Hebrews. "Some hold that these two terms are used indiscriminately by the author. This however is not the case. When Psalm 110 is quoted, it is necessary to speak of Christ as *priest*, with reference to Melchizedek."[2] Wherever he is called *high priest*, the context

---

[1] F. C. Synge, *Hebrews*, p. 20, tries to bridge the relationship between Jesus and Joshua, the son of Nun, by means of the word "apostle" (Heb. 3:1). It is true that both men were sent out by God, and in this respect may bear the name *apostle*. However, it is equally true that the verb $\dot{\alpha}\pi o\sigma\tau\acute{\epsilon}\lambda\lambda\epsilon\iota\nu$, from which the noun *apostle* derives, is very common in the LXX. Further see Grosheide, *Comm.*, p. 96.

[2] Vos, *Teaching*, p. 94.

invariably indicates that Christ represents the Aaronic priesthood.[1]

In order to understand the author's interpretation of these two terms, it is necessary to study the passage from Zech. 6:12,13. These verses contain a prophecy addressed to Joshua, the high priest, but which could only be fulfilled in Christ. It is admitted that the name *Jesus* (Joshua), the son of Jehozadak, is never mentioned in the Epistle to the Hebrews; yet there are several incidents concerning Joshua, the high priest, which are a foreshadowing of fulfilment in Jesus, the Son of God. "What do we know about him that is relevant? He was high priest; he built the temple; he was put to shame, Zech. 3, and then given honour by God."[2] All these things lead up to the prophecy of Zech. 6:12,13, which in the Greek version has expressions parallel to those employed by the author to the Hebrews. The words spoken to Joshua, the high priest, concern the building of the temple (οἶκος), the bearing of glory (δόξα), the sitting and ruling upon the throne (θρόνος), and the position of being "priest at his right hand (ἐκ δεξιῶν αὐτοῦ)." Joshua, the son of Jehozadak, could not fulfill this prophecy, but he in his capacity of high priest foreshadowed his namesake, Jesus, the Son of God.[3] It is Christ, the "high priest, who sat down on the right hand of the throne of the Majesty in heaven" (Heb. 8:1).

The citation from Ps. 40:6–8 (Heb. 10:5–8) does not provide any historical event to which it may refer. Yet the passage as such is a reminder of the whole Levitical rite of sacrificing to Yahweh. Since these sacrifices could never "make perfect them that draw nigh" (Heb. 10:2), it is the sacrifice of Christ himself, which "hath perfected for ever them that are sanctified" (Heb.

---

[1] Even in respect to Heb. 5:10 and 6:20 the term *high priest* refers to the priesthood of Aaron. The clauses in which the term occurs provide a soteriological setting. Since the priesthood of Melchizedek is not soteriological, the phrase, "after the order of Melchizedek," at these places is a reference to the subsequent explanation of Ps. 110:4 in Heb. 7. When in Heb. 10:21 the writer uses the expression "great priest" instead of "high priest," he purposely employs the term *great priest* to emphasize the kingly as well as the priestly aspect of Christ's office. See E. Riggenbach, *Comm.*, p. 315; Grosheide, *Comm.*, p. 239; H. H. Meeter, *Heavenly High Priesthood*, p. 36.

[2] Synge, *Hebrews*, p. 21, and see p. 25.

[3] F. Delitzsch, *Psalmen*, II, p. 206, sees the prophecy concerning the royal priest (Zech. 6:12f.) symbolized in the priestly office of Joshua, the high priest, and in the kingly office of Zerubbabel.

10:14). Jesus fulfilled the psalm passage from Ps. 40 by offering his own body, and by doing the will of God.

Also the other psalm citations referring to certain historical incidents display fulfilment in Jesus Christ. The citation from Ps. 2:7 brings to mind King David and his son Solomon;[1] yet in the context of Heb. 1 and 5 it refers to Jesus. The passage from Ps. 45:6–8 pictures the historical situation in which one of the kings of Israel is celebrating his marriage;[2] the author to the Hebrews applies this Scripture portion to Christ. The last few verses of Ps. 102 undoubtedly call to mind the creation account and the unchangeableness of Yahweh — in the case of Heb. 1:9ff. of the Son. The passage from Ps. 22:23 represents David at the time he was persecuted by Saul; and the words from Ps. 110:1 sketch him as ruler over his enemies. Both verses find their fulfilment in Jesus Christ.

Since the author himself remarks at the close of his Epistle, "... I have written unto you in few words" (Heb. 13:22), it is evident that he has not chosen the quotations from the OT at random. One of the functions of a citation in Hebrews is to represent its historical context. The historical approach to the OT, by means of quotations, is purposely adapted in the Epistle, for "it avoids protracted accounts of events with which the reader is already conversant; it subverses the writer's predilection for using historical figures and historical situations for enforcing spiritual and religious truth; and it becomes a tacit witness to the authority and permanent value of the OT as a prolegomenon to the New."[3] In all these things the writer of the Epistle reveals himself as a man of learning who avoids unnecessary details. "His personal bent in dealing with the Scriptures is towards the reasonable, historic interpretation ...."[4]

The author to the Hebrews and the writers of the Qumran-commentaries agree in purpose: both present the words of the

---

[1] Cf. R. Rendall, "Method," *EvQ*, 27(1955), p. 214; A. Nairne, *Epistle of Priesthood*, p. 249.

[2] E. J. Kissane, *Book of Psalms*, I, p. 196, recognizes the messianic character of Ps. 45, yet he holds to the original setting of the psalm. "But it is now generally agreed that in its literal sense the psalm refers to a historical king, and that it is Messianic only in the typical sense."

[3] Rendall, "Method," *EvQ*, 27(1955), p. 218.

[4] Nairne, *Epistle of Priesthood*, p. 257.

OT as fulfilled; both are of the understanding that the OT prophecies which they interpret refer to the last times, and that these times have come.[1] But in view of sacred history there is a wide difference between the interpretation of Scripture in the *pesharim* of the Qumran-documents and the interpretation of Scripture passages in the Epistle to the Hebrews.

The words of Scripture were regarded by the Qumran-commentators to be shrouded in mystery, with little, if any, historical value for the time in which they were written. This becomes evident *e.g.* in respect to the prophecy of Habakkuk, which conveyed to the mind of the person writing the *pesher* a mysterious meaning devoid of any bearing on the time in which Habakkuk prophesied. The sacred words were understood to refer to the time and circumstances in which the commentator lived. Each sentence or phrase of the inspired text was studied,[2] interpreted, and, in the opinion of the commentator, furnished with the true meaning. "That meaning was inevitably vague and mysterious until the time of fulfilment arrived; with its arrival, the meaning was plain for those who had eyes to see and hearts to understand."[3] Thus in the time of fulfilment, which had already set in when the commentator wrote, the veil of mystery was lifted from the inspired text. And because the true *pesher* of the sacred words had been provided, history pertaining to the time in which the *pesharim* were formed became meaningful.

The author of the Epistle to the Hebrews, on the other hand, found in the OT passages which he quoted a rich source of historical details belonging to the time in which the biblical words were written. His interpretation of the psalm citations has been joined to the historical value of the words quoted. The author linked prophecy in its original setting to its fulfilment

---

[1] Van der Woude, *Bijbelcomm.*, p. 10, in a comment concerning the view of Scripture held by the Qumran-commentators, says: "Doorslaggevend is daarbij de overtuiging, dat de woorden der profeten gesproken zijn met betrekking tot de eindtijd en dat deze eindtijd nu reeds is aangebroken."

[2] In relation to Scripture exegeted in the *pesher* on Habakkuk, Burrows, *Dead Sea Scrolls*, p. 160, adds: "The exposition is governed by the order of the text of Habakkuk; each sentence or phrase brings to the commentator's mind events and persons in the history of his nation and his own religious community, and he mentions them as they occur to him."

[3] F. F. Bruce, *Second Thoughts*, p. 71.

realized in the time when he wrote the Epistle. Therefore those Scripture passages which are taken up in his *Midrash pesher* type of interpretation sparkle with historical perspectives directed towards fulfilment in Jesus Christ.

3. Scriptural Authority

As soon as the term *authority* is mentioned in respect to the OT Scriptures, questions arise pertaining to the validity of the Greek version of the OT, the relation between Scripture and the Word of God, and the assumptions which support the convincingly constructed arguments of the Epistle to the Hebrews.

The author depended for scriptural proof entirely upon a LXX version current in the latter part of the first century A.D.; and he strengthened his arguments with a LXX text which at places departs considerably from the MT.

> No one in these days would argue from or about the Old Testament who did not read it in the Hebrew. There is nothing in this Epistle to show that its author could do so. He is certainly content to quote from the Greek version.... And he read it, in a text which, as far as we can at present judge, does not appear to have been the best text. So much must be allowed, but it cannot be objected that this has, for his purposes, made any real difference.[1]

Seeing then that the author's Bible was the Greek version of the OT, and that any knowledge of the Hebrew tongue was lacking on his part, we are led to believe that the citations quoted in the Epistle were indeed regarded as scriptural proof.[2] More-

---

[1] Nairne, *Epistle of Priesthood*, p. 273.

[2] While G. Harder, "Septuagintazitate," *Theologia Viatorum*, p. 42, asks the question: "Ist es überhaupt möglich diese Zitate des Hebräerbriefs als echten Schriftbeweis zu rechtfertigen?", he does not seem to foster the impression that the author to the Hebrews was devoid of knowledge of the Hebrew tongue. If the writer of the Epistle had been able to discern between the Greek and the Hebrew readings, the problem of the burden of proof would have remained with him. C. Büchel, "Hebräerbrief," *TSK*, 1906, p. 551, tries to solve the problem from the author's point of view in regard to the LXX. "Soll seine Argumentation aber Beweiskraft haben, so muss auch diese griechische Übersetzung inspiriert sein." Granted that the author and his immediate audience considered the Greek version employed

over, we may assume that his method of quoting and applying passages from this Greek version was in harmony with the spirit of his day.¹

The question how the relation between Scripture and the Word of God is to be understood, may best be approached by a study of the evidence found in the writings of the Early Church Fathers. One of the answers given by the Early Fathers is that all of Scripture is the Word of God. But this answer does not remove the basic problem, for God is not always the speaker: also other persons think, speak, and act in Scripture. The problem centers around the normative authority of the thoughts, words, and acts of these people. Clement of Rome quotes a few phrases from the book of Job; although the words cited were originally spoken by Eliphaz, they are designated by Clement as the Word of God.² Justin Martyr asserts that the prophets do not speak on their own initiative; it is the Word of God, the Logos, which moves them and puts the words into their mouths.³ Irenaeus hears a dialogue between the Father and the Son in Ps. 2, in which the Spirit of God speaks for Christ through the mouth of David.⁴

Similarly Irenaeus attributes the authorship of the OT to

---

as authoritative, we cannot say that the *communis opinio* held the LXX version to be inspired. On the contrary, the dawn of our era gave birth to several Greek translations of the Hebrew text. Nevertheless, P. Auvray, "L'inspiration des Septante," *RB*, 59(1952), pp. 321f., asserts that "la foi à l'inspiration de la Septante est générale dans l'Église ancienne."

[1] Nairne, *Epistle of Priesthood*, pp. 275f., claims that the Hellenistic Jews enjoyed a larger measure of freedom in scriptural matters than the straiter sect of religion, i.e., the legal school of the Rabbis. The Early Church enjoyed the same freedom in scriptural study as the Hellenistic Jews. T. W. Manson, "Argument from Prophecy," *JTS*, 46(1945), p. 135, approaches the matter from a different angle: "We tend to think of the text as objective fact and interpretation as subjective opinion. It may be doubted whether the early Jewish and Christian translators and expositors of Scripture made any such sharp distinction. For them the meaning of the text was of primary importance." See P. Padva, *Les Citations*, p. 85; and R. Nicole, "NT Use of the OT," *Revelation and the Bible*, p. 142.

[2] 1 Clem. 39 (Job 4:19ff.; 5:1-5; 15:15). The same phenomenon is found in the NT, where in Gal. 4:30 a word of Sarah (Gen. 21:10) is said to be "scripture."

[3] Justin Martyr, Apol. I, 36. Cf. W. A. van Es, "Schriftgeloof," *GTT*, 35(1934), p. 290; 37(1936), pp. 127ff.; 38(1937), pp. 325f.

[4] Iren. Epid. 49. Cf. Koole, *Overname van het OT*, pp. 144f.

Christ; the writings of Moses are in fact the words of Christ.[1] Also Clement of Rome indicates that the actual speaker in the OT is Christ, who communicates through the Holy Spirit; *e.g.*, with reference to certain psalms he specifies Christ as the speaker, "And again he (Christ) says himself . . . ."[2]

In the Epistle to the Hebrews, on the other hand, the speaker is generally represented as God whenever quotations of the OT are introduced (1:5,13; 4:3,4; 5:5,6; 6:13; 8:8; 12:26,27; 13:5), and even where the words are in the 3rd person singular about God (1:6,7,8; 4:6,7; 7:21; 10:30b). At other times words spoken by God are listed elsewhere as an utterance of the Holy Spirit (3:7). Akin to this phenomenon is the quotation in 8:8, which is introduced as a word spoken by God, but which in 10:15 is rendered as a testimony of the Holy Spirit. Furthermore, there are some citations which are put into the mouth of Christ (2:12; 10:5; 10:30a), and some which are spoken concerning him (1:8; 7:17,21). Also there are two quotations introduced by the indefinite adverb *somewhere* (2:6; 4:4).[3] In the introduction to the quotation from Ps. 8:4-6 (Heb. 2:6) there is also the indefinite pronoun *someone*, which is preceded by the verb *to testify*. The author is not interested in the composer, David, for the psalm does not concern the poet. By omitting the name of the psalmist, he wishes to fix attention on the Word of God, which was once testified by David.[4]

While God is the speaker in Heb. 1:7,8, the preposition πρός in the introductory formula is not to be translated *to*, but rather *with reference to*.[5] In 1:8,10 God does not address the Son with a passage from Ps. 45 and from Ps. 102; instead a few verses of these psalms are applied with reference to the Son. Since the 22nd Psalm is *par excellence* messianic, and even Jesus uttered

---

[1] Iren. IV,2,3.

[2] I Clem. 16,15ff. (Ps. 22:7ff.), and see I Clem. 22,1 (Ps. 34:12-18). Cf. Koole, *Overname van het OT*, pp. 142f.

[3] B. M. Metzger, "Formulas Introducing Quotations," *JBL*, 70(1951), p. 301, asserts that the use of the formula with the indefinite adverb is "generally taken as an Alexandrinism." Both Philo and Clement of Rome employ this type of formula. See Metzger for all the references.

[4] J. A. Bengel, *Gnomon*, II, p. 401.

[5] Arndt & Gingrich, *Lexicon*, p. 717. Cf. Grosheide, *Comm.*, p. 70; Delitzsch, *Comm.*, pp. 29ff.

verses of this psalm (Mt. 27:46), it is understandable that the author to the Hebrews has put its words into the mouth of Jesus (Heb. 2:12).¹ By means of the phrase "it is witnessed" (7:17), in its very context, the author reveals in a direct way that the words from Ps. 110:4 have been uttered with reference to Christ. Heb. 7:21 is analogous to Heb. 1:7,8 in the use of the preposition πρός. Also in this verse it is to be interpreted *with reference to*.

The last quotation attributed to Jesus is the passage from Ps. 40:6–8 (Heb. 10:5–7). Like the citation from Ps. 22:23 the words are direct and employ the 1st person singular. In addition to this personal reference the clause "in the roll of the book it is written of me" is found in the quotation from Ps. 40. The verbal form *it is written* is very common in the other books of the NT, but in the Epistle to the Hebrews the author never appeals to Scripture by means of the perfect tense, denoting resultant state. Only within this quotation the verbal form occurs. It is a bit one-sided to identify the expression *the roll of the book* with the book of Genesis,² or with the Pentateuch. Preferably it includes in a collective way the entire OT, so that messianic prophecies are not limited to any particular section of the Scriptures (cf. John 5:39,46).³

Both Heb. 2:12 and 10:5 have introductory formulas with the same verb of saying (λέγειν) in the present tense. By means of this tense the author wishes to indicate that Christ is still speaking in the Scriptures.

In the Epistle to the Hebrews certain assumptions have been made in the quoting and interpreting of the various psalm citations. Without these assumptions the arguments based on the exegesis of the quotations could never have been presented in their present form. It appears therefore that the author assumes a certain knowledge and acquaintance with scriptural interpretation of OT passages.

---

¹ Grosheide, *Comm.*, p. 88.

² Synge, *Hebrews*, pp. 8f., following the Latin Fathers, interprets the phrase "in the roll of the book" to mean "the head or top or opening of the Book" (p. 9). This would be of course the book of Genesis, which is the beginning of the Scriptures. However, it is questionable whether we should be so specific. What did the prophet Ezekiel (2:9 and see 3:1,2,3) mean when he used the phrase?

³ Riggenbach, *Comm.*, p. 302; Delitzsch, *Comm.*, pp. 460f.

All the quotations cited in Heb. 1 were clearly understood by the early Christians of the latter part of the first century A.D. It is taken for granted that the first addresses were familiar with the messianic interpretation of the psalm citations in chapter 1. In the next chapter the author quotes OT passages on that same assumption. However, the citation from Ps. 8 stands in need of such explanation which will elucidate its relevancy to Ps. 110:1. "Again, he assumes without argument that the passages from which he cites 'I will proclaim thy name among my brothers,' and 'I and the children whom God has given me,' refer to Christ. Here again we seem to discern a common tradition lying behind the original contribution of a single learned author, a tradition which he shared with those to whom he wrote."[1]

Heb. 3 and 4 ostensively indicate that the second half of Ps. 95, which had never been intertwined with Gospel themes, was of vital significance to the recipients of the Epistle.[2] It is the interpretation of Ps. 110:4 (Heb. 7:1–25), which abruptly ends the author's assumptions manifested in previous chapters. With the expression δυσερμήνευτος (Heb. 5:11) he indicates that the implications of Ps. 110:4 represent the heart of his theological argument; he cannot work with assumptions in the exegesis of this psalm passage. This citation called for detailed explication, which was new to the first recipients. The passage from Ps. 40 did not present any difficulty to author and readers of the Epistle to the Hebrews. The use of this psalm passage was based on the assumption that the early Christians were acquainted with the explanation given throughout the OT, instructive of the true sacrifice offered to Yahweh. They also knew that this true sacrifice was fulfilled and exemplified in Jesus Christ, the Son of God.

4. Conclusions

Nothing in the use of the psalm citations indicates that the author to the Hebrews has taken the OT passages at random. Every citation has been chosen to fill out his theological motifs; and every citation manifests this purpose.

---

[1] Dodd, *Acc. to the Scr.*, p. 22.
[2] *Ibid.*

The motif of the difference between the Son and the angels is unfolded by the citations in the first chapter of the Epistle, but it finds its culminating point in the second. Both the Son and the angels have their abode in heaven, but the former is enthroned at God's right hand, while the latter have been given a position of servitude. The angels have been commissioned to be ministering spirits to those who are about to inherit salvation. However, by reason of his divine and human natures, the Son experiences humiliation in the suffering of death, and exaltation by delivering "all them who through fear of death were all their lifetime subject to bondage" (Heb. 2:15).

Every psalm citation serves the purpose of communicating sacred history to the first recipients of the Epistle. This fact reveals the scholarliness of the author, who talentedly writes with economy of words; and it leads to the assumption that a measure of historical knowledge may be expected among the early Christians.

Although the OT came to them in a Greek version, it nevertheless was regarded as the Word of God. Scripture was authoritative to the author and the readers of the Epistle to the Hebrews. To them it was the voice of God, the testimony of the Holy Spirit, and even the direct word of Christ. "God, having of old time spoken unto the fathers in the prophets by divers portions and in divers manners, hath at the end of these days spoken unto us in his Son" (Heb. 1:1,2).

LIST OF ABBREVIATIONS

BA	The Biblical Archeologist
BenMnts	Benediktinische Monatschrift
Bibl	Biblica
BJRL	Bulletin of the John Rylands Library
BT	The Babylonian Talmud
CanJTh	Canadian Journal of Theology
ExpT	The Expository Times
EvQ	Evangelical Quarterly
GCS	Die Griechische Christliche Schriftsteller der Ersten Drei Jahrhunderts
GTT	Gereformeerd Theologisch Tijdschrift
HUCA	Hebrew Union College Annual
ICC	The International Critical Commentary
IEJ	Israel Exploration Journal
JBL	Journal of Biblical Literature
JE	The Jewish Encyclopedia
JTS	Journal of Theological Studies
LCL	The Loeb Classical Library
LXX	Septuagint
MSS	Manuscripts
MT	Masoretic Text
NT	New Testament
NTS	New Testament Studies
NThSt	Nieuwe Theologische Studiën
OT	Old Testament
RB	Revue Biblique
RevQ	Revue de Qumran
ST	Studia Theologica
Str.-Bill.	Strack, H. L. and P. Billerbeck, *Kommentar zum Neuen Testament aus Talmud und Midrasch*, München, C. H. Beck, 1922–25.
ThBl	Theologische Blätter
ThLZ	Theologische Literaturzeitung
ThQ	Theologisch Quartalschrift
TSK	Theologische Studien und Kritiken
TWNT	Theologisches Wörterbuch zum Neuen Testament, (ed. G. Kittel, G. Friedrich), Stuttgart, W. Kohlhammer Verlag, 1933 –.
VoxTh	Vox Theologia
VT	Vetus Testamentum
ZAW	Zeitschrift für die alttestamentliche Wissenschaft
ZdZ	Zwischen den Zeiten
ZNW	Zeitschrift für die neutestamentliche Wissenschaft

BIBLIOGRAPHY

ALLEGRO J. M., "Further Light on the History of the Qumran Sect," *JBL*, 75(1956), pp. 89-95.
—, "Further Messianic References in the Qumran Literature," *JBL*, 75(1956), pp. 174-187.
—, "Fragments of a Qumran Scroll of the Eschatological *Midrashim*," *JBL*, 77(1958), pp. 350-354.
ARNDT W. F. and GINGRICH F. W., *A Greek-English Lexicon of the New Testament*, Chicago, University of Chicago Press, 1957.
AUVRAY P., "Comment se Pose le Probleme de l'Inspiration des Septante," *RB*, 59(1952), pp. 321-336.
BAEHRENS W. A., (ed.), *Origenes Werke*, 7,8, *GCS*, Leipzig, J. C. Hinrichs, 1921–25.
BAKKER A., "Christ an Angel?" *ZNW*, 32(1933), pp. 255–265.
BARBEL J., *Christos Angelos*, Bottrop, W. Postberg, 1941.
BAUERNFEIND O., $καταπαύω$, *TWNT*, III, p. 629.
BEHM J. $ἑρμηνεύω$, *TWNT*, II, pp. 659–662.
BENGEL J. A., *Gnomon Novi Testamenti*, II, Tübingen, 1850.
BLÄSER P., "Schriftverwertung und Schrifterklärung im Rabbinentum und bei Paulus," *ThQ*, 132(1952), pp. 152–169.
BÖHL E., *Die Alttestamentliche Citate im Neuen Testament*, Wien, 1878.
BRAUDE W. G., *The Midrash on Psalms*, I,II, New Haven, Yale University Press, 1959.
BRIGGS E. G., *The Book of Psalms*[5], I,II, *ICC*, Edinburgh, T. & T. Clark, 1952.
BROWN F., DRIVER S. R. and BRIGGS CH. A., *A Hebrew and English Lexicon*, Oxford, Clarendon Press, 1952 (corr. impr.).
BROWNLEE W. H., "Biblical Interpretation among the Sectaries of the Dead Sea Scrolls," *BA*, 14(1951), pp. 54–76.
BRUCE F. F., *Second Thoughts on the Dead Sea Scrolls*, London, Paternoster Press, 1956.
—, *Biblical Exegesis in the Qumran Texts*, (Exegetica III,1), Den Haag, van Keulen, 1959.
BÜCHEL C., "Der Hebräerbrief und das Alte Testament," *TSK*, 1906, pp. 508–591.
BÜCHSEL F., *Die Christologie des Hebräerbriefs*, Gütersloh, C. Bertelsmann, 1922.
BULTMANN R., $ἀπειθέω$, *TWNT*, VI, p. 11.
—, $ἀπιστία$ *TWNT*, VI, p. 205.
BURROWS M., "The Discipline Manual of the Judaean Covenanters," *Oudtest. Studien*, 8(1950), pp. 156–192.
—, *The Dead Sea Scrolls*, New York, Viking Press, 1955.
CAIRD G. B., "The Exegetical Method of the Epistle to the Hebrews," *CanJTh*, 5(1959), pp. 44–51.
CALVIN J., *Commentaries on the Epistle to the Hebrews*, (transl. J. Owen), Grand Rapids, Wm. B. Eerdmans, 1953.

COLSON F. H. and WHITAKER G. H., (edd.) *Philo*, I-VII, *LCL*, London, Wm. Heinemann, 1949–50.
CULLMANN O., *Die Christologie des Neuen Testaments*, Tübingen, J. C. B. Mohr, 1957.
DANA H. E. and MANTEY J. R., *A Manual of the Greek New Testament*, New York, Macmillan Co., 1957.
DANIÉLOU J., *Théologie du Judéo-Christianisme*, Tournai (Belg.), Desclée, 1958.
DAUBE D., "Alexandrian Methods of Interpretation and the Rabbis," *Festschrift Hans Lewald*, Basel, Helbing & Lichtenhahn, 1953, pp. 27–44.
DAVIS W. D., *Paul and Rabbinic Judaism*, London, S.P.C.K., 1948.
DELITZSCH F., *Commentar zum Briefe an die Hebräer*, Leipzig, Dörffling & Francke, 1857.
—, *Die Psalmen*³, I,II, Leipzig, Dörffling & Francke, 1873.
DIBELIUS M., "Der himmlische Kultus nach dem Hebräerbrief," *ThBl*, 21(1942), col. 1–11.
DIESTEL L., *Geschichte des Alten Testaments in der christlichen Kirche*, Jena, Mauke, 1869.
DITTMAR W., *Vetus Testamentum in Novo*, Göttingen, Vandenhoeck & Ruprecht, 1903.
DODD C. H., *According to the Scriptures*, New York, Ch. Scribner's Sons, 1953.
DOEVE J. W., *Jewish Hermeneutics in the Synoptic Gospels and Acts*, Assen, (Holland), van Gorcum, 1953.
DREWS P., *Untersuchungen über die sogen. clementinische Liturgie im VIII Buch der apostol. Konstitutionen*, Tübingen, J. C. B. Mohr, 1906.
DRIVER S. R., *Notes on the Hebrew Text . . . of the Books of Samuel*², Oxford, Clarendon Press, 1913.
DUGMORE C. W., *The Influence of the Synagogue upon the Divine Office*, London, Oxford University Press, 1945(reprint).
ELBOGEN I., *Der Jüdische Gottesdienst*, Frankfurt, J. Kaufmann, 1931.
ELLIGER K., *Studien zum Habakuk-Kommentar vom Toten Meer*, Tübingen, 1953.
ELLIS E. E., *Paul's Use of the Old Testament*, Edinburgh, London, Oliver & Boyd, 1957.
EPSTEIN I., (ed.) *The Babylonian Talmud*, I-XXXV, London, Soncino Press, 1935–52.
ETHERIDGE J. W., (ed.), *The Targums of Onkelos and Jonathan ben Uzziel on the Pentateuch*, London, Longman, Green, 1862–65.
FEINE P., *Theologie des Neuen Testaments*⁸, Berlin, Evang. Verlagsanst. 1953.
FIELD F., *Origenis Hexaplorum*, I,II, Oxford, Clarendon Press, 1875.
FLUSSER D., "Two Notes on the Midrash on 2 Sam. vii," *IEJ*, 9(1959), pp. 99–109.
FOAKES JACKSON F. J. and LAKE K., *The Beginnings of Christianity*, Part. I, I, London, Macmillan and Co., 1920.
FRANKEL Z., *Vorstudien zu der Septuaginta*, Leipzig, F. C. W. Vogel, 1841.
GÄRTNER B., "The Habakkuk Commentary (DSH) and the Gospel of Matthew," *ST*, 8(1954), pp. 1–24.
GASTER T. H., "Psalm 45," *JBL*, 74(1955), pp. 239–251.

GEBHARDT O. DE, HARNACK A., and ZAHN TH., (edd.) *Patrum Apostolicorum Opera*, Leipzig, J. C. Hinrichs, 1876.
GESENIUS W., *Hebrew and Chaldee Lexicon*, (transl. S. R. Tregelles), Grand Rapids, Wm. B. Eerdmans, 1952.
GOODSPEED E., *Index Patristicus*, Leipzig, J. C. Hinrichs, 1907.
—, *Die ältesten Apologeten*, Göttingen, Vandenhoeck & Ruprecht, 1914.
GORDIS R., "Quotations as a Literary Usage in Biblical, Oriental and Rabbinic Literature," *HUCA*, 22(1949), pp. 157–220.
GREIJDANUS S., *Schriftbeginselen ter Schriftverklaring*, Kampen, J. H. Kok, 1946.
GROSHEIDE F. W., *Opmerkingen over Hebr. 1:1–4*, Kampen, J. H. Kok, 1910.
—, *Beknopte Grammatica*, Kampen, J. H. Kok, 1912.
—, *De Beteekenis van de Uitdrukking Zoon des Menschen*, Amsterdam, W. Kirchner, 1921.
—, *Hermeneutiek*, Amsterdam, H. A. van Bottenburg, 1929.
—, *De Brief aan de Hebreeën en de Brief van Jakobus²*, Kampen, J. H. Kok, 1955.
GRUBE K., "Die Hermeneutische Grundsätze Justins des Martyrs," *Der Katholik*, 66(1880), I, pp. 1–42.
HADDAS M., *The Third and Fourth Books of Maccabees*, New York, Harper & Brothers, 1953.
HARDER G., "Die Septuagintazitate des Hebräerbriefs," *Theologia Viatorum*, München, Chr. Kaiser, 1939, pp. 33–52.
HARRIS R., *Testimonies*, II, Cambridge, University Press, 1920.
— and MINGANA A., *The Odes and Psalmes of Solomon*, London, Longmans, Green & Co., 1920.
HENNECKE E., *Neutestamentliche Apokryphen*, (ed. W. Schneemelcher), I, Evangelien, Tübingen, J. C. B. Mohr, 1959.
HERKENNE H., "Ps. 110(109) 'Dixit Dominus Domino Meo' in neuer Textkritischer Beleuchtung," *Bibl.* 11(1930), pp. 450–457.
HERRMANN J. and BÜCHSEL F., ἱλάσκομαι, *TWNT*, III, pp. 300–324.
HIGGINS A. J. B., "The Old Testament and Some Aspects of New Testament Christology," *CanJTh*, 6(1960), pp. 200–210.
HOH J., *Die Lehre des Hl. Irenäus über das Neue Testament*, (Ntliche Abhl.), Münster, 1919.
HOMMES N. J., *Het Testimoniaboek*, Amsterdam, N. Holl. Uitg. Mij, 1935.
HOSKIER H. C., *Text of the Epistle to the Hebrews in the Chester-Beatty Papyrus*, London, B. Quaritch, 1938.
ISRAELSTAM J. and SLOTKI J. J., (edd.) *Midrash Rabbah*, Leviticus, London, Soncino Press, 1939.
JAMES M. R., *The Apocryphal New Testament*, Oxford, Clarendon Press, 1953 (corrected).
JEREMIAS J., *Die Gleichnisse Jesu⁴*, Göttingen, Vandenhoeck & Ruprecht, 1956.
KADUSHIN M., *The Rabbinic Mind*, New York, Jew. Theol. Sem., 1952.
KÄSEMANN E., *Das Wandernde Gottesvolk²*, Göttingen, Vandenhoeck & Ruprecht, 1957.
KATZ P., *Philo's Bible*, Cambridge, University Press, 1950.
—, "οὐ μή σε ἀνῶ... Hebr. xiii.5. The Biblical Source of the Quotation," *Bibl.* 33(1952), pp. 523–525.

—, "ἐν πυρὶ φλογός," ZNW, 46(1955), pp. 133-138.
—, "The Quotations from Deuteronomy in Hebrews," ZNW, 49(1958), pp. 213-223.
KAUTZSCH E., *Die Apokryphen und Pseudepigraphen des Alten Testaments*, II, Tübingen, J. C. B. Mohr, 1900.
KISSANE E. J., *The Book of Psalms*, I, Dublin, Brown & Nolan, 1953.
KITTEL G., GRUNDMANN W. and VON RAD G., ἄγγελος, *TWNT*, I, pp. 72-87.
KITTEL R., *Die Psalmen*[4], Leipzig, Erlangen, A. Deichert, 1922.
—, *Biblia Hebraica*[3], Stuttgart, Priv. Württ. Bibelanst., 1953.
KÖGEL J., *Der Sohn und die Söhne*, Gütersloh, C. Bertelsmann, 1904.
—, "Der Begriff τελειοῦν im Hebräerbrief," *Theologische Studien*, Martin Kähler dargebracht, Leipzig, A. Deichert, 1905.
KÖNIG E., *Die Psalmen*, Gütersloh, C. Bertelsmann, 1927.
KOOLE J. L., *De Overname van het Oude Testament door de Christelijke Kerk*, Hilversum (Holland), J. Schipper Jr., 1938.
KOSMALA H., *Hebräer-Essener-Christen*, Leiden, E. J. Brill, 1959.
KROEZE J. H., *Genesis Veertien*, Hilversum (Holland), J. Schipper Jr., 1937.
KUHN K. G., "Der gegenwärtige Stand der Erforschung der in Palästina neu gefundenen hebräischen Handschriften," *ThLZ*, 85(1960), col. 649-658.
LAKE K., (ed.) *The Apostolic Fathers*, I,II, LCL, London, Wm. Heinemann, 1952.
LAUTERBACH J. Z., "Talmud Hermeneutics," *JE*, XII, pp. 30-33.
LENSKI R. C. H., *The Interpretation of the Epistle to the Hebrews and the Epistle of James*, Columbus (Ohio), Wartburg Press, 1946.
LIDDELL H. G. and SCOTT R., *A Greek-English Lexicon*, (I,II), Oxford, Clarendon Press, 1953 (reprint).
LUEKEN W., *Michael*, Göttingen, Vandenhoeck & Ruprecht, 1898.
MANSON T. W., "The Argument from Prophecy," *JTS*, 46(1945), pp. 129-136.
MANSON W., *Jesus, the Messiah*, London, 1944 (reprint).
MEETER H. H., *The Heavenly High Priesthood of Christ*, Grand Rapids, Eerdmans-Sevensma, 1916.
METZGER B. M., "The Formulas Introducing Quotations of Scripture in the NT and the Mishnah," *JBL*, 70(1951), pp. 297-307.
MEYBOOM H. U., (ed.), *Evangeliën buiten het Nieuwe Testament*, (Oud-Chr. Geschr.), Leiden, A. W. Sijthoff, 1907.
—, (ed.), *Irenaeus, Aanwijzingen der Apostolischen Verkondiging*, (Oud-Chr. Geschr.), Leiden, A. W. Sijthoff, 1920.
MICHAELIS W., *Die Apokryphen Schriften zum Neuen Testament*, Bremen, C. Schünemann, 1956.
—, πάσχω, *TWNT*, V, pp. 903-939.
—, παραπικραίνω, *TWNT*, VI, p. 127.
MICHEL O., "Die Lehre von der christlichen Vollkommenheit nach der Anschauung des Hebräerbriefes," *TSK*, 106(1935), pp. 333-335.
—, *Der Brief an die Hebräer*[11], Göttingen, Vandenhoeck & Ruprecht, 1959.
MICKELSEN A. B., *Methods of Interpretation in the Epistle to the Hebrews*, Chicago, 1959.
MOFFATT J., *Epistle to the Hebrews*, ICC, Edinburgh, T. & T. Clark, 1952 (reprint).

MOORE G. F., *Judaism in the First Centuries of the Christian Era*[6], Cambridge, Harvard University Press, 1950.
MOULTON J. H., *A Grammar of New Testament Greek*[3], I, Edinburgh, T. & T. Clark, 1949 (reprint).
— and MILLIGAN G., *The Vocabulary of the Greek Testament*, London, Hodder and Stoughton, 1952 (reprint).
MOULTON W. F. and GEDEN A. S., *A Concordance to the Greek Testament*[3], Edinburgh, T. & T. Clark, 1953 (reprint).
NAIRNE A., *The Epistle of Priesthood*[2], Edinburgh, T. & T. Clark, 1915.
NESTLE E., "Hebrews iii,8,15," *ExpT*, 21(1910), p. 94.
NESTLE E. and ALAND K., *Novum Testamentum Graece*[23], Stuttgart, Priv. Württ. Bibelanst., 1957.
NICOLE R., "New Testament Use of the Old Testament," *Revelation and the Bible*, (ed. C. F. Henry), Grand Rapids, Baker, 1958, pp. 137–151.
OSSWALD E., "Zur Hermeneutik des Habakuk-Kommentars," *ZAW*, 68, NF 27(1956), pp. 243–256.
PADVA P., *Les Citations de l'Ancien Testament dans l'Épître aux Hébreux*, Paris, N. L. Danzig, 1904.
PLOOY D., "The Baptism of Jesus," *Amicitiae Corolla*, (ed. H. G. Wood), London, University of London Press, 1933, pp. 239–252.
PROCKSCH O. and KUHN K. G., $\dot{\alpha}\gamma\iota\dot{\alpha}\zeta\omega$, *TWNT*, I, pp. 87–116.
RAHLFS A., *Septuaginta*, Societas Scientiarum Gottingensis, *Psalmi cum Odis*, X, Göttingen, Vandenhoeck & Ruprecht, 1931.
—, *Septuaginta*[6], I,II, Stuttgart, Priv. Württ, Bibelanst., 1958.
REITZENSTEIN R., "Eine frühchristliche Schrift von den dreierlei Früchten des christlichen Lebens," *ZNW*, 15(1914), pp. 60–90.
RENDALL R., "The Method of the Writer to the Hebrews in Using OT Quotations," *EvQ*, 27(1955), pp. 214–220.
RIDDERBOS N. H., "Christus in de Psalmen," *GTT*, 44(1943), pp. 129–149.
—, "Het Lied van den Priester-Koning," *VoxTh*, 15(1944), pp. 98–104.
RIGGENBACH E., *Der Brief an die Hebräer*, (Kommentar, Th. Zahn), Leipzig, A. Deichert, 1913.
—, *Der Brief an die Hebräer*, (Bibl. Z. und Strf.), Berlin Lichterfelde, E. Runge, 1916.
ROBERTS B. J., "Some Observations on the Damascus Document and the Dead Sea Scrolls," *BJRL*, 34(1951–52), pp. 366–387.
ROBERTSON A. T., *A Grammar of the Greek New Testament*[4], Nashville, (Tenn.), Broadman Press, 1934.
ROTH C., "The Subject Matter of Qumran Exegesis," *VT*, 10(1960), pp. 51–68.
SCHILDENBERGER J., "Psalm 109(110): Christus, König und Priester," *BenMnts*, 20(1938), pp. 361–374.
SCHIPPERS R., *Het Evangelie van Thomas*, Kampen, J. H. Kok, 1960.
SCHNEIDER J., $\dot{o}\mu\nu\dot{\nu}\omega$, *TWNT*, V, pp. 177–185.
—, $\dot{o}\mu o\iota\dot{o}\omega$, *TWNT*, V, pp. 186–198.
SCHNEIDER H., "Die biblischen Oden im christlichen Altertum," *Bibl.* 30(1949), pp. 28–65.
SCHRENK G., $\dot{\alpha}\varrho\chi\iota\varepsilon\varrho\varepsilon\dot{\upsilon}\varsigma$, *TWNT*, III, pp. 265–284.
SCHÜRER E., *Geschichte des Jüdischen Volkes*[4], II, Leipzig, J. C. Hinrichs, 1907.

SCOTT E. F., *The Epistle to the Hebrews*, Edinburgh, T. & T. Clark, 1922.
SEELIGMANN I. L., "Voraussetzungen der Midraschexegese," Supplement to *VT*, I, *Congress Volume, Copenhagen*, Leiden, E. J. Brill, 1953, pp. 150–181.
SELWYN E. G., *The First Epistle of St. Peter*, London, Macmillan, 1947.
SIEGFRIED C., *Philo von Alexandria*, Jena, H. Dufft, 1875.
SLOT W., *De Letterkundige Vorm van de Brief aan de Hebreeën*, Groningen, J. B. Wolters, 1912.
SPICQ C., *L'Épître aux Hébreux*[3], I.-Introduction; II.-Commentaire; Paris, J. Gabalda, 1953.
—, "L'Épître aux Hébreux, Apollos, Jean-Baptiste, Les Hellénistes et Qumran," *RevQ*, 1(1959), pp. 365–390.
STARFELT E., *Studier i Rabbinsk och Nytestamentlic Skrifttolkning*, Lund, H. Ohlssons, 1959, (Eng. summary pp. 260–288).
STENDAHL K., *The School of St. Matthew*, Uppsala, 1954.
STIEREN A., (ed.), *Irenaeus, Opera*, I, Leipzig, 1853.
STRACK H. L., *Einleitung in Talmud und Midrasch*[5], München, C. H. Beck, 1921.
STRATHMANN H., *Der Brief an die Hebräer*, (Neue Testament Deutsch), Göttingen, Vandenhoeck & Ruprecht, 1956.
SYNGE F. C., *Hebrews and the Scriptures*, London, S.P.C.K., 1959.
THACKERAY H. ST. J., (ed.), *Josephus*, I-VII, *LCL*, London, W. Heinemann, 1950–56.
THOMAS K. J., *The Use of the Septuagint in the Epistle to the Hebrews*, (unpublished dissertation at the University of Manchester), 1959.
TORRANCE T., "The Last of the Hallel Psalms," *EvQ*, 28(1956), pp. 101–108.
UBBINK J. TH., "De Hoogepriester en zijn Offer in de Brief aan de Hebreën," *NThSt*, 22(1939), pp. 172–184.
—, "De Messiaansche Uitlegging van Psalm 8:5–7 LXX in Hebreën 2:9," *NThSt*, 24(1941), pp. 181–185.
VAN DER PLOEG J., "L'Éxégèse de l'Ancien Testament dans l'Épître aux Hébreux," *RB*, 54(1947), pp. 187–228.
VAN DER WOUDE A. S., *Die Messianische Vorstellungen der Gemeinde von Qumran*, Assen (Holland), van Gorcum, 1957.
—, *Bijbelcommentaren en Bijbelse Verhalen*, Amsterdam, Proost & Brandt, 1958.
VAN ES W. A., "De Grond van het Schriftgeloof bij de 'Apologeten' van de tweede eeuw," *GTT*, 35(1934), pp. 282–310; 37(1936), pp. 113–142; 38(1937), pp. 305–330.
VENARD L., "L'utilisation des Psaumes dans l'Épître aux Hébreux," *Mélanges E. Podechard*, Lyon, Facultés Catholiques, 1945, pp. 253–264.
VIS A., *The Messianic Psalm Quotations in the New Testament*, Amsterdam, 1936.
—, "Is Ps. CX een Messiaansche Psalm?" *VoxTh*, 15(1944), pp. 91–93.
VON LOEWENICH W., Zum Verständnis des Opfergedankes im Hebräerbrief, *ThBl*, 12(1933), col. 167–172.
VON RAD G., "Er ist noch eine Ruhe vorhanden dem Volke Gottes," *ZdZ*, 11(1933), pp. 104–111.
VOS G., *Biblical Theology*, Grand Rapids, Wm. B. Eerdmans, 1954.

—, *The Teaching of the Epistle to the Hebrews*, Grand Rapids, Wm. B. Eerdmans, 1956.
VRIEZEN TH. C., "Psalm 110," *VoxTh*, 15(1944), pp. 81–85.
WERNER E., *The Sacred Bridge*, London, D. Dobson, 1959.
WESTCOTT B. F., *The Epistle to the Hebrews*, Grand Rapids, Wm. B. Eerdmans, 1952 (reprint).
WINDISCH H., *Der Hebräerbrief* [2], (Hdb. zum NT, H. Lietzmann), Tübingen, J. C. B. Mohr, 1931.
WINTER P., "Der Begriff 'Söhne Gottes' im Moselied, Dtn. 32,1–43," *ZAW*, 67, NF 26(1955), pp. 40–48.
WUTTKE G., *Melchisedech der Priesterkönig von Salem*, Giessen, A. Töpelmann, 1927.
YADIN Y., "The Dead Sea Scrolls and the Epistle to the Hebrews," *Scripta Hierosolymitana*, IV, Jerusalem, Magnes Press, 1958, pp. 36–45.
—, "A Midrash on 2 Sam. vii and Ps. i-ii (4QFlorilegium)," *IEJ*, 9(1959), pp. 95–98.
ZIEGLER J., *Isaias*, (Septuaginta, XIV), Göttingen, Vandenhoeck & Ruprecht, 1939.
ZUNTZ G., *The Text of the Epistles*, London, Oxford University Press, 1953.

INDEX OF BIBLICAL PASSAGES

Genesis
1:28 . . . . 103f.,141
2:1ff. 36
2:2 113,115,131
3 103
4:17-22 120
5:11 120
6:2 137
14:17-20 38
14:17 16
14:18ff. 16,119ff.,131,138
21:10 147
21:12 . . . . 50f.,73
22:16f. 38
23:1 120
25:7,17 120
28:15 . . . . 55f.
35:28 120
36:1-43 120
47:28 120
47:31 17
50:26 120

Exodus
3:6 53
5:21 115
9:16 31
14:11 115
15:1-19 47
15:24 115
16:2 115
17:2f. 115
17:3ff. 72
17:11 63
19:13 52
19:19 53
20:8,12,19 63
23:30 82
24:8 41,137
25:40 39
28-29 121
32:1 115

Leviticus
1:2 63

8-10 121
13:2 63
17:13 63
19:1-15 63
19:11 63

Numbers
11:1,4 115
12:1 115
12:7 34
12:14 63
14 115
14:2 115
14:9,11ff. 112
14:22,30 115
16-18 121
20:2ff. 72
21:8 63
24:17 70

Deuteronomy
3:20 115
3:21-43 47
3:36 46
4:24 17
7:22 82
9:19 . . . . 16,52f.
9:23f. 112
12:9f. 113
12:9 115
18:15ff. 69
25:19 115
31:6 . . . . 54ff.
32 15
32:35 . . . . 45f.,55
32:36 . . . . 45f.
32:43 . . . . 20ff.,77,137

Joshua
1:5 . . . . 55f.
21:43ff. 115
23:1 115

Judges
13:6 32

I Samuel

1-2	50
15:22	126

II Samuel

7	77f.
7:6-16	76
7:12ff.	69
7:13	78
7:14	19f.,70,75f.,92
7:16	78
7:17	80
16:1	82
22	33f.
22:3	32,34,84

I Kings

2:1-10	47
8:56	115

II Kings

10:18	82

I Chronicles

16:23	31
17:13	20
23:25	115
28:20	56

II Chronicles

6:41	115
32:33	106

Ezra

2:61ff.	121

Nehemiah

7:63ff.	121
8:8	61,93

Job

1:6	136
2:1	136
4:19ff.	147
5:1-5	147
10:20	82
15:15	147
37:22	106
38:7	136
40:5	106

Psalms

1	69
2	17f.,37,69,77,79,136,147
2:2	18
2:7	17ff.,28,37,75f.,80,82,86,97f.,116,136,144
2:8	18,80
2:9	18
8	29f.,74,82ff.,99,101ff.,104,107,130,132
8:4ff.	12,29,81,96,102,130,139ff.,148,150
8:4	82f.
8:5f.	83
8:5	82f.,88,98,106
8:6-9	103
8:6	30,81,107
8:7	83,91
9:15	31
11	53
18	33
22	31f.,84
22:2,6	84
22:7ff.	148
22:8f.,16,19	84
22:23	31,83ff.,139,144,148f.
29:1	106,137
34:12-18	148
35:14	15
37	140
40	43,87,101,132
40:6ff.	12,43,57,87,124ff.,127,143,149f.
40:6	43,88f.,126
40:8	137
40:10	43
45	78f.
45:3	24
45:6ff.	116,144,148
45:6f.	24,78
45:6	88,98
50:8ff.	126
50:14	15
50:23	15

51:16f.	126
55:18	32
69:9	15
78	114
89:6	137
89:50f.	15
94-110	59
95	35ff.,79,85,101,108, 110,112,114ff.,132
95:7-11	12,35,85,108,114,130, 141,150
95:11	36,88,113,115,119
96	35
96:3	31
96:7	106
97:7	22
102	30,79f.,144,148
102:22	31
102:25ff.	26,29,116
102:25	88f.,98
103:4	137f.
104:2	77
104:4	23ff.,77,88f.
104:12,35	23
106	114
107:26	14
110	27,37f.,78f.,101,132,135
110:1	16,18,27ff.,37,80ff., 86,91,98f.,116f.,144,150
110:3	136
110:4	12,20,37,86,97,116ff., 130f.,141ff.,149f.
118	57,90
118:6	56,88
118:18	51
118:22	90
135:14	46
141:5	51

Ecclesiastes

8:1	65
4:8	82

Proverbs

3:1-12	51
3:11ff.	131
3:11f.	51

Isaiah

1:10ff.	126
5:1-9	47
6:1-9:7	32f.
6	32
6:9f.	32
7:14	33
8	34
8:8ff.,14	33
8:17f.	33f.
8:17	43,84
8:18	34,84,137,139
8:23	33
9:1	33
13:22	48
21:14	121
26	47
26:9-20	47f.
26:9	46
26:17ff.	47
26:18f.	48
26:20	47
28:16	33
34:4	27
38:10-20	47
43:6	20
57:2	20

Jeremiah

7:21ff.	126
30:21	117
31	41,87,132
31:31-34	40f.,131
31:31f.	41
31:33f.	87
31:33	57,129
31:34	57
38:33(LXX)	129
51:10	31

Ezekiel

2:9	149
3:1ff.	149
3:12,14	138
8:3	138
11:16	82
11:24	138

43:5	138
44:3	20

Daniel

3:25	136
3:26-45(LXX)	47
3:27	106
3:52-88(LXX)	47
3:92(LXX)	137
4:27	160
7:13	30,81f.
7:14	82
7:26	20

Hosea

6:6	126

Amos

5:21ff.	126
5:26f.	68

Jonah

2:3-10	47

Habakkuk

2	47f.
2:1-4	48
2:3f.	47
2:3	48
2:4	49
2:17	65
3:2-19	47

Haggai

2:6	53,88

Zechariah

1:15	82
6:12	143
6:13	116
13:3	143

Malachi

3:1	48

Matthew

3:17	19,91
4:3,6	76
4:15f.	33
7:11	71
10:25	71
11:3	49
11:7ff.	109
11:16	36
12:2-6	71
12:41f.	36
12:42	20
12:45	36
13:14f.	32
13:32	23
13:52	71
21:16	29
22:44	28,117,124
23:34	71
24:30	30
26:28	41
26:63	76
26:64	30
27:11	117
27:35	84
27:37	117
27:39	84
27:40	76
27:42	117
27:43	76,84
27:46	84,149
27:54	76

Mark

1:11	18f.
4:32	23
8:12	36
12:36	28
13:32	134
14:24	41
14:62	28
15:24,29,34	84

Luke

1:32f.	20
1:46-55	47
1:55	38
1:68-79	47
1:73	38
2:29-32	47
3:22	18f.,28
7:20	49
7:24ff.	109

11:13	71
11:29	36
11:49	71
12:28	71
13:19	23
17:7ff.	109
20:42f.	28
21:22	21,45
22:20	41
22:69	81
23:34f.	84
24:26	106
24:27	89,114
24:39,41ff.	138

John

1:19ff.	69
3:36	112
4:25	69
5:27	30
5:39,46	149
5:46f.	71
6:14	69
7:40	69
7:42	20,69
7:52	69
14:19	48
16:16	48
17:5	106
19:24,28	84
19:37	20

Acts

2:34f.	28
3:1	15
4:11	90
4:25	18
7	114
7:2	15
7:30	23
7:32	53
7:44	39
7:55	28
7:56	82
13:17-23	76
13:33	18,28,76
14:1f.	112
28:24	112
28:26f.	32

Romans

1	75
1:2ff.	75
1:3	77
1:17	49
5:5	84
7:9f.	73
8:14,17	96
8:34	28,121
9	50
9:7	51
9:52f.	33
10:4	125
10:5-9	73
10:7	14
10:19	21
11:11	21
11:12,24	73
12:19	21,45f.
15:10ff.	20
15:10	21

I Corinthians

1:9,28	107
3:20	20
10:1ff.	72
10:20	21
11	42
11:25	42
15	107
15:20-28	107
15:21	107f.
15:25	29,81,107
15:26	107
15:27	29,81
15:28	107

II Corinthians

6:18	20

Galatians

3:11	49
4	50
4:30	147

Ephesians

1:20	28f.,81
1:22	29,81
5:2	43

5:14	48

Philippians

2:15	21

Colossians

2:12	134
3:1	28
3:16	58

II Thessalonians

1:8	24

I Timothy

2:5f.	121
3:16	106

Hebrews

1:1-10:18	96
1	75,77f.,80,86,98,130,139,150
1:1	75,113,131,151
1:2f.	26
1:2	75,96,137f.,151
1:3	28,80,98f.,106,138
1:4ff.	134
1:4	73,134,136
1:5	17ff.,19f.,74f.,80, 96,130,137,144,148
1:6	20ff.,46,74,83,137f.148
1:7	22ff.,24,78f.,138,148f.
1:8	24f.,58,78f.,96,137,148f.
1:9	24ff.,79,137,144
1:10ff.	26,79
1:10	25,30,138,148
1:11f.	58
1:12	27
1:13	27ff.,74f.,80f.,98,102, 106,138,148
1:14	138
2-10	98
2	99,116,139f.,150
2:3f.	88
2:5-10	107
2:5f.	108
2:5	102ff.,105,139
2:6ff.	74,130
2:6	54,90,96,148
2:7	30,83,102,104f.
2:8f.	141
2:8	81,83,102ff.
2:9	83,96,98ff.,102f.,105f.,127
2:10f.	83,99
2:10	96f.,100,107,129,139,142
2:11	84,96,99,129
2:12f.	130
2:12	31,137,148f.
2:13	25,29,31ff.,34
2:14	99,107,114,127,139
2:15	126,151
2:16	149f.
2:17ff.	124
2:17	99,101,115f.,118,125, 127f.,129,131
2:18	99f.
3-4	101,108
3	131,150
3:1	106,116,142
3:2	34,108
3:3	73,106
3:5f.	129
3:5	34f.,108
3:6	96f.
3:7-4:11	116
3:7-11	35,74,130
3:7	85,148
3:8f.	111
3:10	86
3:12-4:11	108,111
3:12	85,108f.,111
3:13	108,110ff.
3:14	112
3:15	108
3:16-19	108,114
3:16ff.	142
3:16	114ff.
3:17	111f.,115
3:18	111f.,119
3:19	111
4	131,150
4:1	109
4:2f.	113
4:2	111f.
4:3f.	148
4:3	109ff.,112,119
4:4	36,90,110
4:6	109,111,148
4:8	132f.,142

165

Reference	Pages	Reference	Pages
4:9	110,113,115,131	7:15-25	118
4:10	113	7:15-19	119
4:11	109,111	7:15	122
4:14-5:10	101,118,124	7:17	37,148,150
4:14ff.	116	7:20ff.	119
4:14	96f.,106	7:21	37,131,148,150
4:15	99,101,127	7:22	106
5	86	7:23ff.	119
5:1-10	101,116	7:23f.	127
5:3	127	7:25	119
5:4	106	7:27	101
5:5f.	97,148	7:28	96f.,99f.,127
5:5	17ff.,96,106	8	129
5:6	37,117,131	8:1	28,80,87,125,138,143
5:7f.	100	8:4	129
5:7	100	8:5	39,122
5:8	96f.,117,127	8:6	73,125
5:9f.	86	8:7	128,132f.
5:9	99f.,139	8:8-12	40ff.,129,131
5:10	118,143	8:8	41,148
5:11	117,150	8:9	41,124f.
5:12	117	8:10	41,129
6:1f.	117	8:13	128f.
6:6	96	9:1-10:18	101
6:13-18	131	9:1f.,6	128
6:13ff.	119	9:7f.	127f.
6:13f.	38	9:12	126f.
6:13	148	9:13f.	73
6:20	106,118,143	9:14f.	125
7-10	127	9:15	128
7	98,143	9:17f.	125
7:1-25	118,150	9:18	128
7:1-12	118	9:19	129
7:1ff.	118	9:20	41,137
7:1f.	16,38	9:22	125,129
7:2f.	133	9:24-28	101
7:2	74	9:25f.	126
7:3	96f.,122f.,127,142	9:26	99f.
7:4-11	118	9:27	99,126
7:4	74,123	10	43
7:5f.	123	10:1-18	127,129
7:5	97,129	10:1-4	126
7:8	99,123	10:1	122,129
7:9f.	133	10:2	125,143
7:11ff.	118f.	10:5-18	131
7:11	132f.	10:5-10	75,88
7:13-25	118	10:5-9	44
7:13f.	118f.	10:5-8	143,150

Reference	Pages
10:5ff.	43f.,131
10:5	87,99,127,148,150
10:7	127,129,137
10:8ff.	43f.,57
10:8	127ff.
10:9	128
10:10	100f.,126,128
10:12f.	138
10:12	16,28,80,87,99,127
10:14	100f.,129,144
10:15	148
10:16f.	57f.,87,129
10:16	41,129
10:18	99,126
10:19-13:25	131
10:19	129,143
10:28f.	73
10:28	94,129
10:29	96
10:30	21,25,34
10:37f.	16,45ff.,74
10:38	25,49f.,58
11:1-32	114
11:4	99
11:8	111
11:13	99
11:18	50f.
11:21	17
11:26	15
11:37	99
12	52
12:1	129
12:2ff.	106
12:2	28,80,99,106,138
12:3	99
12:5-11	97
12:5-8	75
12:5f.	51,131
12:5	51
12:14	15
12:20	52
12:21	52f.
12:22	136
12:26f.	148
12:26	53f.
12:29	17
13:5	54ff.,148
13:6	56
13:12	99,106
13:15	15
13:17ff.	59
13:20	106
13:21	129
13:22-25	59
13:22	144
13:23	59
13:24	94
13:25	131

I Peter

Reference	Pages
1:11,21	106
2:5	121
3:22	28f.

I John

Reference	Pages
2:12ff.	41

Jude

Reference	Pages
9	135

Revelation

Reference	Pages
1:4	49
1:6	121
1:8	49
1:14	24
2:18	24
4:8	32,49
5:10	121
5:12	29
6:10	21
9:20	46
10:5	21
12:7	135
15:3	21
18:20	21
19:1	23
19:2	21
19:3	23
19:5	46
19:6	23
19:10	134
19:12	24
20:6	121
21:7	20
22:8f.	134

www.ingramcontent.com/pod-product-compliance
Lightning Source LLC
Chambersburg PA
CBHW070943160426
43193CB00011B/1794